The God That Failed

Liberalism and the Destruction of the West

John Q. Publius

BLACK
HOUSE
PUBLISHING

The God That Failed
Liberalism and the Destruction of the West

John Q. Publius

ISBN-13: 978-1-912759-34-7
1st Edition May, 2020.
This 2nd Edition, September 2020.

Black House Publishing Ltd
Kemp House
152 City Road
London
United Kingdom
EC1V 2NX

www.blackhousepublishing.com
Email: info@blackhousepublishing.com

BLACK
HOUSE
PUBLISHING

The central feature of the corrosive system destroying the West, neo-liberalism, is its "namelessness," that is to say that it largely operates anonymously, in the shadows, or by not calling something by its real name: "human rights," "liberal democracy," et cetera. It is a power for cowards.

Contents

Exordium

"The ideology that dominates our lives has, for most of us, no name...Its anonymity is both a symptom and cause of its power. It has played a major role in a remarkable variety of crises: the financial meltdown of 2007-8, the offshoring of wealth and power...the slow collapse of public health and education, resurgent child poverty, the epidemic of loneliness, the collapse of ecosystems...But we respond to these crises as if they emerge in isolation, apparently unaware that they have all been either catalysed or exacerbated by the same coherent philosophy; a philosophy that has – or had – a name...So pervasive has neoliberalism become that we seldom even recognise it as an ideology. We appear to accept the proposition that this utopian, millenarian faith describes a neutral force; a kind of biological law, like Darwin's theory of evolution. But the philosophy arose as a conscious attempt to reshape human life and shift the locus of power."- George Monbiot

Something's not right. All around us, society seems to be sinking into decay, and we don't recognize, let alone even know, the people living right next door to us. The media sells illusory progress with the latest gadgets and fads, and for all the talk of "social justice," there's scant justice to be had. Filth, violence, dereliction, and despair fester as the wounds turn septic, and the people are sick to death – literally.

Look at the results in the United States: "The latest CDC data show that the U.S. life expectancy has declined over the past few years. Tragically, this troubling trend is largely driven by deaths from drug overdose and suicide," CDC Director Dr. Robert Redfield states. Suicides and drug overdoses are among the leading causes of death in the US for people under fifty. The odds of dying from an accidental opioid overdose in the US are greater than those of dying in a car accident, according to findings from the National Safety Council (NSC). The lifetime odds of death by suicide are 1 in 88. The lifetime odds of an accidental opioid overdose are 1 in 96 compared with 1 in 103 for vehicular death. Drug overdoses killed almost 64,000 people in 2016 (over 42,000 of which were from opioids). Drug overdose deaths rose above 70,000 in 2017, at least 47,000 of which have been attributed to opioids.

For all Americans, the mortality rate for drug overdoses in 2016 was 19.8 per 100,000, an increase from 16.3 per 100,000 in 2015. The drug-related mortality rate per 100,000 in 2016 for whites was 25.3, blacks 17.1, and Hispanics 9.5, meaning whites are much more likely to die from drug overdoses than blacks and Hispanics, respectively.[1] Of the over 42,000 opioid overdose deaths in 2016, 33,450 of the victims (79.6%) were white, and for whites, there are roughly 6 suicides for every 1 homicide; among blacks, there are about 3.5 homicides for each suicide; and the ratio among Hispanics is roughly 1:1.

In 2018, the highest US age-adjusted suicide rate was among whites (16.84 per 100,000) and the second highest rate was among American Indians and Alaskan Inuit (14.12). This contrasts sharply with Hispanics (7.2), Asians and Pacific Islanders (7.16), and blacks (7.03).

The rate of suicide is highest in middle-aged white men in particular and white males of all age groups accounted for 69.67% of suicide deaths in 2018.[2] Also from the CDC:

- 36% of men aged 20 and over are overweight (2013-2016)

- 38% of women aged 20 and over are overweight (2013-2016)

- 35% of men aged 20 and over have hypertension. (2013-2016)

- 34% of women aged 20 and over have hypertension. (2013-2016)[3]

1   Centers for Disease Control and Prevention National Center for Health Statistics. Available at: www.cdc.gov/nchs/fastats/white-health.htm.

2   "Suicide Statistics," American Foundation for Suicide Prevention, 2018. Available at: https://afsp.org/about-suicide/suicide-statistics/.

3   Centers for Disease Control and Prevention National Center for Health

The people are clearly sick, which is also clearly by design. This begs the essential question: what is the purpose of a government if its rulers do not govern in the interests of its people?

For the ruling class, the answer is to protect and expand their profits and to act out their warped grievances and disdain. They are at best haughty and unconcerned, but there is something darker lurking within many of them, perhaps best exemplified by the comments made by Purdue Pharma's former President and Chairman Richard Sackler at the OxyContin launch party: "The prescription blizzard will be so deep, dense, and white." It's people like the Sacklers and vulture capitalist Paul Singer who are killing this country and getting unfathomably rich in the process. It is not a stretch to say that their behavior is not just malicious but downright lethal.

What we are dealing with here are a number of mutually reinforcing and often-inextricable phenomena. Many of these effects also intersect with the consequences of atomization and demoralization, leading to an explosion of white "deaths by despair." The members of the ruling class don't care about you. In fact, they hate you. How else to explain the massive mark-ups on prescription painkillers in the middle of the worst drug epidemic in American history, or the media's silent complicity,[4] or the fact that advertisers of these terrible drugs specifically targeted the elderly and veterans, who are disproportionately white?

Things are going so well for rural and working-class people in this country that heroin overdoses among persons aged 25–34 more than quadrupled in the time period 2010-2015. As Josh Bloom explains:

Statistics. Available at: www.cdc.gov/nchs/fastats/white-health.htm.

4   On the few occasions they thought it worth mentioning, it was dismissed away as a symptom of "racism." Yes, unbelievably from PBS to *The New York Times* to *The Guardian* "systemic racism" apparently made it easier for whites to be prescribed opioids in the first place, and thus the implication is that these poor and working-class whites, the elderly, and veterans mostly affected by the epidemic – and with virtually no public representation – are getting just what they deserve because of their racism and backwards views. This exemplifies just how thoroughly corrupted and reprehensible the media gatekeepers are in protecting the even worse primary actors behind the scenes.

In 2010 Purdue Pharma, after years of formulation research, got FDA approval for a new version of OxyContin – a high-dose, extended release form of oxycodone. Prior to that, addicts knew that by simply grinding up the pill, they could defeat the extended release formulation, and get as much as 80 mg (16 Percocet pills) of pure oxycodone. The new formulation put a stop to this, since when users tried to grind up the pills, they got a gum which could not be easily used. OxyContin use fell off of a cliff, as desired, but the solution was problematic. Addiction is a demon, cutting off one supply does not cure it, and addicts switched en masse to heroin, and the number of overdoses more than doubled in just three years.[5]

From the CDC:

During 2006, there were 2,088 drug overdose deaths involving heroin (age-adjusted rate of 0.7 per 100,000 population); during 2015, there were 12,989 deaths (age-adjusted rate of 4.1). The rate of drug overdose deaths involving heroin increased slightly during 2006–2010 but more than tripled during 2010–2015; the rates increased from 1.2 to 3.8 per 100,000 for persons aged 15–24 years, from 2.2 to 9.7 for persons aged 25–34 years, from 1.6 to 7.4 for persons aged 35–44 years, from 1.4 to 5.6 for persons aged 45–54 years, and from 0.7 to 3.4 for persons aged 55–64 years. In 2015, the rate of drug overdose deaths involving heroin was highest for persons aged 25–34.[6]

Yet, as bad as all of this is, drug overdose fatalities have gotten even worse since then, primarily due to synthetic opioids. We are now at

5   Bloom, Josh, "Prince Was Killed By 'The Devil in the Room,'" June 3, 2016. American Council on Science and Health. Available at: www.acsh.org/news/2016/06/03/prince-was-killed-by-the-devil-in-the-room.

6   Hedegaard, Holly, Margaret Warner, and Arialdi Mininio, "Rates of Drug Overdose Deaths Involving Heroin, by Selected Age Groups – United States 2006-2015," January 6, 2017. US Department of Health and Human Services/Centers for Disease Control and Prevention. *Morbidity and Mortality Weekly Report*, Vol. 65, No. 52. Available at: www.cdc.gov/mmwr/volumes/65/wr/pdfs/mm6552a12.pdf.

the point where we are talking about the annual death toll from drug overdoses exceeding the number of American soldiers killed in the entirety of the Vietnam War.

In 2017, "an estimated 1.7 million people in the United States suffered from substance use disorders related to prescription opioid pain relievers, and 652,000 suffered from a heroin use disorder (not mutually exclusive)."[7] About 80% of people who use heroin first misused prescription opioids.[8] Fentanyl is 50-100 times more potent than even morphine. Fentanyl is often substituted for heroin, which explains the spike in fatalities. A fatal ingested dose of fentanyl for those without opioid tolerance is about 2 milligrams – the weight of a few grains of salt. Most fentanyl comes from Mexico and China, and because of its size-to-potency ratio, it is extremely easy to smuggle. This is made even easier by the fact that the United States effectively does not have borders.

Deaths from fentanyl increased a whopping 45% from 2016 to 2017 alone. One out of every 12 deaths among people aged 25-34 can be blamed on heroin. 130 Americans die each day after overdosing on opioids, according to the Centers for Disease Control and Prevention, and yet in volume and pitch, the opioid crisis in this country barely registers compared to the HIV/AIDS and crack epidemics of the 1980s and 1990s. The brunt of the opioid epidemic's toll has been felt most heavily in vulnerable populations, particularly those in economically depressed and/or rural areas of the country, and yet the media drum beats steadily for those poor illegal aliens who somehow have the means and contacts to travel thousands of miles unmolested to the United States and gain instant entry – in the process becoming far more American than you are.

---

7   "2017 National Survey on Drug Use and Health: Detailed Tables," 2018. Center for Behavioral Health Statistics and Quality (CBHSQ), Rockville, MD: Substance Abuse and Mental Health Services Administration. Available at: www. samhsa.gov/data/sites/default/files/cbhsq-reports/NSDUHDetailedTabs2017/ NSDUHDetailedTabs2017.pdf.

8   Muhuri P.K., J.C. Gfroerer, and M.C. Davies, "Associations of Nonmedical Pain Reliever Use and Initiation of Heroin Use in the United States," August, 2013. *CBHSQ Data Review*. Available at: www. samhsa.gov/data/sites/default/files/DR006/DR006/nonmedical-pain-reliever-use-2013.htm.

Drug overdoses are just one kind of what are called "deaths by despair," and for too many Americans, they are exploding out of control. The suicide rate in rural America increased over 40% from 1999-2015. The CDC's National Center for Health Statistics shows an increase in the death rates from 1999 to 2014 for young whites; 25-year-old white women experienced an average increase in mortality of 3% every year over that time period, while 25-year-old white men had an average annual increase of 1.9%. Mortality rates also went up for whites in the age groups 40 to 50 and 62 to 64. In the last few years, the average life expectancy for whites as a population group has been in decline. *Every other ethnic group, save Amerindians, experienced declines in mortality for all ages over the same time period.* The rural and working-class populations of America are floundering and from our leadership to the media, *no one says a word.*

Here in America, opiates are the opium of the masses, and deaths-by-despair continue to skyrocket in all that red space between the enlightened blue metropoles. This doesn't happen in a country where things are going well, and it certainly isn't not just allowed to get worse but *enabled* to do so by the ruling class and their lackeys. Only the most depraved and morally bankrupt profit from – and take a certain amount of satisfaction if not joy in – the suffering of others. R.R. Reno observes:

> That is indeed shocking. It's the sort of rise that only occurs during periods of social crisis or collapse. Russia after the collapse of the Soviet Union is one instance. Europe during and in the immediate aftermath of World War II is another. The crisis, however, has been plain to see. It's a judgment on the moral myopia of today's academic culture and mainstream media that anyone would be blind-sided by this report of rising death rates among poor whites.[9]

---

9   Reno, R.R., "Deadly Progressivism," November 4, 2015. *First Things.* Available at: www.firstthings.com/web-exclusives/2015/11/deadly-progressivism.

The negative effects of this runaway globalism are being felt the hardest in rural America, which has been hollowed-out by decades of outsourcing, youth and "brain-drain" due to urbanization and the neo-liberal economic structure, and of course immigration. As a case-in-point of what Reno is talking about, Carol Graham and Sergio Pinto write in "Unhappiness in America: Desperation in White Towns, Resilience and Diversity in the Cities":

> The starkest marker of desperation is the trend of increasing mortality rates – driven by preventable deaths – among middle-aged, uneducated whites. That stands in sharp contrast to gradual improvements in health and well-being of blacks and Hispanics over the past decades, and high levels of optimism about the future among these same groups. The trends among poor whites – and the frustrations that they are generating – have complex causes that we do not fully understand.[10]

Could you imagine being so disconnected from your fellow Americans that you "do not fully understand" why working-class whites – generally now poor thanks to generations of mass immigration, out-sourcing, targeted destruction, and neo-liberal decadence – feel desperate? And why ascendant blacks and Hispanics – who are catered to and indulged by the ruling class at the expense of working-class and poor whites – might feel good about the future?

To their credit at least the authors have endeavored to understand whites as an interest group and a legitimate identity, which is beyond the pale for most, and the causes are actually much more complex than "acceptable" discourse would ever entertain, yet the fundamental flaw of any neo-liberal starting point is that the premise – neo-liberalism as good and a given – dooms the analysis to failure. Furthermore, the authors decry "the surprising level of political support for a populist platform rife with nativism, racism, and unrealistic proposals."

---

10   Graham, Carol and Sergio Pinto, "Unhappiness in America: Desperation in White Towns, Resilience and Diversity in the Cities," September 29, 2016. The Brookings Institution. Available at: www.brookings.edu/research/unhappiness-in-america-desperation-in-white-towns-resilience-and-diversity-in-the-cities/.

White identity is acknowledged, but is also summarily dismissed as inherently negative. The proposals, such as not importing the entire planet while simultaneously out-sourcing industry and denigrating the host population, and prosecuting the people responsible for the opioid crisis (for starters), are anything but "unrealistic." They are eminently reasonable and, if we want to have a country, necessary.

Contrary to, or the exact opposite of, the claims of "systemic racism," at least by whites against non-whites, there are clear and identifiable reasons for white despair, and all are traceable to the source: neo-liberalism. Understanding that anti-white animus and intense in-group favoritism of the controlling cabal undergirds so much neo-liberal policy, it is also vital to understand that without financial motive and the ability to gain and consolidate control through this particular vector, said anti-white policies would not have the chance to be implemented in the first place and the post-industrial nepotism of "our" so-called "elites" would not have the ramifications that it does.

Neo-liberalism must be understood as both an economic system and an ideology; in fact, the two are inextricably intertwined. Its progenitors sought to fuse political and social views of liberalism with laissez-faire capitalism. The emphasis was on privatization, de-regulation, and the removal of barriers to free trade. The state would advance "social progress" legalistically, and "the market" would be allowed to "go to work" with minimal government interference. While all of that has for the most part occurred, the government only steps out of the room when it proves beneficial to the oligopoly. Otherwise it's perfectly happy to pick winners and losers, or at the very least ensure the insiders get to stay on the inside track. Confiscatory taxation serves as a mass wealth transfer, and the government, rather than letting the market work itself out in truly laissez-faire fashion, ensures outcomes.

As one example, in the United States, the same factory farms that employ illegal labor, pollute the environment, treat animals deplorably, and kill off small family-owned farms are given lavish subsidies so generously provided by people like you and me. Between 1995 and 2016, the top 10% of farmers received 77% of subsidies, with the top 1% getting 26%. From 1995-2010, more than 6% of the subsidies went toward corn syrup, high-fructose corn syrup, corn starch, and soy oils.[11] According to the Cato Institute, the US government uses roughly $100 billion of taxpayer funds every year on "corporate welfare," and this is before considering the massive bail-out of the Fannie Mae and Freddie Mac mortgage lenders in 2008 which ultimately cost taxpayers $187 billion, the AIG bailout of $182 billion, or the $700 billion authorized with the Troubled Asset Relief Program (TARP) in October 2008 which bailed-out predominantly financial institutions and auto manufacturers (eventually reduced down to a still-huge almost $440 billion),12 among others. Reaganomics was so successful that half of America's savings and loan institutions failed between 1986 and 1995; Congress enacted the Financial Institutions Reform, Recovery and Enforcement Act of 1989 which cost taxpayers $124 billion. The UK authorized approximately £500 billion for its financial sector bail-out in October 2008. The wonders of the free market!

The Federal Reserve has conducted several rounds of asset purchases that included purchases of securities of the housing government-sponsored enterprises (GSEs). The Federal Reserve announced the first round in November 2008, which resulted in the purchase of $1.25 trillion of mortgage-backed securities (MBSs) guaranteed by Fannie Mae, Freddie Mac, and Ginnie Mae, and $172 billion of debt securities issued by the housing GSEs between January 2009 and March 2010. In September 2011, the Federal Reserve announced the second round of purchases through the reinvesting of principal payments from its holdings of GSE and Ginnie Mae securities in GSE and Ginnie Mae MBSs. In September 2012, the Federal Reserve announced that it would purchase additional agency MBSs at a pace of $40 billion a month and continue to reinvest principal payments in GSE and Ginnie MBSs.[12]

---

11   Amadeo, Kimberly, "Government Subsidies (Farm, Oil, Export, Etc)," January 16, 2020. *The Balance*. Available at: www.thebalance.com/government-subsidies-definition-farm-oil-export-etc-3305788.

12   Available at: www.fhfa.gov/DataTools/Downloads/Documents/Market-Data/Current_Market_Data-2016-02-19.pdf.

Then you also get colossal piles of garbage like the $831 billion "stimulus package" of 2009[13] based on Keynesian economic theory. To quote George Monbiot, "Every invocation of Lord Keynes is an admission of failure," and he is exactly right. Exhuming Keynes to paper over the systemic failures of neo-liberalism is hardly any kind of solution, and it's obviously proven to not even be a band-aid, unless of course you happen to be part of the infinitesimally small percentage of profiteers at the top, which is the whole point. The fact that Martin Feldstein, Larry Summers, Paul Krugman, and Joe Stiglitz all felt that the "stimulus package" was not large enough should tell you everything you need to know.

The hand-in-glove government and mega-corporations are so progressive, in fact, that billions of dollars are spent on employees – from the public trough. That's right, companies like Wal-Mart and Amazon pay their employees so little that a large percentage have to turn to public assistance to survive. In states like Arizona, one-third of Amazon employees rely on food stamps. Walmart's abysmally low wages forced workers to turn to public assistance to the tune of an estimated $6.2 billion. The American fast food industry represented a $7 billion drain in costs to taxpayers – and these are some of the nation's largest employers!

Many of these companies – not to mention some of the largest financial institutions as well – are given generous taxpayer subsidies to pad their already ludicrous profits; these include Boeing (over $13 billion), Alcoa (over $5.6 billion), Intel (almost $3.9 billion), GM ($3.5 billion), Ford (over $2.5 billion), Fiat, Nike, and Royal Dutch Shell (over $2 billion each), Nissan ($1.8 billion), and Berkshire Hathaway and IBM (over $1 billion each). Other major beneficiaries of taxpayer subsidies to the tune of hundreds of millions of dollars each include: Goldman Sachs, JP Morgan Chase, Google, Apple, Silver Lake, Disney, Morgan Stanley, Cabela's, Eli Lilly, the Blackstone Group, Comcast, Prudential, Amazon, Pfizer, ConAgra Foods, Bank of

---

13   Available at: www.cbo.gov/sites/default/files/cbofiles/attachments/02-22-ARRA.pdf.

America, Jackson Labs, Citigroup, and Nestlé.[14] Amazon has a larger net worth than all but sixteen countries on earth, and yet they paid no corporate tax in 2018[15] and had a tax rate of just 1.2% for 2019.[16] What was your income tax rate? Exactly.

Neo-liberalism as an articulated concept can be traced to Austrian Economics godfathers F.A. Hayek and Ludwig von Mises, among others, at the 1938 Walter Lippmann Colloquium. There was a divide from the beginning as a number of attendees did not see an issue with a strong state or with state intervention in quite the same way as others, especially as the ideology evolved later in the century, but the more laissez-faire camp largely predominated, at least until recently. Neo-liberalism first started gaining major traction in the 1960s, and by the 1970s, neo-liberal monetary policy had gained a foothold in Britain and America; by the 1980s with the cooption of conservatism by "neo-conservatives" and following the policies enacted by the administrations of Ronald Reagan and Margaret Thatcher, the convergence was on. As George Monbiot writes:

> After Margaret Thatcher and Ronald Reagan took power, the rest of the package soon followed: massive tax cuts for the rich, the crushing of trade unions, deregulation, privatisation, outsourcing and competition in public services. Through the IMF, the World Bank, the Maastricht treaty and the World Trade Organisation, neoliberal policies were imposed – often without democratic consent – on much of the world.[17]

---

14 Mattera, Philip, "Subsidizing the Corporate One Percent," February 2014. Good Jobs First. Available at: http://www.goodjobsfirst.org/sites/default/files/docs/pdf/subsidizingthecorporateonepercent.pdf.

15 Huddleston, Tom, "Amazon will pay $0 in federal taxes this year – and it's partially thanks to Trump," February 15, 2019. CNBC. Available at: www.cnbc.com/2019/02/15/amazon-will-pay-0-in-federal-taxes-this-year.html.

16 Myers, Kristin, "Amazon paid a 1.2% tax rate on 13,285,000,000 in profit for 2019," February 5, 2020. Yahoo Finance. Available at: https://finance.yahoo.com/news/amazon-paid-a-12-tax-rate-on-13285000000-in-profit-for-2019-210847927.html.

17 Monbiot, George, "The Zombie Doctrine," April 16, 2016. *The Guardian.* Accessed via: www.monbiot.com/2016/04/15/the-zombie-doctrine/.

There became less and less daylight between "liberal" and "conservative," especially in the Anglosphere, however many more dominoes have since fallen. It was at the turn of the millennium with the explosion of digitized mass communication aided by technological innovation, especially in the form of the internet, that neo-liberalism was sent into hyper-drive – but when by rights it should have been put to rest and forgotten in a seldom-visited graveyard in the sticks after the horrific crash of 2008 and the subsequent Great Recession, that did not happen. The Great Recession should have been catastrophic, and in a sense it was – for the middle, and working-classes. The financial fat cats made out just fine. In fact, things are going better than ever for them. All of the true costs were shunted on to the thoroughly un-exotic middle- and working-class people, and before the casket could even be closed, the gray-skinned zombie of neo-liberal economics was ambulatory with stimulus and bailout money, jaws working in anticipation of living flesh to tear into and devour.

According to Pew Research, the median net worth of American families in 2007 just prior to the housing market crash was $137,955. Just six years later, this figure had declined precipitously to $82,756.[18] In 2015, the middle class ceased being a majority in the United States for the first time. Without this inherently conservative bedrock (conservative in the truest sense) of middle- and working-class people who own property, who are invested in their community and work toward a shared destiny, and who generally reinforce traditional values, there can be no solid foundation for the nation. The profiteers do not concern themselves with the inculcation of these values from one generation to the next, though: they have no skin in the game. They can always take off and find a soft landing spot somewhere else. In their present form, most Western nation-states are not reflections of their people but rather reflections of their bureaucracies and the moneyed globalist cosmopolitans who control them. Thus the United States, for example, does not function like a traditional nation but rather as a proxy for and increasingly an extension of the defense

---

18   "The American Middle Class Is Losing Ground," December 9, 2015. Pew Research Center. Available at: www.pewsocialtrends.org/2015/12/09/5-wealth-gap-between-middle-income-and-upper-income-families-reaches-record-high/#fn-21084-46.com.

contractors, financial institutions, multi-nationals, and of course Israel. There is no respect for national sovereignty when there is money to be made, or an agenda to be executed. For the ruling class, quoting Tucker Carlson, "America is an economy with land attached; it's a massive private equity scheme from which they are benefiting, its people interchangeable human widgets to be discarded and replaced," where under the auspices of this ruthlessly exploitative system a small cabal of globalists has become unfathomably wealthy and powerful. Carlson says it best: "There is nothing free about this market."

It is confiscatory taxation that goes to subsidize mass Third World immigration to drive down labor costs and atomize communities. It is confiscatory taxation that finances deluxe professional sports stadiums and it is confiscatory taxation that builds Amazon's second headquarters – not to mention welfare for all of the Amazon and Uber employees who are unable to even earn a living wage. In short, the government is subsidizing your destruction with your time and money, which is to say that *you* are subsidizing your own destruction. Does Nike really need over $2 billion in taxpayer subsidies, or could that money be spent better elsewhere? Do Americans really need to spend between $4,000-$6,500 per illegal alien[19] to elevate crime, drive down wages and take jobs (when they have them), use the emergency room as healthcare, push out anchor babies, and send huge sums of money out of the country? In 2010, remittances to Mexico represented 2.1% of that country's GDP.[20] According to the World Bank, migrants in the West sent home $466 billion in 2017 and $485 billion in 2018. The US has been the top source of outgoing remittances for over thirty-five years; in 2017 alone, $148 billion in remittances left the country.

---

19   Bedard, Paul, "Illegal immigrants cost taxpayers $6.5k a year: Report," February 5, 2020. *Washington Examiner*. Available at: www.washingtonexaminer.com/washington-secrets/report-illegal-immigrants-cost-taxpayers-6-500-a-year-each.

20   Swanson, Ana, "Remittances: An Economist's Remedy for Organized Crime in Mexico," September 30, 2014. *Forbes*. Available at: www.forbes.com/sites/anaswanson/2014/09/30/remittances-an-economists-remedy-for-organized-crime-in-mexico/#7549eble6e6c.

In his 2018 tome *Suicide of the West,* Jonah Goldberg refers to the miracle of Western civilization as "capitalism." Capitalism is anything but a miracle, and it is telling that Goldberg uses revelatory and religious language to describe an economic system. We live today in the midst of a globalist revolution that would turn the entire planet into a strip-mall and all people like Goldberg and Ben Shapiro can do is extol the virtues of "civility" and "markets." Quoting Tucker Carlson:

Market capitalism is not a religion. Market capitalism is a tool, like a staple gun or a toaster. You'd have to be a fool to worship it. Our system was created by human beings for the benefit of human beings. We do not exist to serve markets. Just the opposite…[For Republican leaders] questioning markets feels like apostasy…For our ruling class, more investment banking is always the answer. They teach us it's more virtuous to devote your life to some soulless corporation than it is to raise your own kids…As if putting a corporation first is empowerment. It is not. It is bondage… Not all commerce is good. Why is it defensible to loan people money they can't possibly repay? Or charge them interest that impoverishes them?…Under our current system, an American who works for a salary pays about twice the tax rate as someone who's living off inherited money and doesn't work at all. We tax capital at half of what we tax labor. It's a sweet deal if you work in finance, as many of our rich people do. In 2010, for example, Mitt Romney made about $22 million dollars in investment income. He paid an effective federal tax rate of 14 percent. For normal upper-middle-class wage earners, the federal tax rate is nearly 40 percent…Our leaders rarely mention any of this. They tell us our multi-tiered tax code is based on the principles of the free market. Please. It's based on laws that the Congress passed, laws that companies lobbied for in order to increase their economic advantage. It worked well for those people. They did increase their economic advantage. But for everyone else, it came at a big cost.[21]

---

21   Carlson, Tucker, "Mitt Romney supports the status quo. But for everyone else, it's infuriating," January 3, 2019. Fox News. Available at: www.foxnews.com/opinion/tucker-carlson-mitt-romney-supports-the-status-quo-but-for-everyone-else-its-infuriating.

These neo-conservatives are particularly invested in this model of gigantic, exploitative multi-national corporations and shadowy hedge funds, but they couch this support in an appeal to the "greater good" of the planet's rising standard of living. This is a disingenuous argument on several fronts: a) this increase is from abject poverty to relative poverty; b) it comes at great cost to billions of people for the benefit, all told, of the few; and c) most of the growth is illusory, a product of proprietary trading formulas and fractional-reserve banking. In the end, the spread of unbridled capitalism comes at the ultimate price as we become even less than the sum of our parts, our very humanity stripped from us as cogs in the machine.

Even if we went full laissez-faire with no controls whatsoever, as sure as any "ideal" without a failsafe will become corrupted, the "free market" will become an oligopoly, and there are no considerations for "externalities" like the environment or social harmony besides; in its present incarnation, neo-liberalism has just seen governments hasten the process. We're now in this weird limbo of selective laissez-faire market capitalism glomming on to Keynesian solutions as a kind of duct tape to prevent the whole crony system from coming coming apart at the seams, one foot in each of the Walter Lippmann Colloquium camps as the worst of both worlds with the worm-eaten brain of the Frankfurt School.

I have an alternate title to propose for Mr. Goldberg: *The Soul-Killing Guide to Conservatism.* The introduction would be a haughty dismissal of the white working class, possibly going so far as to advocate for their complete replacement a la Bill Kristol, or for their death a la Kevin Williamson. Next: the virtues of global free trade, endless wars for Israel, de-stabilizing regime change, open borders, and identity politics for me but not for thee. Oh, that's what the book *is* about. Never mind. As Paul Gottfried brutally excoriated Goldberg's nonsense for the Unz Review:

For his newest venture into deep thought, Goldberg has crassly stolen the title of James Burnham's great work, *Suicide of the West* published in 1964 at the height of the Cold War. That is where the similarity ends. Unlike Burnham's scalding indictment of liberalism as "the ideology of Western suicide," Goldberg's random opinions represent the very pathology that Burnham railed against. Goldberg hates national identities (although he makes an exception for Israel), opponents of the Deep State, immigration patriots, and those who imagine that democracy has something to do with the popular will. Rather his "conservative" view of democracy privileges public administration, the operation of multinational corporations, and socially sophisticated journalists such as himself.[22]

Naturally Goldberg would not bite the hand that feeds, and as an extension of the Establishment pretending to be the opposition, he, like Shapiro and the Turning Point USA and UK groups, is able to funnel productive energies in opposition to the unhinged Left into what several commentators have referred to as transformation at the speed limit. Turning Point UK's leadership actually favors increased immigration. With its acceptance of transgenderism and warm embrace of intersectionality, it is just neo-liberalism without the abortions and some of the most extreme rhetorical excesses.

The globalists view our nations as carcasses to be stripped bare and then reanimated as neo-liberal zombies. "Conservatives" offer no resistance. They simply accept the premises of corrosive liberalism at a decade-and-a-half delay. There is nothing conservative about sacrificing your progeny to the open-mouthed furnace of Baal. What we are witnessing, then, is at once The Convergence (in ideology, in the locus of control) and The Divergence (of man from community, man from identity, man from self, man from meaning). "Diversity" signals a complete uniformity. Multi-culturalism makes everywhere exactly the same. War is peace. Freedom is slavery. Ignorance is strength. Repeat the talking points *ad infinitum*. The One Percent, which is more appropriately the Naught-Point-Two Percent, stands to gain while everyone else loses.

---

22 Gottfried, Paul, "'Suicide of the West' – or of Conservatism?" May 16, 2018. *Unz Review*. Available at: www.unz.com/pgottfried/gottfried-on-goldberg-suicide-of-the-west-or-of-conservatism/.

This is a system that, when it isn't neglecting the people it's supposed to protect, is actively working to dispossess and even replace them. Far be it from the founding ideals of a government for the people by the people, its endless bureaucracies and the professional political and pundit class run cover for the plutocrats. These people live a life a world away from their countrymen, and have grown so estranged they no longer view themselves as citizens of the same country. Many of them, in fact, are not, but what unites these "citizens of the world" is not just the belief that they have transcended borders, but nature itself.

The white working class that actually builds the infrastructure, fights the wars for, and feeds the country is reviled by these cosmopolitan "elites." So divorced are they from any of the negative ramifications of their terribly destructive policies that the plight of their countrymen in the blasted mid-sized cities, coal country, and steel country, the men and women who make their living with their hands, on a boat, under a car – they register not, unless as a subject of gleeful derision and mockery. They *hate* you, but – projection and displacement – *you* are the hater for wanting a job and a country to call your own, and for the temerity of asking to be treated with dignity. Perhaps we ought to stop being so polite.

While conservatives of yore sought to combat the very real and very significant threat of communism, they failed to notice two things: one, that its practitioners had also colonized their own countries, and two, who, exactly, was behind the introduction of these spores of communism. While the West ultimately triumphed over the USSR, it may well be that the ghosts of Lenin and company have the last laugh. In many ways, life in the West is worse than it was in the Eastern Bloc. Such a comparison may seem totally baseless – we have plenty of *stuff* after all – but advance just one unpopular opinion about race, sex, and the like and watch what happens to your gainful employment, your placid home life, and your ability to even cash a check. The totalitarianism is more sinister precisely because it is more covert and because it is more invasive. Don't like it? Build your own platform. Ask the founders of Gab how that went when the "free" market is an oligopoly with government-guaranteed winners and losers.

On the other side, the Left has taken a triple-shower in "critical theory," whereby the economic issues were more or less washed off and social, racial, and cosmic inequalities became the center of their grievances. Actual concern for labor vanished, and the modern Left has become medievalist with its notions of original sin ("privilege" and "whiteness"), and its support for plantation economics. They literally want to own you. The Left is comprised of the extremely wealthy and the throngs of dependents and hyper-consumers they would deign to rule. They support a system where capital is only taxed at half the rate of labor and the ever-shrinking middle- and working-classes bear an ever-increasing share of the burden. These cosmic scapegoats finance their own dispossession through onerous taxes and wealth redistribution while they are harried and harassed into oblivion from above *and* below.

This is not to rail against taxation as such, but rather to point out that when a government is working *against* you, not for you, taxation can be seen in no other light. Like many former libertarians, I once believed strongly that limited government was the only answer to ensure maximal individual liberty, failing to consider that: a) a limited government is not necessarily a just government; b) government is not the only source of tyranny; c) the cultural default to at least nominal liberalism inevitably deteriorates into naked self-interest and the abdication of responsibility and duty; d) voluntarily abdicating power only leaves a power vacuum someone else will fill; and finally, e) power itself is the ultimate guarantor of rights, and the derivation or source of power is through superior force. For any power to be legitimate, however, its source must be the people it would deign to rule. In other words, the only legitimate government for any nation must not only come from the people who comprise that nation, it must govern for the people who comprise that nation. Any other government is illegitimate. As such, nationalism, localism, and particularism are anathema to neo-liberalism.

The "antiquated" nation-state has no place in this new paradigm where nations are considered nothing but markets; in light of the recent populist revolution in Italy, European Union Budget Commissioner Gunther

Oettinger announced his displeasure at the rise of Italian populist parties stating the economics would "signal to voters not to hand power to populists" before re-tweeting, "The markets will teach Italy to vote for the right thing." Ah yes, the markets. According to the International Monetary Fund (IMF), Spain needs five-and-a-half million additional "migrants" to pay for its pensions, despite the fact that the country's youth unemployment rate is consistently north of 40% and eclipsed 50% from 2012-2015 with a high of nearly 58% in 2014, and with 4.23 million total Spaniards unemployed at the end of 2016, but still they "need" millions more migrants. Why?

This also despite the fact that Europe's "migrants," far from being a boon to the economy, represent a lead weight on the state's checkbook. In order to circumvent the illegality of collecting ethnic statistics, a group of French economists used national origin on the country's census to estimate youth unemployment amongst African immigrants at 32%. The French bureaucrats don't make anything, aside from enabling migrants to torch Citroens (about 40,000 cars are burned a year) and rape women (a sexual assault occurs every forty minutes), easy. Granted, France is suffering from extremely high levels of unemployment in general, and youth unemployment specifically, and indeed the bulk of the Mediterranean nations are being slammed by sky-high youth unemployment rates, but the migrant trend toward unemployment and receiving of state benefits is consistent across Europe and the West. Additionally, the OECD found that 40% of the youth unemployment in France is attributable to "migrants."[23]

85% of "migrants" in the Netherlands were unemployed as of mid-2018, and of the paltry 15% actually employed, most of those were in part-time work.[24] In mid-June 2017, the German unemployment rate for

23 Tomlinson, Chris, "France: Migrants Make Up 40% of Unemployed Youth," January 22, 2019. *Breitbart*. Available at: www.breitbart.com/ europe/2019/01/22/migrants-make-up-40-percent-french-unemployed-youth/.

24 Hale, Virginia, "Netherlands: 85% of refugees still unemployed," May 8, 2018. *Breitbart*. Available at: www.breitbart.com/europe/2018/05/02/netherlands-85-refugees-unemployed/.

their "refugees" was 83%.[25] Economist Bernd Raffelhüschen estimates the long-term cost of the 2015 "migrants" to Germany alone to be €878 billion, and a second major economist, Hans-Werner Sinn, has come out and pinned the long-term cost of the 2015 "migrant crisis" at potentially almost €1 trillion. Raffelhüschen believes that this figure could possibly balloon up to €1.5 trillion.[26] Of all "totally dependent families" in Denmark (married couples where both partners are on welfare), 84% are "non-Western origin migrants."[27] The most extreme case is the 99.7% unemployment rate from that particular batch of faux-refugees in Sweden measured the year after their influx.[28] That is 494 employed asylum-seekers out of almost 163,000. Perhaps more have found steady employment since, but the numbers suggest if they did, it was not in large numbers.

According to the OECD, the average asylum applicant in Europe costs around €10,000 per application for the first year, but "this figure can be significantly higher if integration support is already provided during the asylum phase." For refugees, the OECD admits the costs are higher.[29] German "migrant" expenses increased 11% in 2018 from 2017; housing and "integration" costs rose 14% and expenses aimed at keeping these migrants out rose 16%.[30] Oddly, still they come. It

---

25   Chazan, Guy, "Most refugees to be jobless for years, German minister warns," June 22, 2017. *Financial Times*. Available at: www.ft.com/content/022de0a4-54f4-11e7-9fed-c19e2700005f.

26   Oliphant, Vickiie and Monika Pallenberg, "Germany Woes Continues: Migrant crisis to cost Merkel's government over a trillion pounds," July 21, 2016. *Express*. Available at: www.express.co.uk/news/world/691638/Germany-migrant-crisis-immigration-economy-trillion-pounds.

27   Lane, Oliver J.J., "In Denmark, 84 Per Cent of Welfare Recipients are 'Non-Western Immigrants,'" March 17, 2016. *Breitbart*. Available at: www.breitbart.com/europe/2016/03/17/in-denmark-84-per-cent-of-welfare-recipients-are-non-western-immigrants/.

28   Available at: www.thelocal.se/20160531/fewer-than-500-of-163000-asylum-seekers-found-jobs.

29   "Who bears the cost of integrating refugees?" January 2017. OECD. *Migration Policy Debates*, No. 13. Available at: www.oecd.org/els/mig/migration-policy-debates-13.pdf.

30   Nienaber, Michael, "Germany spends record 23 bln euros on refugees: document," May 20, 2019. Reuters. Available at: www.reuters.com/article/

can't be the lavish benefits they can expect to receive, right? 19% of Sweden's annual budget (3.2% of its GDP) was ear-marked for "refugee benefits" in 2017, or $58,490 per "refugee." As a point of contrast, Swedes have an average of $28,859 in annual disposable income.[31] In Germany, an average of $48,000 is spent per migrant on housing subsidies. Almost a full quarter of the Danish budget goes toward its "migrants." Supposedly these costs are meant to decline over time as the refugees integrate, but do they? Per Morten Uhrskov Jensen, third-generation immigrants to Denmark are *still* less self-sufficient than native Danes, utterly obliterating the narrative that migration is necessary to prop up the welfare state, as they represent a multi-generational drain on taxpayer resources before even considering the tremendous social costs and, most importantly, whether they have any right to be there in the first place.

Neo-liberalism is predicated on exponential growth, swelling and consuming everything in its outward expansion, but on a finite planet with finite resources, this is an obvious problem, with consequences ranging from the relatively minor (longer commutes and other inconveniences) to the potentially catastrophic (finite resources and space combined with artificially-subsidized mass population growth, dysgenic reproductive habits, and excess consumption equating to a veritable Malthusian nightmare of ecological devastation, mass die-offs, and extinction). It increasingly subsists on the intangible, from the ideological ("invisible structures of racism") to the economic (carbon trading). All become articles of faith, a curious quirk in an irreligious and materialist system that seeks to sever roots and, indeed, play God with the very fabric of reality.

We might even go so far as to say that the implementation and expansion of neo-liberalism has proven apocalyptic, at least in the sense that its demise is now guaranteed. The liberal moment

us-germany-budget-refugees/germany-spends-record-23-billion-euros-on-refugees-migration-document-idUSKCN1SQ182.

31 Morrison, Spencer P., "Refugees Will Cost Sweden $18.6 Billion This Year – 9.3x Its Budget," February 10, 2017. *National Economics Editorial.* Available at: https://nationaleconomicseditorial.com/2017/02/10/sweden-migrant-crime-cost/.

is already passing, done in by its own worst excesses. The truly apocalyptic in the form of racial and civilizational extinction is not off the table, though. Things really do have the potential to get that bad. Consider that although a red giant star, for example, has greatly expanded in radius, this is not a harbinger of growth as we might understand it, but is actually an indication that the star is dying. In times of great instability – at the ends of eras – millenarian movements often proliferate; the spread of millenarian movements and ideologies, from "social justice" to the Islamic State, reflects a period of growing instability across the globe as the old social order rapidly comes undone. Paradoxically, power and control are increasingly in the hands of the few.

On some level, the average person intrinsically understands that despite the absurdity of Council on Foreign Relations member Francis Fukuyama's claim that the demise of the Soviet Union represented "the end of history" and the ultimate victory of the obscene misnomer "liberal democracy," that is far from the truth. It was the end of an era, to be sure, and a temporary triumph allowing "liberal democracy" to run roughshod over the globe, but that era is, too, drawing to a close. The world is becoming tri-polar as opposed to uni-polar; "liberal democracy" is but one pole and a decreasingly cohesive one at that. Russia and its pro-nationalist axis, including Syria and Iran, is another, and the managed economy of China is the third. Where China is aggressively expansionist at the expense of other ethnic groups, Russia appears to be pursuing a policy more along the lines of 1930s Germany, with an emphasis on ethnic re-unification and an autarkic economy.

Of the three, neo-liberalism under the guise of liberal democracy is very clearly the most insidious. The wholesale replacement of populations as occurs under the banner of "free trade" or "human rights" is unprecedented in human history and produces a level of misery and genocide the likes of which humanity may never recover from. This is not to excuse or ignore the Han Chinese expansion project, but rather that it must be understood in context; Han expansion is enabled by the neo-liberal system they exploit to their benefit.

The much-vaunted "democracy" of neo-liberalism is only democratic when it aligns with the goals and desires of the ruling class. Otherwise it is an impediment to "progress" and the will of the people is subverted (think: Brexit, the Mueller investigation of so-called Russian Collusion in the election of Donald Trump and the subsequent impeachment fiasco, and even the attempt to depose Bashar al-Assad). Majority rule is conveniently supported when there is a white minority to destroy, such as in South Africa or Rhodesia, but minority rights are the order of the day in white nations – until those white populations are themselves a minority, in which case the script will flip.

There is no democratic solution within the confines of the system as it is constructed today because the game is rigged. Access to power is restricted and information control remains the exclusive province of the Establishment. We have no institutional power, and even more crucially in the neo-liberal system, we have no *financial* power.

The neo-liberal model is in practice defined by its combination of crony capitalist economics with extreme Cultural Marxist social reengineering and wholesale population replacement. It cultivates and encourages all of the worst impulses of humanity with the constant refrain of more, more, *more*. Its engine runs on lust for power and control, greed, extreme in-group favoritism, and a dark undercurrent of spite few want to acknowledge for the truth is so ugly. But confront it we must, and that, Dear Reader, is the essence of the book in your hands.

This book will be divided into the two major aspects of the neo-liberal system: ideology and economics. Neo-liberalism as an economic system and liberalism as a social ideology work brilliantly together, and they amplify each other and work synergistically. In the case of the 2007-08 financial crisis, the housing market crash, and the Great Recession, the government was able to use taxpayers' largesse to off-set the damage done to the corporations and the lenders, CEOs awarded themselves giant pay raises for a job well done, and the permanent bureaucracy and politicians made sure all the right people were taken care of, including themselves. It is the worst of both worlds: a government unafraid to "play God" – going so far as to generate an entirely new population amenable to their designs – and an oligarchic set of international bankers and businessmen who've seen to it that the game is rigged in their favor.

The 2007 tremors in the financial world became the global earthquake of 2008, but the ruling class rebuilt on the same site with the same rickety foundation. The coronavirus pandemic of 2020 showed once again just how fragile the whole system is, and how much of the economy is built on a house of cards: the growth of money from money, of compound interest compounding fantastical unsustainable delusions, but it's just rearranging deck chairs on the Titanic. Most people know that something is deeply wrong, but they haven't the vocabulary or full understanding of this invisible system that wants to keep them tethered to the sinking "unsinkable" ship.

It is my aim with this book to drag the hideous "nameless" system causing such devastation into the light so that this heretofore largely-invisible engine of destruction can finally be seen in all its grisly detail. Only when we have identified our enemy can we ever hope to launch a successful counter-attack.

Part One: Ideology

Chapter 1 - The Equality Lie

"Reality must take precedence over public relations, for nature cannot be fooled."— Richard Feynman

The first and most obvious lie of liberalism is that which, albeit increasingly selectively, undergirds the whole ideology: that all people are equal. No two people are equal, let alone entire population groups. We all have different strengths and weaknesses, and yet we are incessantly treated to the usual pablum about diversity right alongside equality. It makes no sense, because even if we were talking about equal worth – equal in God's eyes – the relativistic nature of our "discourse" (insofar as the idiocy that passes for mainstream discourse can be called that) is a moonscape of cratered unevenness. The whole thing is fraught with contradiction. The notion of equality-as-interchangeable is brilliant for the ruling class from a neo-liberal economics perspective, one which the social aspect greases the skids for, but we will get to that later.

Today, any kind of frank realism – about race, about sex, about economics – the Left wants to obfuscate. Read any academic journal and most of the jargon is incomprehensible, the logic circular, the theses hyper-specific yet oddly abstract. There are inherent contradictions built in to the model that go unchallenged when the entire cultural default has been set to universalism-with-an-asterisk. Today's orthodoxy holds that human beings are exactly the same and thus inter-changeable, unless of course they happen to bear the White Mark of Cain; by the same token the unique and "diverse" non-white and non-hetero-normative possess a kind of divine spark in their equality. It makes no sense on its face when divorced from the obvious agenda. Race, sex, and the like are not scientifically-measurable barometers that can help explain why, say, men are stronger than women, or why European men are responsible for such a large percentage of the globe's discoveries and innovations – only the ubiquitous White Male's evil

27

machinations will suffice as an explanation. Ironically, most of the delusions that presently animate the social aspect of neo-liberalism are derived from an Enlightenment tradition of white male thinkers; these men generally did not have the entire globe's populations in mind – let alone replacing their own – when they set quill to paper. Additionally, there was far more of a dialogue on the nature of man than someone like Dave Rubin would have you believe – for every John Locke there was a Thomas Hobbes. Granted, even the most damaging ideas put forth by Jean-Jacques Rousseau and the Sephardic Baruch Spinoza are not directly taught in school anymore as DEMs (Dead European Males) are rendered persona non grata, but the ideological basis for liberalism was provided by these men centuries ago.

What's become of liberalism is a grotesque distortion such that the majority of Enlightenment thinkers would find it unrecognizable, which is not to say that all or even most of the premises were correct in the first place, but cherry-picked and often corrupted Enlightenment ideals of liberty and equality, along with a reversion to the inherent universalism of Christianity minus the infusion of indigenous European energies (and paradoxically a concomitant *abandonment* of Christianity by many), the transference of the religious impulse to "social justice," the late-stage empire blues, the ennui and apathy of material excess, whites' natural predispositions to altruism and a relatively weaker sense of kinship ties, and the profoundly negative influence of subversive interlopers at every level of society, among other factors, have all contributed to the mutation before us today.

There are many convergent factors that have contributed to our civilizational ennui, factors that have, in varying degrees, been acting upon the West for at least a century, if not all the way back into the Enlightenment. Diversity and multi-culturalism may be more recent, but they are symptoms born from the same disease. The rank-and-file "progressives" believe that we are in a post-tribal society; we have post-tribal means of transport and post-tribal technologies in this increasingly inter-connected world, but our brains are very, very far from being post-tribal. It's a nice sentiment, this One World-ism, but in application it leads only to conflict, dereliction, and misery.

The moral imperative of eliminating slavery as an institution was spear-headed by Western nations, who committed great time, energy, and resources to bringing about its terminus, though you would be hard-pressed to say they have been justly rewarded for their trouble. Instead, they find themselves in the position of cosmic scapegoat for any and all ills befalling and shortcomings of the deified "people of color." We're told to just shut up and move aside, or even more macabre, just die already.

The Left uses idealism and utopian rhetoric in order to mask their cravenness, greed, and malice. The Left has been wildly successful in not only framing the "debate," but in defining its terminology. This is particularly vital when we consider that the highest ethical organization of peoples is along hereditary national lines (ie-Hungary for Hungarians, Quebec for Quebecois, Scotland for Scottish, etc.), but the frame is that the highly disruptive movement of peoples – which is also terrible for the environment – and "humanitarian" regime change wars are defined as moral and virtuous; similarly, the Chinese, with their deplorable human rights record, highly censorious regime, and mass amount of pollution are given a pass simply because they have moneyed interests in the West and they are not white or Christian.

As both Joe Sobran and Peter Brimelow have noted, there is little conception of or true linguistic equivalent to white racism or "xenophobia" – the immigration and diversity conversation is only ever allowed to exist in one particular context, one where Ricardo Duchesne says, "negative effects on whites count as evidence that whites are not accepting diversity and that they need more education on the merits of diversity and the perils of racism." This kind of dis-arming propaganda has deep roots, and it has been devastatingly effective. Civilization is inextricable from its people. Maybe a minority adapt and even come to cherish a civilization that is not "theirs" as such, but a majority never have and never will accept what is fundamentally alien to them. And why would they? They are not "of" the people that built it. Before we decide to "restore our civilization with someone else's babies," to borrow from Iowa Representative Steve King, we should look long and hard at the reality of what we are importing en masse.

Coming less than two weeks after news that the Nigerian Mafia butchered and possibly dined on a young Italian girl in early 2018, another horrific story of cannibalism emerged, this time from the Parisian suburbs. Three men were arrested on February 19th in Clichy-sous-Bois, a notorious No-Go Zone, after a back-alley altercation allegedly over money resulted in pieces of a fourth man's ears and lips being bitten off and swallowed. The perpetrators all hail from Cape Verde, an island country off the west coast of Africa. The ethnicity of the victim, due to typical French bureaucratic obscurantism, is unknown. While it would be tempting to dismiss these gruesome events as outliers, the preponderance of evidence suggests otherwise. The Leopard Society, operating out of West Africa – Sierra Leone, Nigeria, the Ivory Coast, and Liberia primarily – would capture and dismember people, and share the flesh with each other, in the belief that they could absorb energy from the victim and it would strengthen them as warriors. In countries like Tanzania, the dismemberment of albinos, and often ingestion of their flesh, is conducted by witch doctors, and the deceased albinos' limbs are sold as good luck charms. Ugandan dictator Idi Amin was very fond of human flesh, and the Lord's Resistance Army operating out of that nation and several others has been known to practice "magical cannibalism." On October 24th, 1986, the self-declared Emperor of the Central African Empire, Jean-Bédel Bokassa (Emperor Bokassa I), stood trial, though was never convicted, of eating several people. In the years since, the Muslim minority has routinely been victimized by cannibalism in the Central African Republic. Forced cannibalism was common practice during the Liberian, Congolese, Sierra Leonean, and Sudanese civil wars.

There have been several reports out of the Congo that the Mbuti Pygmies are being treated as a perverse kind of delicacy – and that these Pygmies are typically eaten alive. Seven South African men were arrested and tried in 2017 for working with a traditional healer to lure women, rape them, and then consume their flesh. They allegedly fed this flesh to as many as three hundred other people. Dr. Gwyn Campbell, writing in *The South African Medical Journal*, notes that traditionally in South Africa and Madagascar, people would (and often continue to) practice two kinds of cannibalism, "Exocannibalism, where enemies were consumed, and endocannibalism, where dead relatives were eaten to assist their passing to the world of the ancestors, or to prolong contact with beloved and admired family members and absorb their good qualities." Endocannibalism is widely practiced in Burundi, where deceased relatives are eaten in the belief that doing so will also allow for the ingestion of said relative's hunting prowess. In parts of Kenya, like Tanzania, albino cannibalism is practiced under the belief that it will bring wealth and good fortune. Among the Luhya tribe in Kenya, it is believed that eating the genitals of a young virgin male will cure AIDS. In 2016, Eritrean human trafficker "The General" Medhanie Yehdego Mered was apprehended carrying a cellphone that featured graphic images and video of migrants' executions and the consumption of their flesh and sale of their organs. Mered is associated with a substantial trafficking network primarily operating out of Africa and into Italy.

Back in 2003, eleven arrests were made of "black magic" practitioners in Cameroon who had murdered and eaten the organs of seventeen victims. Eleven arrests were made in Nigeria in 2014 at a restaurant that was serving roasted human heads as a delicacy. In 2017, a South African man was executed by police after he refused to stop eating a woman that he had decapitated. Also that year in South Africa, an uncle killed his four-year-old nephew and made him into a stew. Teodoro Obiang Nguema Mbasogo, the resident dictator of Equatorial Guinea, has been known to torture political opponents to death and eat their testicles and brains.

Cannibalism is of course not limited to Africa, either. There have been recent reports of its practice in Syria, Iraq, India, Laos, Cambodia, Indonesia, Myanmar, and Pakistan, and we are all likely familiar with the long-standing Papua New Guinean tradition of exocannibalism (often witnessed throughout Polynesia). So in addition to soaring crime rates, acid attacks, sexual assaults, pedophilia, the erosion of cultural capital, plus bestiality brothels and the depressingly regular little horrors like a Syrian migrant being detained for raping a pony at a children's petting zoo in Germany, we also have another "benefit" of diversity to add to the list—cannibalism! This is precisely what you can expect when your leaders decide your replacement population will be the same people who waltz with the dead as the Madagascans do during Famadihana – which unsurprisingly has led to several recurrences of the Black Death.

Speaking of the Black Death, diseases like the bubonic plague and others have made a roaring comeback in the United States since borders stopped being a thing. Hepatitis A and semen-tainted flutes carrying who-knows-what in California, tuberculosis and leprosy in West Texas, the bubonic plague in New Mexico...Long-eradicated or steeply declining diseases are re-emerging in the United States for one primary reason: un-trammeled immigration. We certainly should not lament our ability to globe-trot, and there are wont to be exotic diseases contracted by travelers even if precautions are taken, but the central concern is that there has been a sharp rise in communicable diseases that no Westerner should ever be exposed to on their home soil. The core of the problem is that our non-existent borders can allow anyone to just waltz on in. Strong borders are vital to national survival for many reasons, not least of which is the health of a nation's citizens. If you import the Third World, you become the Third World. It really is that simple.

Globally about half of all Muslim marriages are consanguineous (blood related), usually between first cousins or an uncle and niece, while the rate is about 1% in Europe (largely attributable to the "migrants") and 0.2% in the US. The consequences can be severe. Medical data show that while British Pakistanis are 3% of all births in the country, they account for over 30% of children in the UK born with genetic illnesses, costing the NHS at least about £600 million per annum.[1] A 2005 survey found that 55% of Britain's Pakistani population was married to a first cousin;[2] in Pakistan itself, 70% of all marriages are consanguineous. British geneticist Steve Jones explains:

---

1   Gardham, Duncan, "Warning over births to first cousin marriage," December 29, 2008. *The Telegraph*. Available at: www.telegraph.co.uk/women/mother-tongue/4014743/Warning-over-births-to-first-cousin-marriages.html.

2   Lall, Rashmee Roshan, "Ban UK Pakistanis from marrying cousins," November 16, 2005. *The Times of India*. Available at: https://timesofindia. indiatimes.com/world/rest-of-world/Ban-UK-Pakistanis-from-marrying-cousins/articleshow/1298135.cms?.

It is common in the Islamic world to marry your brother's daughter, which is actually closer than marrying your cousin. We should be concerned about that as there can be a lot of hidden genetic damage. Children are much more likely to get two copies of a damaged gene.[3]

Consanguineous marriages result in an average IQ deficit of about 15 points. The risk for having an IQ lower than 70 increases by 400% among the offspring of first cousin marriages. It also increases aggression, lowers impulse control, and dramatically elevates the risk of a whole host of medical disorders. The Danish "migrant" community offers another illuminating case study. From the newspaper *Jydskevestkysten*:

> Immigrant children are clearly overrepresented on Copenhagen's schools for retarded children and children with physical handicaps...51% of the children in the three schools in Copenhagen for children with physical and mental handicaps have an immigrant background and in one of the schools the amount is 70 percent...These amounts are significantly higher than the share of immigrant children in the municipality, which is 33 percent. The many handicapped children provide clear evidence that there are many intermarried parents in the immigrant families.[4]

From *B.T.:*

> Disabled immigrant children cost Danish municipalities millions. In Copenhagen County alone, the number of disabled children has increased 100% in 10 years...[Social worker] Meredith Lefelt has contacted 330 families with disabled children in Copenhagen. She estimates that one third of their clients have a foreign cultural background.[5]

---

3   Wynne-Jones, Jonathan, "Hay Festival 2011: Professor risks political storm over Muslim 'inbreeding,'" May 29, 2011. *The Telegraph*. Available at: www. telegraph.co.uk/culture/hay-festival/8544359/Hay-Festival-2011-Professor-risks-political-storm-over-Muslim-inbreeding.html.

4   Available at: https://nordjyske.dk/indland/forside?ctrl=10&data=2%2c3195839 %2c5%2c2&count=1.

5   Available at: www.bt.dk/nyheder/indvandreres-indavl-koster-millioner.

The Rockwool Foundation Research Unit found that:

Those who speak Arabic with their parents have an extreme tendency to lack reading abilities – 64% are illiterate. ... No matter if it concerns reading abilities, mathematics or science, the pattern is the same: The bilingual (largely Muslim) immigrants' skills are exceedingly poor compared to their Danish classmates.[6]

From *Kristeligt Dagblad*:

In Sct. Hans Hospital, which has the biggest ward for clinically insane criminals in Denmark, more than 40% of the patients have an immigrant background.[7]

In Denmark, the number of inbred Muslims ranges from Pakistanis at 40% to Turks at 15%. The rate of inbreeding in Turkey itself is about 25-30%. For Islam, this is pretty low. While in India, the Muslim rate of cousin marriage is 22%, the rate spikes to 40% in Jammu and Kashmir. Between 20-28% of Morocco's marriages are of the cousin variety. 34% of all marriages in Algeria are consanguine, with Tunisia at 39% and Syria at 40%. About 40% of the population marries a cousin in Egypt, according to a 2016 report in *The Economist*. "Rates are thought to be even higher in tribal countries such as Iraq and the Gulf states of Saudi Arabia, Yemen and Kuwait," says *The Economist*.

Statistical research on Muslim-majority countries shows that up to 42% of all marriages in Lebanon are consanguine (blood related), as are 45% in Yemen, 46% in Bahrain, 47% in Mauritania, 48% in Libya, 54% in Qatar, 54% in the United Arabic Emirates, 56% in Oman, 60% in Iraq, 63% in Sudan, 64% in Jordan, 64% in Kuwait, 66% in Palestine, and 68% in Saudi Arabia. In the region of Nubia, it is an astronomical 80%. Arabs have one of the world's highest rates of genetic disorders, with 66% of the abnormalities linked to cousin marriage. A Saudi study discovered that "90% of couples detected as

---

6   Available at: http://www.bkchefer.dk/uploads/File/Rockwoolfonden.pdf.

7   Available   at: www.kristeligt-dagblad.dk/liv-sj%C3%A6l/etniske-minoriteter-overrepr%C3%A6senteret-i-retspsykiatrien.

carriers did not follow the advice they were given and went ahead with their marriages."[8] Executive Director of the Prince Salman Center for Disability Research, geneticist Dr. Stephen R. Schroeder, stated:

Saudi Arabia is a living genetics laboratory. Here you can look at 10 families to study genetic disorders, where you would need 10,000 families to study disorders in the United States.[9]

In Afghanistan, where 46% of the marriages are consanguineous,[10] Danish psychologist Nicolai Sennels discusses some of the consequences:

A study from Kabul, Afghanistan, based on autopsies of the remains of suicide bombers, shows that close to 90% were suffering from severe illnesses or deficiencies such as blindness, cancer, missing limbs or leprosy. Many Muslim societies, including that of Afghanistan, have a low social acceptance of handicaps and mental illness. Being physically handicapped or mentally retarded often leads to exclusion. Becoming a martyr may be the only chance of achieving social recognition and honor. Some cases of Down's syndrome may be another unpleasant effect of inbreeding and al-Qaeda has been known to use people afflicted with it.[11]

The numbers for consanguinity in some Muslim nations such as Indonesia, Niger, Djibouti, Somalia, and Bangladesh are woefully incomplete, though we do know that 17.6% of marriages in the Teknaf region of Bangladesh are consanguineous. 37.5% of Iran's marriages are consanguineous, as are between 65.8% and 71% of Burkina Faso's

---

8   Available at: http://jms.rsmjournals.com/content/16/1/22.full.

9   Kershaw, Sarah, "Saudi Arabia Awakes to the Perils of Inbreeding," May 1, 2003. *The New York Times*. Available at: www.nytimes.com/2003/05/01/world/saudi-arabia-awakes-to-the-perils-of-inbreeding.html.

10   Saify, K. and M. Saadat, "Consanguineous marriages in Afghanistan," January 2012. *Journal of Biosocial Science*, 44 (1). Available at: www.ncbi.nlm.nih.gov/pubmed/21729362.

11   Available at: https://muslimstatistics.wordpress.com/2013/05/28/danish-psychologist-serious-consequences-of-muslim-inbreeding/.

Fulani's and 27% of Mali's (admittedly a small sample at just 600 persons).[12,13,14] We do not know the percentage of Azerbaijani marriages of this kind, but there is a tradition of inter-marriage, and a prevalence of certain diseases and disorders common to this practice.[15] 30-35% of birth defects in Tajikistan are attributable to kin marriage.[16] 35-50% of sub-Saharan African marriages regardless of religion are estimated to be between blood relations, although Islam may be viewed as an exacerbating factor; Nigeria's rate, for example, is highly variable depending on the tribe: Hausa (percentage unknown) and Yoruba (51.2%) practice it; the Igbo ban it.

Rima Khalaf Hunaidi, Assistant Secretary-General and Director of the Regional Bureau for Arab States (RBAS) at the United Nations Development Program (UNDP), and her team of Arab researchers found that roughly the same number of books are translated within the country of Spain annually as have been translated into Arabic in the last 1,200 years. Their 2002 Arab Human Development Report (AHDR), citing the 1999 study Translation in the Arab Homeland: Reality and Challenge, states that, "The Arab world translates about 330 books annually, one fifth of the number that Greece translates. The cumulative total of translated books since the Caliph Maa'moun's time [813-833 AD] is about 100,000, almost the average that Spain

12   Saadat, M., M. Ansari-Lari, and D.D. Farhud, "Consanguineous marriage in Iran," 2004. *Annals of Human Biology*, Vol. 31. Available at: www.tandfonline.com/doi/abs/10.1080/03014460310001652211?journalCode=iahb20.

13   Hampshire, Kate and Malcolm T. Smith, "Consanguineous Marriage among the Fulani," September 2001. *Human Biology* 73 (4). Available at: www.researchgate.net/publication/11832150_Consanguineous_Marriage_among_the_Fulani.

14   Landoure, Guida, et al., "Genetics and genomic medicine in Mali: challenges and future perspectives," March 2016. *Molecular Genetic Genomic Medicine*, March 2016 4 (2). Available at: www.ncbi.nlm.nih.gov/pmc/articles/PMC4799869/#__ffn_sectitle.

15   Aghayeva, Izolda, "Inter-family marriages in Azerbaijan: a dangerous tradition," August 22, 2017. *JAM News*. Available at: https://jam-news.net/inter-family-marriages-in-azerbaijan-a-dangerous-tradition/.

16   Karim, Orzu, "Couples Rush To Altar To Beat Tajik Marriage Ban," June 30, 2016. Radio Free Europe. Available at: www.rferl.org/a/tajikistan-weddings-between-cousins-new-law-marriage/27830125.html.

translates in one year." From the *Nature International Journal of Science:*

> In 2003, the world average for production of articles per million inhabitants was 137, whereas none of the 47 OIC countries for which there were data achieved production above 107 per million inhabitants. The OIC average was just 13.[17]

Minus a few outliers, our indiscriminate immigration policy means that we are not importing the engineers of tomorrow, and despite all protestations to the contrary, mass immigration *does* make our countries dirtier and more diseased and violent. The twenty worst cities globally for air pollution are: Onitsha (Nigeria), Peshawar (Pakistan), Zabol (Iran), Rawalpindi (Pakistan), Kaduna (Nigeria), Aba (Nigeria), Riyadh (Saudi Arabia), Al Jubail (Saudi Arabia), Mazar-e Sharif (Afghanistan), Gwalior (India), Hamad Town (Bahrain), Allahabad (India), Shijiazhuang (China), Karachi (Pakistan), Dammam (Saudi Arabia), Umuahia (Nigeria), Raipur (India), Kabul (Afghanistan), Ma'ameer (Bahrain), and Boshehr (Iran). The nations with the highest levels of air pollution are: Saudi Arabia, Qatar, Egypt, Bangladesh, Kuwait, Cameroon, United Arab Emirates, Nepal, India, and Libya. The top five nations with the highest carbon dioxide emissions per capita are: Qatar, Kuwait, Bahrain, United Arab Emirates, and Trinidad and Tobago. The nations with the most deaths from air pollution are: Turkmenistan, Tajikistan, Uzbekistan, Egypt, China, Mongolia, Kazakhstan, India, Iraq, and Saudi Arabia. The twenty countries with the most polluted urban areas are: Pakistan, Qatar, Afghanistan, Bangladesh, Egypt, United Arab Emirates, Mongolia, India, Bahrain, Nepal, Ghana, Jordan, China, Senegal, Turkey, Bulgaria, Mauritius, Peru, Serbia, and Iran.

According to the World Health Organization data spanning from 2008-2016, eleven of the twelve worst cities in the world for mean concentration of particulate matter in the air were in India, with the

---

17 Butler, Declan, "Islam and science: The data gap," November 2006. *Nature* 444. Available at: www.nature.com/articles/444026a.

other in Cameroon. The majority of the top three hundred cities were found in China alone. 95% of the plastic waste choking our oceans comes from just ten rivers, eight of which are in Asia, while the other two are in Africa; among the primary offenders are the Yangtze River (727 million pounds of plastic waste per year), the Xi, Dong, and Zhujiang Rivers (233 million pounds), and the Ganges River (1.2 billion pounds). China produces by far the most plastic waste that winds up in the world's oceans – a whopping thirty times more than the United States! Countries such as Laos, Vietnam, Burma, Mozambique, Zambia, Indonesia, Tanzania, and Thailand are doing very poorly in their efforts to protect endangered species, as evidenced on the World Wildlife Fund's scorecard. The demand for exotic animal parts, such as rhinoceros horn, is primarily driven by the Asian market, especially in China.

According to Yale's Environmental Performance Index, the top ten nations in the world for environmental stewardship and conservation are, in order: Finland, Iceland, Sweden, Denmark, Slovenia, Spain, Portugal, Estonia, Malta, and France. The bottom ten are: the Democratic Republic of the Congo, Mozambique, Bangladesh, Mali, Chad, Afghanistan, Niger, Madagascar, Eritrea, and Somalia as the worst. The nations with the lowest levels of air pollution are: New Zealand, Brunei, Sweden, Australia, Canada, Finland, the United States, Iceland, Estonia, and Spain. The nations with the fewest deaths from air pollution arc: Sweden, Australia, Brunei, New Zealand, Finland, Cameroon, Iceland, Norway, the United States, and Spain. The twenty countries with the least polluted urban areas are: Australia, Brunei, New Zealand, Estonia, Finland, Canada, Iceland, Sweden, Ireland, Liberia, Japan, Bhutan, Norway, Malta, Portugal, Spain, the United States, Monaco, Malaysia, and Luxembourg. Lithuania, Latvia, Russia, and the United States have the strongest environmental democracy laws, whereas Belize, Cambodia, and Jordan have the worst. Haiti has clear-cut over 99% of its primal forest.

We'd like the saying "demography is destiny" to not be true, to think that all people could eventually come to cherish the ideals of the Enlightenment and live peacefully alongside others who may not be like them, and in the micro sense we can find many examples of this being the case. Unfortunately, in the macro, the saying almost always holds true, and this is something fundamental about human nature that we must understand. Not all groups of people have the same values or behave the same. This can be good or bad, but we need to be realistic about the kinds of societies certain peoples create and the carry-over to ours.

A facility in Artesia, New Mexico, meant to house illegal alien families, offers a glimpse in microcosm of what the United States is allowing to pass through its indefensibly undefended southern border. Per the *Washington Times,* from October 2014:

> Communicable diseases continue to be a problem at the New Mexico facility built to house illegal immigrant families surging across the U.S.-Mexico border, and the immigrants themselves aren't taking their own health care very seriously, according to an audit. "Family unit illnesses and unfamiliarity with bathroom facilities continued to result in unsanitary conditions," Inspector General John Roth wrote in a memo to Homeland Security Secretary Jeh Johnson. Mr. Roth said the illnesses – which put the facility in Artesia, New Mexico, on lockdown earlier this year, preventing any immigrants from being transferred in or out – have proved to be a continuing problem. Part of the issue is the immigrants themselves, some of whom have never seen a doctor before, don't follow up afterward, either for themselves or their children.[18]

Sounds like the kind of people you want forming the nucleus of a strong, republican-minded constituency, eh, conservatives? *Unfamiliarity with bathroom facilities?* This is what we are allowing to occur on our own soil – adults who are not potty trained. This is absolutely disgusting, and it facilitates the spread of diseases like E. coli and Hepatitis A. Incidentally, California recently wrestled with a huge Hepatitis A outbreak originating in San Diego County, most likely attributable

---

18   Dinan, Stephen, "Disease plagues illegal immigrants; lack of medications, basic hygiene blamed," October 6, 2014. *The Washington Times.* Available at: www.washingtontimes.com/news/2014/oct/6/diseases-still-problem-illegal-immigrant-families/.

to a) the burgeoning homeless population the state ignores, and b) unchecked illegals inter-mingling – and for both, a lack of access to and/ or unwillingness to use public toilet facilities. The outbreak spread as far afield as Sacramento, and at least six hundred people were infected. Hepatitis A is most commonly spread by feces-to-mouth contact, often through contaminated food. According to Dr. Monique Foster of the CDC: "It's not unusual for [outbreaks] to last quite some time – usually over a year." As Santa Cruz public health manager Jessica Randolph stated at the time: "I don't think the worst is over."

I can assure you, on our current trajectory, it's not. It is now no longer a felony to knowingly expose a sexual partner to HIV (or give HIV-positive blood) without prior notification in the State of California. The bill, signed by Governor Jerry Brown and introduced by gay Jewish State Senator Scott Wiener of San Francisco, is aimed at "de-stigmatizing" the communicable disease, its genesis prompted by what Wiener believed was the "irrational and discriminatory" nature of the existing law. This is truly a sign of the times if there ever was one.

It might surprise you to learn that California, America's most diverse state, also has the worst air quality, the greatest wealth disparity, and was ranked as the worst state to live in by *US News* based on health care, education, economy, opportunity, infrastructure, crime and corrections, fiscal stability, and quality of life. This ranking merely echoes what Robert Putnam's research revealed about Los Angeles, what was then "the most diverse human habitation in human history" and the "crown jewel" of the multi-cultural mess that is California today and our future tomorrow if we don't turn the tide, and soon.

Incidents like the following in Maputo, Mozambique in February 2018 will become increasingly commonplace, as well: following heavy rains, a three-story mountain of garbage collapsed and killed seventeen people. According to officials, people often comb through the garbage looking for food and discarded items to re-sell. Ghana loses almost $300 million a year due to the costs associated with poor sanitation and 90% of human excreta ends up in the same rivers and lakes the country gets its drinking water from. Port-au-Prince, Haiti, has no sewer system at all to service its three million people. According to the World Bank, around one-seventh of the world's population still defecates out in the open where the human waste often finds its way back into the water supply and the fecal bacteria spread disease. Listed here by percentage of the population still practicing "open defecation," see if you can notice a pattern:

1. Eritrea: 76%
2. Niger: 71%
3. Chad: 68%
4. South Sudan: 61%
5. Benin: 55%
6. Togo: 51%
7. Namibia: 50%
8. Burkina Faso: 48%
9. Madagascar: 44%
10. Liberia: 42%

According to the World Health Organization, 56% of deaths in sub-Saharan Africa are attributable to communicable diseases, many of which would be preventable with proper sanitation.

In 2010, Haiti suffered a severe cholera outbreak that killed around 10,000 people and sickened close to a million more; although according to the CDC the last cholera outbreak in the U.S. was over a century ago, countries like Malawi, Burundi, Guinea-Bissau, Mozambique, Ghana, Sierra Leone, Tanzania, Somalia, the Democratic Republic of the Congo, Zimbabwe, Sudan, Niger, Nigeria, Angola, Ethiopia, and Uganda have all wrestled with cholera outbreaks this past decade.

In 1994, over 12,000 people in what was then Zaire died from a cholera epidemic. Approximately half-a-million people have been afflicted with cholera in Yemen since 2016, though this is primarily a result of the conflict-induced devastation there. Other countries that have had issues with cholera in the last few years include India, Pakistan, Cuba, Mexico, Malaysia, Iraq, Bangladesh, Namibia, Kenya, Liberia, Burkina Faso, and Cameroon. Britannica defines cholera as, "an intestinal disease that is the archetype of waterborne illnesses. It spreads by the fecal-oral route: infection spreads through a population when feces containing the bacterium contaminate water that is then ingested by individuals."[19] From National Public Radio's *All Things Considered*:

> Public health authorities say cholera will stay in the environment for a long time, because Haiti has the worst sanitation in this hemisphere. It's hard for Americans to imagine what this means. The cumulative sewage of 3 million people flows through open ditches. It mixes with ubiquitous piles of garbage...Follow pediatrician Vanessa Rouzier on a tour of a Port-au-Prince slum called Cite de Dieu – City of God – to get an idea of what it means to live in a city sans sanitation...We cross over a wide canal that cuts through the slum. The garbage-clogged channel brings sewage down from the hillside precincts of the capital. "So you can imagine that if human waste goes through there, and if it rains, [it] just really spills into the environment and ends up in the sea," Rouzier says. She takes us down to a small, garbage-cluttered beach on the edge of the slum and points to a ramshackle structure perched on stilts over the water. Those who have seen the movie *Slumdog Millionaire* will know what it is – an outhouse. "If you live close by the water, you may use these over-the-sea hanging toilets during the daytime," Rouzier says. "But at night you wouldn't come out in the dark to use that. You would have a bowel movement in some sort of plastic bag and... throw it out during the day out here."[20]

---

19 I offer here an ancient example contrasted with these modern ones. The first sewers were laid in Rome well over 2,000 years ago; Strabo, writing around the time of Christ stated: "The sewers, covered with a vault of tightly fitted stones, have room in some places for hay wagons to drive through them. And the quantity of water brought into the city by aqueducts is so great that rivers, as it were, flow through the city and the sewers; almost every house has water tanks, and service pipes, and plentiful streams of water." In the year 100 AD, an early form of indoor plumbing was implemented by the Romans, and their waste and their potable drinking water from the aqueducts, several of which are still presently in operation over two thousand years later, never came into contact.

20 Knox, Richard, "Port-Au-Prince: A City Of Millions, With No Sewer System," April

As a woman, the primary reason you would not use the outhouse at night is that many women in the Third World, especially Africa, have expressed fears that using a public toilet alone, or even going to the bathroom in the bush privately, will result in their sexual assault, and the data support this fear. Reports from refugee camps in Greece routinely reveal the few women there wearing adult diapers for fear of being raped while going to the toilet at night. Numbers ranging from 20-50% of African women report having been sexually assaulted in the last year, with 40-70% reporting sexual abuse at some time in their lives. Ethiopia – never colonized by the West save a brief five-year Italian occupation – is particularly bad. Per Ejaz Khan:

Ethiopia is estimated to have one of the highest rates of violence against women in the world. A report by the UN found that nearly 60% of Ethiopian women were subjected to sexual violence. Rape is a very serious problem in Ethiopia. The country is infamous for the practice of marriage by abduction, with the prevalence of this practice in Ethiopia being one of the highest in the world. In many parts of Ethiopia, it is common for a man, working in co-ordination with his friends, to kidnap a girl or woman, sometimes using a horse to ease the escape. The abductor will then hide his intended bride and rape her until she becomes pregnant. Girls as young as eleven years old are reported to have been kidnapped for the purpose of marriage. Also the Ethiopian military has been accused of committing systematic rapes against civilians.[21]

This kind of systematic rape is common when an invading army is attempting to occupy a territory and demoralize and/or eradicate its population. For all of the talk of compassion that comes from the Left, even a cursory glance at the horrors being perpetrated against the women of Europe reveal these claims to be at best ignorantly one-sided and at worst deliberately duplicitous.

13, 2012. NPR. Available at: www.npr.org/sections/health-shots/2013/01/29/150501695/port-au-prince-a-city-of-millions-with-no-sewer-system.

21   Khan, Ejaz, "Top 10 Countries With Highest Rape Crime," April 12, 2017. Katehon. Available at: https://katehon.com/389-top-10-countries-with-highest-rape-crime.html.

By 2030, it is estimated that one in four Swedish women and girls will have been sexually assaulted (the number presently stands at one in eight). The culprits are obvious: rape in Sweden has risen *1,666%* since 1975, the first year of large-scale immigration – though the numbers from back then look sublimely small by comparison.[22] 80% of molestations in Sweden's public baths have been committed by men of foreign origin. Patrik Jonasson's survey of rulings regarding sex-related crimes passed by 40 Swedish courts between 2012 and 2014 indicated that 95.6% of rapes were committed by men of foreign descent.[23] Approximately 40% of the rapes in Sweden are of minors (10% of whom are boys). Afghanis are seventy-nine times more likely to rape than native Swedes.[24]

Sweden had to shut down its largest annual music festival due to rampant sexual assaults committed by "migrants." The Rinkeby subway station in Stockholm, Sweden was recently categorized as a place too dangerous to work without a police escort due to the security risk created by "migrant" gangs. In 2016, 15.6% of people suffered one or more offences against the person (defined in the National Council for Crime Prevention's survey as assault, threats, sexual offences, robbery, fraud or harassment), up from 13.3% the year prior, and the numbers both in total offenses and per capita continue to rise as immigration does. This is apparently not evidence enough to stop the mass importation of hostile aliens.

This trend is not isolated to Sweden, either. It seems like every day brings some fresh horror – a Somali attempting to rape a woman going into labor in Italy; a Pakistani raping a woman in a coma, also in Italy; mass rape and sexual assault by at least 2,000 "migrant" men in Cologne, Germany and several other cities on one New Year's Eve (Cologne's mayor dismissed concerns by stating that the women shouldn't have dressed so provocatively); a thirty-three year-old

---

22   Available at: www.friatider.se/v-ldt-kterna-har-kat-med-1666-procent-sedan-1975.

23   Available at: https://pjjonasson.files.wordpress.com/2017/10/sexualbrottslighet_bland_man_fodda_i_sverige_och_i_utlandet_v3.pdf.

24   Available at: http://avpixlat.info/2017/06/12/statistik-halften-av-alla-sexbrottslingar-har-utomeuropeisk-harkomst/.

Iranian pretending to be sixteen raping and murdering a woman, also in Germany; and on it goes. Not even animals are safe! A Syrian raped a pony at a petting zoo in Berlin in front of a group of children in 2017. Regarding the May 2018 savage rape and murder of young Susanna Maria Feldman by "migrant" Iraqi Kurd Ali Bashar, AfD co-leader Alice Weidel said:

> Susanna is dead. Maria from Freiburg; Mia from Kandel; Mireille from Flensburg; and now Susanna from Mainz... Susanna's death is not a blind stroke of fate. Susanna's death is the result of many years of organized irresponsibility and the scandalous failure of our asylum and immigration policies. Susanna is victim of an out-of-control leftwing multicultural ideology that stops at nothing to impose its sense of moral superiority. Susanna is also another victim of Chancellor Angela Merkel's hypocritical and selfish welcome policy. Legally, Ali Bashar should never have been allowed into Germany. His asylum request was rejected more than two years ago, and he should have been deported. Bashar was known to police for physical assault, attacking police officers, and possessing illegal weapons. In March 2018, he was suspected of raping an 11-year-old girl at a refugee shelter. According to the law, Bashar should have had to leave Germany a long time ago or be arrested. An absurd asylum law and a grotesque asylum policy...it is lenient toward asylum cheaters and criminals but ignores the genuine concerns of German citizens. Ali Bashar, his parents and five siblings lived here on the taxpayer's dime, they could not be deported, but after his Ali's crime, they somehow found the money to flee Germany on falsified documents. No problem in a Germany with open borders. On the day of Susanna's murder, [Merkel] testified in parliament that you have handled the migrant crisis responsibly.[25]

25 Weidel, Alice, "Was sagen Sie den Eltern der ermordeten #Susanna, Frau Merkel," June 7, 2018. Available at: https://twitter.com/Alice_Weidel/status/1004792858325454849.

The data can often be hard to come by given governmental and bureaucratic obscurantism, but the numbers we do have are damning. For Germany, as Soeren Kern informs:

A quarterly report – Criminality in the Context of Migration (*Kriminalität im Kontext von Zuwanderung*) – published by the Federal Criminal Police Office (*Bundeskriminalamt, BKA*) showed that migrants (*Zuwanderer*, defined as asylum seekers, refugees and illegal immigrants) committed 3,466 sex crimes during the first nine months of 2017 – or around 13 a day. (Final crime statistics for 2017 will not be publicly available until the second quarter of 2018.) By comparison, in all of 2016 migrants committed 3,404 sex crimes, or around nine a day; in 2015, 1,683 sex crimes, or around five a day; in 2014, 949 sex crimes, or around three a day; and in 2013, 599 sex crimes, or around two a day. The actual number of migrant-related sex crimes in Germany, however, is believed to be far higher than the official number...The director of the Criminal Police Association (*Bund Deutscher Kriminalbeamter, BDK*), André Schulz, estimates that up to 90% of the sex crimes committed in Germany do not appear in the official statistics. German police frequently omit any references to migrants in crime reports. When they do, they often refer to migrant criminals with politically correct euphemisms.[26]

According to the Rape, Abuse, and Incest National Network (RAINN), 27% of all perpetrators of sexual violence in the United States are black. According to US Justice Department figures, over 34,460 white women are sexually assaulted or raped by black males each year, and most authorities believe that the actual rape figures are at least twice the reported number. The number of black female rapes by white men is "statistically negligible" because there are consistently fewer than ten cases nationally per annum. In fact, because white-on-black rape is so statistically insignificant and rare, the FBI has simply

---

26 Kern, Soeren, "Germany: Migrant Rape Crisis Still Sowing Terror and Destruction," March 20, 2018. Gatestone Institute. Available at: www.gatestoneinstitute.org/12066/germany-rape-crisis.

stopped tracking it altogether. According to the 2016 New York Police Department *Crime and Enforcement Activity* report, 84.7% of all rapes in the city had a black or Hispanic suspect. Per the same NYPD report:

Blacks made up 47.6% of suspects, but only 40.6% of the suspects arrested. For petite larceny, 51.1% of suspects were black, but only 43.7% of the people arrested were black. 53.3% of the people stopped by the NYPD under the "Stop and Frisk" initiative were black. 59.7% of the people who were targeted that turned out to be a suspect in a violent crime were black. Whites and Asians were over-targeted while blacks were under-targeted.[27]

42% of rapes in Italy are perpetrated by "migrants," who account for 8% of the population.[28] Sex crimes increased 133% in one year alone from 2015 to 2016 in Austria almost solely as a result of the "refugee" influx.[29] In Oslo, Norway, from 2005-2010, "a total of 86 sexual assaults involving rape was (sic) reported in 83 cases the man was described as having 'non-western appearance.'" In 2001, an article in *Aftenposten* stated that in Oslo, "While 65% of those charged with rape are classed as coming from a non-western background, this segment makes up only 14.3% of Oslo's population. Norwegian women were the victims in 80% of the cases."[30] Rapes in Belgium have ballooned to 27.9 per 100,000 courtesy of its Third World "refugees," and a Greece awash in "migrants" has seen its number of annual reported rapes eclipse 5,000.

27 O'Neill, James P. (Commissioner), "Crime and Enforcement Activity in New York City," January 1-December 31, 2016. New York Police Department. Available at: http://www.nyc.gov/html/nypd/downloads/pdf/analysis_and_planning/year-end-2016-enforcement-report.pdf.

28 Tomlinson, Chris, "Migrants Account for Nearly Half of Rapists in Italy," December 7, 2019. *Breitbart.* Available at: www.breitbart.com/europe/2019/12/07/migrants-account-for-nearly-half-of-rapists-in-italy/.

29 Robinson, Belinda, "'There are big problems' Outrage as migrant rapes soar by 133%--in just ONE YEAR," December 9, 2016. *Express.* Available at: www.express.co.uk/news/world/741840/Outrage-as-migrant-rapes-soar-by-133-in-just-ONE-YEAR.

30 Kirkwood, R. Cort, "'Non-Western' Men Dominate Sex Crimes in Norway," June 2, 2011. *The New American.* Available at: www.thenewamerican.com/world-news/europe/item/8755-non-western-men-dominate-sex-crimes-in-norway.

In Finland, individuals of foreign origin represent about 6% of the population, but they account for 24% of the country's rapes. 80% of "migrants'" sexual assaults are perpetrated against Finnish women, with about half of those being minors. The assailants' predominant countries of origins were Iraq, Somalia, Iran, Bangladesh, Afghanistan, Morocco, Syria, and Algeria.[31]

According to the official statistics from 2010-2014, we know that in that time period Somalis were almost thirty-six times more likely than native Danes to commit rape; Afghanis were almost twenty-six times more likely than native Danes to commit rape, and Iranians, Iraqis, and Lebanese were over fifteen times more likely than native Danes to commit rape. Over half of all convicted Danish rapists have immigrant backgrounds, with Iranians, Iraqis, Somalis, and Turks dramatically overrepresented. One in three persons convicted of sexual assault in Denmark are Muslim, despite constituting less than 5% of the population. According to the Danish Ministry of Justice, since the onset in June 2015 of the "migrant crisis," reported rapes have exploded by 196%. From 2015-2016, rapes in Denmark increased 163%![32]

It is worth noting here that the average migrant is a male in his late-20s or early 30s – in other words, fighting age – and that there are scarcely any women or children to be found. Sweden's National Board of Forensic Medicine reported that in 83% of the cases where it had stated an opinion about the age of the asylum applicant, the applicant had not been a minor. A recent survey of Greece's largest refugee camp, the Moria camp on Lesbos, found that out of a total population of 5,206 there were just 162 unaccompanied children and 216 women, meaning up to 92.8% of the camp's inhabitants were men, per *Iefimerida*.[33] According to the UN High Commissioner for Refugees (UNHCR), in Italy in 2016, only 2.65% of the record-level 181,436 persons arriving

---

31   Available   at: www.alandsnyheter.com/brott/valdtakt/finskor-offer-i-80-av-asylinvandrares-sexbrott-halften-av-dem-flickor-under-18/ and https://helda.helsinki.fi/bitstream/handle/10138/156334/Katsauksia_4_Rikollisuustilanne_2014_2015.pdf.

32   Available at: http://www.dst.dk/da/statistik/nyt/NytHtml?cid=20879.

33   Available at: www.iefimerida.gr/news/391553/iefimerida-sti-moria-se-skines-kai-konteiner-paramenoyn-ekatontades-asynodeyta-anilika.

were actually deemed to have met the qualifications for refugee status.[34] For the UNHCR in 2015: "548 individuals, or less than one per cent of the overall figure of 134,044, were submitted under the emergency priority." Further, as a percentage of total resettlement submissions by the UNHCR, emergency cases were 0.8% of all submissions for 2011, 1.4% for 2012, 1.2% for 2013, and 0.8% for 2014.[35] For 2017, "Some 869 individuals, or just over 1 per cent of all submissions, were submitted under the emergency priority, an increase of 66 per cent compared to 2016."[36] So virtually none of these people – who are mostly fighting age males – are even refugees.

What we know is that of the (at bare minimum) seven million migrants who entered Europe between the period of 2010 and 2016, somewhere in the ballpark of 55-60% hail from Islamic countries, making the Islamization of Europe an extremely pressing issue. Pew Research projects Sweden, for example, will be 30% Muslim by mid-century in its High Migration projection. These are not problems that are going away. In fact, we are most likely seeing the first ripples of a coming bloodbath, and I say this without being hyperbolic in the slightest. Consider that according to the EU Terrorism Situation and Trend Report the number of people killed by terrorist attacks from the year before the "migrant crisis" (2014) to the year of the onset of the "migrant crisis" (2015) rose an astronomical *3,000%!* These terror attacks are almost exclusively driven by religious fanaticism coming in – and financed – from abroad. Countries like Switzerland, however, seem to prefer their own "don't ask, don't tell" of radicalization, as Judith Bergman reports:

> Several experts have pointed out the foreign Muslim networks at work in Switzerland. In 2016, Reinhard Schulze, professor of Islamic Studies at the University of Bern, pointed out that donations from the Muslim World League, based in Saudi

---

34 Available at: www.dailymail.co.uk/news/article-4442910/Less-3-migrants-reached-Italy-refugees.html.

35 Available at: www.unhcr.org/575836267.pdf.

36 Available at: www.unhcr.org/protection/resettlement/5b28a7df4/projected-global-resettlement-needs-2019.html.

Arabia, and other funds from Saudi Arabia were flowing to "those mosques and organizations that are open to the Wahhabi tradition." Another expert on Islam in Switzerland, Saïda Keller-Messahli, has spoken and written widely on how "Huge sums of money from Saudi Arabia, the United Arab Emirates, Qatar, Kuwait and Turkey are flowing to Switzerland," and how the Saudi-based Muslim World League is behind "a whole network of radically-oriented mosques in Switzerland...with the clear intention of spreading Salafist thought here."[37]

This is a long-standing Wahhabi practice; Saudi Arabia has been funding radical mosques across Europe from the UK to Bulgaria, from France to Russia for decades, as well as funding NGOs with direct ties to extremist activity. In 1994, Saudi donations to Islamic NGOs in Bosnia totaled $150 million. From WikiLeaks:

> In Bulgaria, Taiba (Taibah), supported by donations from Saudi Arabia, was registered in 1995 as a successor to two NGOs (Dar al-Irshad and Al Waqf al-Islamiyya) which were closed in 1994 for supporting Islamic extremism. Bulgarian security services report that the organization's objective is to radicalize Bulgaria's Muslim population, in part by encouraging central institutions such as the Muftiship to become financially dependent on its contributions. The founder of Taiba, Abdurahman Takan, was expelled from Bulgaria for illegally preaching against the state.[38]

Further east at the edge of Europe, Lawrence A. Franklin writes:

> Dagestan, the largest republic of the north Caucasus, can best be described in negative superlatives. It is probably the most violent spot in the entire Russian Federation. The administrative

---

37 Bergman, Judith, "Switzerland Welcomes Radicalization," June 20, 2018. Gatestone Institute. Available at: www.gatestoneinstitute.org/12558/switzerland-islam-radicalization.

38 "Islam and Islamic Extremism in Bulgaria," July 14, 2011. WikiLeaks. Accessed via: www.novinite.com/articles/130230/WikiLeaks:+Islam+and+Islamic+Extremism+in+Bulgaria.

bureaucracy of the republic's capital, Makhachkala, is among the most corrupt. The ethnic and linguistic diversity of Dagestan is the most complex among Russia's Republics... Religiously, it is also the most radical Muslim entity in the Russian state... This Salafist ascendency has been fueled, allegedly, by Arabian Gulf states' financial support for mosque construction and the hiring of fundamentalist imams as preachers throughout the Caucasian republics. However, the scholarships for Dagestani youth to study in Saudi Arabia have been particularly effective in the Wahabbization of Islam in Dagestan. Riyadh's largesse has helped accelerate the radicalization of the republic's Muslims.[39]

Terrorism of the kind so commonplace in Europe – and increasingly elsewhere as well – is but one aspect, however. Everyday violence, wrought by indiscriminate "diversity," continually erodes trust, cohesion, and social capital, and often is a pre-cursor to ethnic cleansing. In Cyprus, at the most extreme end – and a harbinger of things to come if we do not defend our nations from this invasion – Turkey remains committed to the ethnic cleansing of Greek Cypriots and the European Union and the United Nations say nothing.

Foreigners are 2.5 times more likely to be suspected of crimes than people born in Sweden to Swedish-born parents, and these predominantly young males view their criminality, perpetrated almost exclusively against native Swedes, as war. Don't believe me? Petra Åkesson interviewed young "migrants" in the city of Malmö and reports the following:

> "When we are in the city and robbing we are waging a war against the Swedes." This argument was repeated several times. "Power for me means that the Swedes shall look at me, lie down on the ground and kiss my feet." The boys explain, laughingly, that "there is a thrilling sensation in your body when you're robbing, you feel satisfied and happy, it feels as if you've succeeded, it simply feels good." "It's so easy to rob Swedes, so easy." "We

---

39 Franklin, Lawrence A., "Dagestan: New Epicenter of Muslim Terrorism in Russia," February 14, 2014. Gatestone Institute. Available at: www. gatestoneinstitute.org/4172/dagestan-terrorism-russia.

rob every single day, as often as we want to, whenever we want to." The immigrant youth regard the Swedes as stupid and cowardly: "The Swedes don't do anything, they just give us the stuff. They're so wimpy." The young robbers do not plan their crimes: "No, we just see some Swedes that look rich or have nice mobile phones and then we rob them."[40]

The lack of fight by the Swedes described is deeply disturbing in its own right, but it should be mentioned that should they resist, they would likely be the ones arrested for some concocted crimes pertaining to "racism." The attitude of these criminals speaks volumes, however. They may project strength (in numbers) to the interviewer, but really there's something else (in addition to the clear disdain exhibited for the Swedes): they know they'll get away with it, or at the very least the punishment will be so light as to be a slap on the wrist.

In Finland, the precedent has now been established that raping a ten-year-old white girl is acceptable if you are a member of the protected migrant class. The Supreme Court stated that Juusuf Muhamed Abbudin, aged 23, did not force the ten-year-old into the act or coerce her with fear, and thus it was not rape.

In 2017 in Austria, a ten-year-old boy was raped by an Iraqi man at a public pool, and surprisingly the man was convicted – but it was a four-year sentence. Senate President Thomas Philipp supported the decision, saying, "Four years are appropriate here." A Swedish mother was gang-raped by three Afghani "youths" in September 2017; they took photographs of the incident, and yet one was apparently never identified and the other two received sentences of eleven months and fourteen months. The grooming and abuse of a twelve-year-old in Dundee, Scotland netted the perpetrator Rana Irfan Aslam, in his thirties at the time, a mere one-year sentence.

A recent report from the UK found that Muslim men are over *two hundred times* more likely than non-Muslim men to sexually assault

---

40   Åkesson, Petra. Available at: www.sociologi.lu.se/krim/vi_krigar.pdf.

children. An inquest into the Newcastle grooming gang scandal in the UK found that the perpetrators acted with "arrogant persistence" as many of their seven hundred victims, not the perpetrators, were punished by the police as, to quote the report, the authorities used, "deterrent punishments of victims for being drunk and disorderly or for making false allegations when accounts were changed. This sent an unhelpful message to perpetrators – they were unlikely to be prosecuted or prevented from continuing to abuse." One member of the Newcastle gang, Badrul Hussain, once told a white female ticket inspector: "All white women are only good for one thing – for men like me to fuck and use like trash. That's all women like you are worth." Undeterred by authorities, attitudes like Hussain's are allowed to flourish under tacit protection from and by the law. A delightful 2017 probe into a grooming network in Glasgow revealed that the Four Corners area is "rife with child exploitation problems." According to a relative of one of the girls who had been groomed and gang raped:

This really is just our worst nightmare, it's this Rochdale and Rotherham-type stuff but it's happening in Glasgow in a big way. Nobody seems to be doing anything to stop it, all the girls have been made to believe these men are their boyfriends. It's white females they are hitting on, ages 14 to 19.[41]

No outrage or concern for sister-kind, feminists? Disgraceful. There have been, to date, over 6,000 reported cases of female genital mutilation in Ireland, 53,000 in Australia, and 70,000 in the UK and just *two cases have ended with convictions*. One estimate was that there have been over 140,000 in Sweden, but once again we run into bureaucratic obscurantism. The British police and governmental apparatus were content to turn a blind eye to what, according to Sarah Champion's estimate, were up to one *million* young white girls groomed, abused, and raped by largely "South Asian" Muslim men.

---

41   Rodger, Hannah, "Grooming ring probe at Glasgow's four corners after teenagers 'exploited for sex' by groups of men," September 26, 2017. *Glasgow Times*. Available at: www.glasgowtimes.co.uk/news/15556999.grooming-ring-probe-at-glasgows-four-corners-after-teenagers-exploited-for-sex-by-groups-of-men/.

Maybe the bogeyman of "racism" really is that potent. The Newcastle perpetrators (with one exception), just like Rochdale, Rotherham, Oxford, Derby, Telford, et cetera, "all appear to come from a non-white, predominantly Asian/British minority ethnic culture or background." Seven individuals only described by the BBC as "Oxford men" were convicted for "predatory... sexual exploitation on a massive scale."

The "Oxford men" are named: Assad Hussain; Moinul Islam; Raheem Ahmed; Kamran Khan; Kameer Iqbal; Alladitta Yousaf; and Khalid Hussain. Not a Smith or Jones among them. Curious. In one positive sign of diversity that Labour MP Naz Shah is sure to love (remember her grooming gang victims need to "shut their mouths for the good of diversity" re-tweet?), the Bristol grooming gang wasn't "Asian" – they were Somali! Nonetheless, it remains of paramount importance for the so-called "elites" to keep a lid on these scandals as much as possible. As just one example, not only was the Telford grooming gang scandal not covered by the national news, it wasn't even covered on the BBC's Shropshire news page! BBC News Editor James Stephenson defended the BBC's decision not to cover the event because, "The initial suggestion was...possibly 1,000 victims, and that was based not on hard information, but on an extrapolation based on work with an academic."

The neo-liberal calculus of Great Britain: Jimmy Saville and Gary Glitter. > Thousands of Muslim, predominantly Pakistani men committing large scale, systemic grooming, sexual abuse, and rape of up to one million under-age native British girls.

Now if you ask Lily Allen, not only does the UK's "attitude toward women...attract men of a predatory nature to want to settle here," the girls victimized by the Rochdale grooming gang, "Would have been raped or abused by somebody else at some point. That's kind of the issue." Lily Allen clearly considers these working-class girls to be little more than trash, utterly disposable in the service of "diversity," but she *is* actually right about one thing, and that is the way a subverted and alienized Western culture degrades and hyper-sexualizes its young women.

In a materialistic society, it's little surprise the first thing that usually attracts these young girls to the men in grooming gangs is their possessions – a nice car, nice clothes, the ability to give them gifts or supply them with the drugs and alcohol so vaunted on television and in popular music. Grooming is a process, and the men in question target girls specifically for their vulnerability as well as their race and religion. The girls frequently come from broken homes or foster care, the result of the decades-long campaign to atomize the nuclear family. With absentee fathers and over-burdened or neglectful mothers, of course these fragile tween and teen psyches are craving positive attention. And when, as Jayne Senior wrote in *Broken and Betrayed*, most social services and certainly the authorities are unwilling to step in on the girls' behalf, leaving them to fend for themselves, where else can they go? Who else can they turn to to protect them from the predations of well-connected and clearly sadistic men who are effectively operating with impunity when most people don't even know their neighbors? Individuals or sitting ducks? This is becoming the state of affairs for entire Occidental populations, both metaphorically and literally, with the streets of many Western cities starting to resemble scenes from the film *28 Days Later*.

It is exceedingly obvious that none of this is about "equality." Were that the case, why are whites discriminated against in every arena from college acceptances to hiring? Why the incessant need to ascribe cosmic guilt to whites for things they didn't even do – often worked against in fact? Why is "treason to whiteness loyalty to humanity," but the Democrats rigging the 2018 mid-term elections is described by *The Forward* as "Hanukkah"? Why the condemnation of asking, "Is it good for whites?" but the celebration of naked self-interest for other groups? Why can you literally get away with murdering someone who called you a naughty word so long as you are a member of a protected class? How exactly does one "flee poverty and crime" when they are of the milieu that produced it in the first place? Surely they bring it with them.

Minorities are treated by the Left as though they have no agency and yet we are expected to acknowledge them as full equals under the auspices of "democracy." If America is simply a set of principles, an idea or ideal if you will, then why is Liberia such a disaster when until 1980 it had a near-carbon-copy of our Constitution?

If diversity is our strength, why does it result in more violence and diminished health by all metrics, from civic to mental to physical? If diversity is a source of such incredible strength – indeed, our *greatest* strength – then it is axiomatic that the world's most ethnically diverse nations, listed below, would be global juggernauts:

1. Papua New Guinea
2. Tanzania
3. The Democratic Republic of the Congo
4. Uganda
5. Liberia
6. Cameroon
7. Togo
8. South Africa
9. Congo-Brazzaville
10. Madagascar
11. Gabon
12. Kenya
13. Ghana
14. Malawi
15. Guinea-Bisseau

Not so much. Instead, they are impoverished and riven with ethnic conflict. And if it's such a natural process, why is it that people naturally self-segregate? Uganda, for example, has 1.25 million refugees, "for which it receives $200 million in aid to allow refugees to farm small plots of land that are donated by rural villages; a third of this refugee aid goes to natives. Natives often live segregated from newcomers, as when natives are in one part of a rural village and refugees in another."[42] Additionally, there is ample data that the more diverse the city, the more segregated it becomes.[43]

---

42 "Europe, Asia," 2019. *Rural Migration News*, Vol. 25, No. 1. UC Davis. Available at: https://migration.ucdavis.edu/rmn/more.php?id=2250.

43 Silver, Nate, "The Most Diverse Cities Are Often The Most Segregated," May 1, 2015. FiveThirtyEight. Available at: https://fivethirtyeight.com/features/the-most-diverse-cities-are-often-the-most-segregated/.

Chapter 2 - The Many
Lies of Diversity

"We have a moral obligation to admit the world's poor, they tell us, even if it makes our own country poorer, and dirtier, and more divided. Immigration is a form of atonement. Previous leaders of our country committed sins—we must pay for those sins by welcoming an endless chain of migrant caravans. That's the argument they make."-Tucker Carlson

The most visibly obvious aspect of neo-liberalism and globalization is the proliferation of alien peoples in formerly homogeneous areas. Racial and ethnic diversity is essential for the advancement of the neo-liberal project. The imported peoples' criminality and sheer alienness are instrumental in the bankrupting of social capital, battering a community, state, or polity, and opening the way for the torrent of horrors that follow while the subverter works to weaken the defenses from within.

Transformative immigration threatens the integrity of a republic or democracy because there can be no common consensus in a tribal landscape, just as a decline in morals and virtue, both civic and personal, creates an environment of self-gratifying individualism. "Liberal democracy" in both cases caters to peoples' worst impulses. Not coincidentally, the degradation of the integrity of the Republic in the United States has coincided with the extension of the franchise from a limited group of men of character who had "skin in the game" to literally everyone, even non-Americans and the deceased. This essentially applies across the West from Australia to Great Britain to Canada: citizenship itself has become corrupted and, increasingly, meaningless, like so much else.

Our homelands are being fundamentally transformed beyond all recognition, as mass immigration is of course transformative. This is axiomatic, but in contemporary discourse, unmentionable. Whites certainly have no right to their own homelands – migration is a human right! Even the estimable United Nations says so! Read the excerpt below from the document entitled, "Replacement Migration: Is It a Solution to Declining and Ageing Populations?" from the United Nations' Department of Economic and Social Affairs: Population Division (since deleted) and ask yourself again, "What conspiracy?":

United Nations projections indicate that over the next 50 years, the populations of virtually all countries of Europe as well as Japan will face population decline and population ageing. The new challenges of declining and ageing populations will require comprehensive reassessments of many established policies and programmes, including those relating to international migration. Focusing on these two striking and critical population trends, the report considers replacement migration for eight low-fertility countries (France, Germany, Italy, Japan, Republic of Korea, Russian Federation, United Kingdom, and United States) and two regions (Europe and the European Union). Replacement migration refers to the international migration that a country would need to offset population decline and population ageing resulting from low fertility and mortality rates.

So there you have it, in black-and-white, the end-game: *replacement migration*. So yes, you *are* being replaced, but one-way migration into white and future select Northeast Asian societies *is a human right*. Clearly this is absurd, and to quote Alexander Solzhenitsyn, "It is time, in the West, to defend not so much human rights as human obligations." What about the obligation to your fellow countrymen? What about the obligation to your posterity? Many whites have opted out of the latter obligation in refusing to have children, but it's worth considering that you can't be a "cool wine aunt" if some thrice-deported illegal runs you over in a crosswalk and takes off leaving you for dead. For the rest, what kind of country do you want to leave your children and your children's children? One that's healthy, happy, and cohesive, or a squalid, disease-ridden hell-hole? The perpetrators cry foul while literally trying to erase whiteness through genocidal policies including: mass non-white immigration; white reproductive suppression through propaganda and onerous taxes; demoralization of whites and pressure to self-medicate with harmful substances; incessant anti-white propaganda; and the normalization of weird sexual proclivities, gender fluidity, and "trans." One study from Cornell University recommended dating app algorithms be altered so as to essentially force whites to date outside their own race. No such proposal exists for other groups to the best of my knowledge. Also, according to *The Guardian*, using a dating app to meet members of your own race is "racist." White eradication has to be the ultimate goal. Google "white couple" and see what comes up.

Anushka Asthana writes in *The Guardian* with no apparent agenda that, "Color-blind love is the mark of a healthy and dynamic society," using only the anecdotal evidence of the fact that she is in an interracial marriage as evidence to prove her hypothesis.[1]

The "ideal" of a mongrelized population having "less racism" is belied by the mystery-meat experiment that is Brazil, where according to the 2010 census, 50.7% is mixed-race; far from racial issues being non-existent in a country with a white plurality and a whole lot of what the blacks call "swirling," race remains an intractable obstacle to paradisal post-racial utopianism. In fact, Brazil is fraught with racial tension and is one of the most violent countries on earth.

Growing diversity in Asthana's adopted nation of Great Britain has seen its quality of life decline dramatically in exact correlation with its increasing diversity. Her prescription is to just have all the native Britons and their racially-distinct replacements mix and mix until we have heaven-on-earth. But besides the many impediments to a "café con leche" future society oft fantasized about by many an ardent Leftist, most people do not want to date outside their own race, and

1   Asthana, Anushka, "Colour-blind love is the mark of a healthy and dynamic society," July 6, 2014. *The Guardian*. Available at: www.theguardian.com/commentisfree/2014/jul/06/mixed-marriage-interracial-partnerships-multiculturalism-society-class.

furthermore, the more diverse an area becomes, the *less* interaction there is. Simply put, their own project is confounded by itself as people will inevitably self-segregate. Forcing school integration at gun-point was gang-busters so why not those we pair-bond with? The following from City Lab gives the game away:

> Although 11% of white newlyweds are now married to someone of a different race or ethnicity, white people are still the least likely of all major racial or ethnic groups to intermarry. Black newlyweds, meanwhile, have seen the most dramatic increases of any group, from 5% in 1980 to 18% today. The gap between metropolitan and non-metropolitan areas, however, "is driven entirely by whites," according to the report… 83% of newlyweds in non-metro areas are white, compared to 62% in metro areas.[2]

Channeling her inner Anushka Asthana, Lionel Shriver believes Vin Diesel-ing the population may well short-circuit the dreaded identity politics game, for whites of course.[3]

For people who make such a big deal about "fighting hate," it is curious, then, that Harvard University found acceptable the vile hatred spewed out by a journal called *Race Traitor*, founded by its own lecturer and fellow Noel Ignatiev, where "treason to whiteness is loyalty to humanity": "Make no mistake about it: we intend to keep bashing the dead white males, and the live ones, and the females too, until the social construct known as 'the white race' is destroyed – not 'deconstructed' but destroyed." Well then.

The definition of a pogrom is "an attack, accompanied by destruction, looting of property, murder, and rape, perpetrated by one section of the population against another." The word pogrom itself literally means "devastation," and is related to the Russian pogromit, "to create a

---

2   Balwit, Natasha, "The Urban-Rural Divide in Interracial Marriage," May 18, 2017. City Lab. Available at: www.citylab.com/equity/2017/05/interracial-marriage-in-cities-pew-report/527217/.

3   "Will racial blending undermine identity politics? Let's hope so," *The Spectator,* December 8, 2018

desert." From Encyclopedia.com, a pogrom will result in "plunder... persecution and dispossession." It also, from the YIVO Encyclopedia, "usually implies central instigation and control, or at minimum the passivity of local authorities." The victims of these neo-progroms, perversely, are those portrayed to be the perpetrators. That sounds an awful lot like Soviet Russia in the 1920s and 1930s, or the Eurowestern world today.

The Soviets also committed themselves to infiltrating social clubs and organizations, even the Boy Scouts, by attaining leadership positions in order to purge ideological foes and politicize these organizations, essentially rendering the ideology of The New Soviet Man inescapable. The parallels with the modern West are disconcerting, to put it mildly. There was no respite even in one's personal life – for example, one in three East Germans was a government informant, so the odds that your spouse or one of your siblings, offspring, parents, or friends was reporting directly to the Stasi were quite good; in the interests of self-preservation it was best to never voice any displeasure with the regime, even to those closest to you. In Soviet Russia, during the Stalin era, 200,000 people were sent to the gulag for telling what Mark Steyn characterizes as "ideologically unsound gags."

The Soviet Union was also big on population replacement. The new totalitarian system in Europe is a variation on a theme. We've seen this game played before. For example, in 1945, the percentage of the Estonian population that was ethnically Estonian was 97%. In 1959, it was 74.6%. In 1989 it was 61.5%, all courtesy of the Soviet Union's mass deportations and executions of native Estonians, and mass importation of ethnic Russians, Ukrainians, and Belarusians, in order to dissolve the country's national character and identity, and to erase any sense of an "Estonia" that was anything more than just an administrative district in the Soviet Union. Deprived of positions of seniority in the soviet and subject to "reforms" to the education system biased against the Estonian language and their national history, Estonians, like Latvians, Ukrainians, Lithuanians, and so many other ethnicities in the USSR, were ear-marked for oblivion to be replaced by the crushing uniformity of the New Soviet Man. The parallels with the modern era are truly terrifying, but to voice any kind of opposition to the modern Bolshevik population replacement of Europe…well, that would be *racist*.

Not long after World War II, Germany began importing hundreds of thousands of Turkish migrant workers who proved to be neither migrants as they ultimately stuck around nor workers as few worked – the Turkish population to this day has an unemployment rate three times that of the native Germans. With three-quarters of a century of proof that, as even Reuters acknowledges, the Turks remain Germany's least-integrated minority, German Chancellor Angela Merkel decided to recklessly "invite" millions more unassimilable "migrants," with Muslims representing 86% of those who arrived in the country between mid-2014 and mid-2016. The justification has been a thin and convoluted mixture of apologism, economic necessity, and compassion for the global downtrodden. The results have been predictably disastrous for a continent that's ill-equipped for such an influx, particularly of the violent and unassimilable variety that's flooded Europe in increasing numbers. Such a population group would be a challenge for anyone, as can be readily witnessed regardless of the context.

According to Germany's own 2017 crime statistics, more than 1,100 foreigners were charged with murder or manslaughter, as opposed to around 1,500 Germans. In 2016 the numbers were: 1,137 foreigners charged with homicides compared to 1,638 Germans. Regarding violent crimes, in 2017 police charged 69,163 foreigners compared to 112,346 Germans. In 2016, the government reported 67,869 foreigners committed violent crimes compared to 110,494 Germans. This is an astounding overrepresentation of foreign criminality but it is not an outlier. More than 90% of the 10.4% increase in reported violent crimes in Germany's southern state of Lower Saxony was attributed to young male migrants, according to a study from the Zurich University of Applied Sciences. North Africans were overrepresented by over 1,600%! Nationally, German victims of immigrant crime hit a new high in 2017, rising 23.7% in one year, and these are just the recorded numbers.

In 2015 in Denmark, Lebanese men were measured to have at over 250 the highest crime index among the studied populations in the country; the index was standardized at 100 for all males in Denmark that year. Male offspring of Lebanese immigrants were measured to have an astronomical crime index approaching 400. Moroccan and Somali male offspring had crime indexes over 300. The lowest crime index was recorded among immigrants originating from the United States.

Crime index 2015 of immigrant men to Denmark
Index 100: All males in Denmark 2015

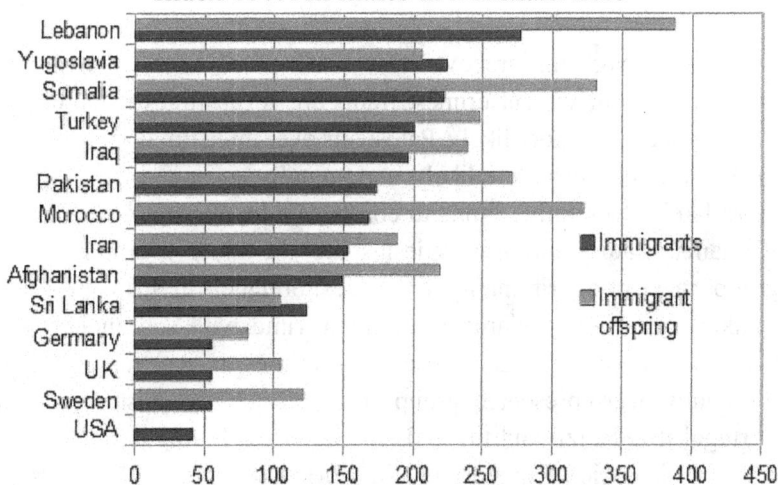

Iraqis and Pakistanis have rates of conviction for felonies greater than native Norwegians by factors of 3 and 2.6, respectively. Overall, Iraqis are four times more likely than native Norwegians to commit violent crimes. Afghanis are two-and-a-half times more likely than native Norwegians to commit violent crimes, and Turks and Iranians are twice as likely. First-generation African immigrants/"migrants" are three times more likely than native Norwegians to be convicted of a felony, with Somalis the worst offenders at 4.4 times more likely to be convicted of a felony than a native Norwegian.

In 2010, it was reported that first generation immigrants are over-represented by a factor of 1.7 for sex crimes. Nevertheless, in January 2020, the Norwegian government unilaterally decided to take 600 "refugees" from sub-Saharan Africa to "send a message." Message received.

Interestingly, second-generation African and Asian immigrants have a higher rate of convictions for felonies than first-generation immigrants in Norway. First-generation African immigrants have conviction rates for felonies of 16.7 per 1,000 individuals over the age of 15, whereas for second-generation immigrants the rate is 28 per 1,000 – an increase of over 60%. For Asians there is an increase from 9.3 per 1,000 to 17.1 per 1,000.

In Finland, Afghanis are over five times more likely than native Finns to commit violent crimes. Iraqis are seven times more likely, Iranians six times more likely, Pakistanis over three times more likely, Turks over six times more likely, and Somalis seven-and-a-half times more likely than native Finns to commit violent crimes.[4] Pakistanis, Afghanis, Iraqis, and Bangladeshis are the most overrepresented groups in terms of criminality in Greece. Foreigners in Spain are twice as likely as native Spaniards to commit a crime, with Venezuelans and Colombians the most likely to commit crimes. In Austria, the most criminally-overrepresented group comes from Afghanistan, and in Portugal it is Brazil and the PALOP countries (Portuguese-speaking countries in Africa: Equatorial Guinea, Mozambique, Guinea-Bissau, Cape Verde, Angola, and São Tomé and Príncipe).

In Italy, a 2013 report stated that "immigrants accounted for almost 23% of the criminal charges although they represented only 6-7% of the resident population" at that time. In the Netherlands, almost one-in-five individuals of a foreign background between the ages of 18-24 have been investigated for crimes, and in a report published in 2009, 63% of all teenagers arrested for a serious crime had a foreign background.

---

4   Skardhamar, Torbjorn, Mikko Aaltonen, and Martti Lehti, "Immigrant crime in Norway and Finland," July 2014. *Journal of Scandinavian Studies in Criminology and Crime Prevention*, 15 (2). Available at: www.researchgate. net/publication/266400120_Immigrant_crime_in_Norway_and_Finland.

Asylum seekers are at least fourteen times more likely than native Swiss to be arrested. Angolans, Nigerians, and Algerians all have crimes rates multiples higher than those of the native Swiss. The following chart shows the numbers for criminal representation among the various populations of Switzerland:[5]

Rank	Country of Origin	Crime Rate (relative value)	Registered Population (thousands)	Male Young Adults (thousands)
1	Angola	6.3	4.4	0.54
2	Nigeria	6.2	2.9	1.5
3	Algeria	6.0	4.1	1.2
4	Ivory Coast	5.9	1.7	0.44
5	Dominican Republic	5.8	5.9	1.0
6	Sri Lanka	4.7	31	4.4
7	Congo	4.7	5.8	0.78
8	Cameroon	4.4	4.3	0.97
9	Morocco	4.3	7.4	1.6
10	Tunisia	4.2	6.3	2.1
11	Iraq	3.7	8.0	2.9
12	Colombia	3.2	4.2	0.71
13	Turkey	3.2	73	16
14	Kosovo	3.1	188	36
15	Brazil	3.0	17	2.5
16	Egypt	2.7	2.1	0.81
17	Croatia	2.4	35	5.0
18	Bosnia and Herzegovina	2.3	37	6.2
19	Macedonia	2.3	60	12
	Total Foreign National Population	1.6	1,714	330
20	Portugal	1.3	213	46
21	Italy	1.2	294	49

---

5   Available at: www.blick.ch/news/schweiz/auslaender-statistik-angolaner-sind-die-top-kriminellen-in-der-schweiz-id58723.html.

22	Switzerland	1.0	6,072	710
23	Austria	0.8	38	5.8
24	France	0.7	95	21
25	Germany	0.6	266	62

Blacks comprise about 13% of the US population, but commit 52.5% of its homicides. Blacks are far more likely to commit violent crimes against whites and Hispanics much more likely than the other way around, contrary to what the media would have you believe. Worse, writes Heather MacDonald, "That ratio is becoming more skewed, despite the Democratic claim of Trump-inspired white violence. In 2012-13, blacks committed 85 percent of all interracial victimizations between blacks and whites; whites committed 15 percent."

Interracial Violent Crime Incidents 2018

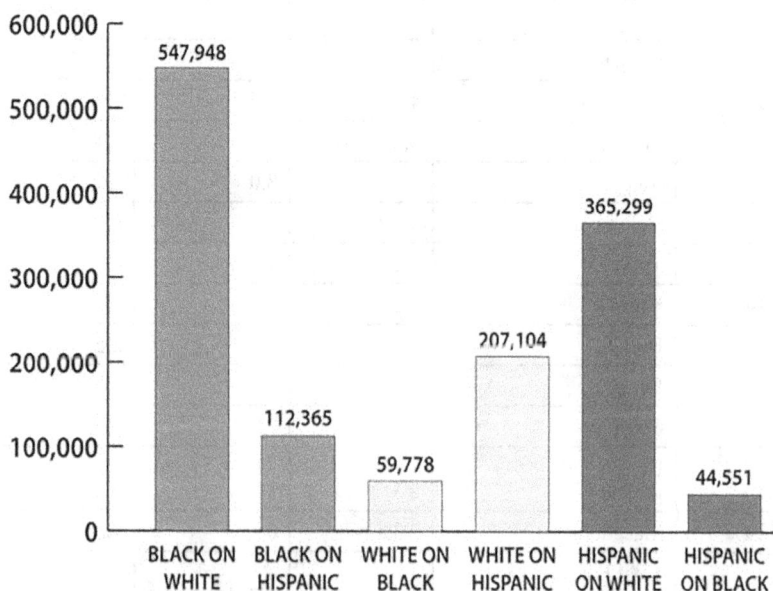

As Edwin S. Rubenstein recorded in *The Color of Crime* (2016 Edition):

- In 2014 in New York City, a black was 31 times more likely than a white to be arrested for murder

- The overwhelming majority of black homicide victims (93% from 1980 to 2008) were killed by other blacks.

- There are dramatic race differences in crime rates. Asians have the lowest rates, followed by whites, and then Hispanics. Blacks have notably high crime rates. This pattern holds true for virtually all crime categories and for virtually all age groups.

- In 2013, a black was six times more likely than a non-black to commit murder, and 12 times more likely to murder someone of another race than to be murdered by someone of another race.

- For the crime of "shooting" – defined as firing a bullet that hits someone – a black was *98.4 times* more likely than a white to be arrested.

- In an all-white Chicago, murder would decline 90 percent, rape by 81 percent, and robbery by 90 percent. Blacks in Chicago are 23.8 times more likely to be arrested for murder than whites.

- In Milwaukee in 2014 (the most recent year available), blacks were 12 times more likely to be murder suspects than whites.

- In Pittsburgh in 2012 (the most recent year available), blacks were 26.6 times more likely than whites to be arrested for murder.

- In California in 2013, blacks were 5.35 times more likely than whites to be arrested for violent crimes, and 4.24 times more likely to be arrested for property crimes.

- High crime rates among blacks are not limited to the United States. Statistics released by the Metropolitan Police in London, England, show that in 2009-10 blacks accounted for 54% of arrests for street crimes, 59% for robbery, and 67% for gun crimes. Blacks accounted for just over 12% of London's population of 7.5 million. Likewise, according to information that had to be sought through a freedom-of-information request, in 2002, blacks were 8.1% of the population of Toronto, Canada, but accounted for 27% of all charges for violent crimes.[6]

---

6   Rubenstein, Edwin S., *The Color of Crime*, 2016 Revised Edition. Available at: www.amren.com/the-color-of-crime/.

In 1993, blacks committed an even higher percentage of US homicides at an astronomical 57.6%. Blacks in Missouri have a murder rate 16.3 times that of whites per capita, a rape rate five times that of whites per capita, an assault rate 5.3 times that of whites per capita, and a robbery rate 22.2 times that of whites per capita. In Virginia for the year 2008, blacks committed 64% of the state's murders, 38% of its forcible sex offenses, 42% of rapes, 82% of robberies, 45% of burglaries, 52% of aggravated assaults, 36% of incidents of vandalism, 47% of drug/narcotics violations, 49% of motor vehicle thefts, 70% of purse snatchings, 36% of incidents of counterfeiting/forgery, 45.5% of shoplifting offenses, 66% of incidents of extortion/blackmail, 44.4% of "simple assaults," 52% of kidnappings, 49% of incidents of welfare fraud, 39% of statutory rapes, 52.4% of instances of bribery, 56% of offenses against the family, and 44% of total larceny. At 9.1% of the population of the state of Connecticut, blacks commit over half of the murders and over one-third of the rapes. A recent study in the United States found that blacks from the top 1% of household income are statistically as likely to commit crime as whites from an average household income of $36,000. So much for the poverty-drives-crime narrative.

For most crimes, blacks make up a larger percentage of reported offenders than they do of those arrested, so systemic bias is off the table. If anything, these figures *downplay* black criminality. From the article "Is There Evidence of Racial Disparity in Police Use of Deadly Force? Analyses of Officer-Involved Fatal Shootings in 2015-2016" by Joseph Cesario, David Johnson, and William Terrill we learn that:

> When adjusting for crime, we find no systemic evidence of anti-black disparities in fatal shootings of unarmed citizens, or fatal shootings involving misidentification of harmless objects. Multiverse analyses showed only one significant anti-black disparity out of 144 possible tests. Exposure to police given crime rate differences likely accounts for the higher per capita rate of fatal police shootings for blacks.[7]

---

7   Cesario, Joseph, David Johnson, and William Terrill, "Is There Evidence of Racial Disparity in Police Use of Deadly Force? Analyses of Officer-Involved Fatal Shootings in 2015-2016," June 13, 2018. Available at: https://journals.sagepub.com/doi/full/10.1177/1948550618775108.

Objective truth must be suppressed at all costs in order to reinforce the narrative. Better to use RACISM as an explanation for the fact that in Australia, Victoria police stated that in 2012 Sudanese (0.1% of the population) and Somali (0.05% of the population) immigrants were approximately five times more likely to commit crimes than other state residents. The rate of offending was 1301.0 per 100,000 for the Victorian average, whereas for the Sudanese it was 7109.1 per 100,000 individuals and 6141.8 per 100,000 for Somalis. The Sudanese and Somalis seem to have a particular affinity for assault, which represents 29.5% for Sudanese and 24.3% for Somalis of their offences. Three years later, Victoria police data showed that male Sudanese "youths" were "vastly over-represented" in criminal behavior, responsible for 7.44% of home invasions, 5.65% of car thefts, and 13.9% of aggravated robberies. Again, keep in mind the Sudanese are 0.1% of Victoria's population, and young males are only maybe a quarter to a sixth of that 0.1%. Additionally, despite constituting just 3% of the population, aborigines make up 28% of Australia's prison population.

Crimes committed per 100,000 of the population, Victoria, Australia, 2012

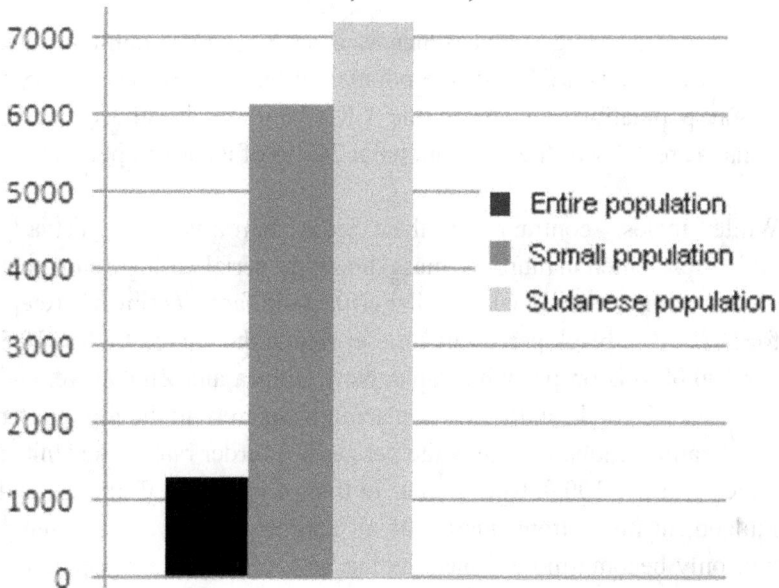

Legend:
- Entire population
- Somali population
- Sudanese population

In England and Wales, whites are arrested at a rate of 12 per 1,000, whereas "Asians" are at 14, mixed-race individuals at 26, and blacks at 38. Blacks comprise 3% of the UK's population, but 10% of its prison population. In 2011, non-whites in the UK committed 51.9% of rapes, 50.1% of sex crimes, 67% of gun crimes, 65% of knife crimes, 71% of personal robberies, and 74% of purse snatchings.

In the United States, according to the Department of Justice's "Felony Defendants in Large Urban Counties," for the year 2009, in the country's 75 largest counties, blacks committed 62% of robberies, 45% of assaults and accounted for 57% of murder defendants. According to the Justice Department, "American Indian women are 10 times more likely to be murdered than other Americans. They are raped or sexually assaulted at a rate four times the national average, with more than one in three having either been raped or experienced an attempted rape." Guam, which is 7.1% white, has the second-highest rape rate in America, behind Alaska, whose rate is driven largely by aborigine peoples; 56% of Amerindian and aborigine women have been victims of sexual assault or sexual violence.

In Canada, as immigration has increased, so, too, has its homicide rate. Black Canadians are 3% of the population but 10% of the country's prison population, just as in the UK. Additionally, aborigines in Canada are 4.3% of the population but 24.4% of its prison population.

White males, contrary to the media narrative, are actually underrepresented in murders, mass shootings, serial killings, and other violent crimes, even in white collar crimes – in fact *all* crimes – except for DUIs. The black per capita murder rate in the United States (10.5 per 100,000) is on par with Papua New Guinea and Zimbabwe, and just below Uganda and Zambia, placing it squarely in the top quarter of all nations globally. The white per capita murder rate in the United States (1.5 per 100,000) is similar to that of Hungary, Romania, and Finland, in the bottom quarter of all nations globally. The country will only become more violent as the bulk of America's population growth comes from Latin American immigration, where despite accounting for just 8% of the world's population, Latin Americans are responsible for 38% of the world's murders. With cities like Toronto and London becoming "majority-minority," their murder rates have now exceeded that of New York City. Acid attacks are now a more common occurrence in London than in Islamabad. How many acid attacks were there in London in 1940? or 1960?

What do you think happened to Ancient Rome? Why do you think Europe sank into the Dark Ages? After cheapening what it meant to be a Roman citizen over an extended period of time, after taxing the citizens into oblivion, after allowing scores of barbarians to serve in the legions and settling tribes wholesale within the boundaries of the empire, it is little wonder the cumulatively corrosive effects of their ancient form of super-state multi-culturalism wore the empire down until it ultimately fell. Centuries later, wandering among the ruins of Rome, the barbarians wondered what gods had built the magnificent structures they beheld. These awe-inspiring monuments were products of a unique civilization, not just representative of that civilization, but singularly *of that civilization*. Our modern Tower of Babel has the charm of a Soviet housing block, all the technical proficiency and nuance of Michael Eric Dyson's work, and the general characteristics of an open sewer, sometimes quite literally.

Even heavily-biased liberals are finding in study after study that "contact theory" is bogus and diversity's greatest strength is alienation and conflict. Harvard researcher Ryan Enos conducted a pair of surveys on white subjects regarding their views on Mexican immigration, asking, among other things, if they favored allowing noncriminal, employed illegal immigrants to remain in the country. Enos did this in two rounds: once before exposing the whites to more Hispanic commuters on train platforms and once after. Support for immigration and allowing the undocumented to stay plunged in the "after" follow-up from what it had been in the "before" survey. As Rich Barlow writes:

> "Diversity" is said to be the sun of our civic solar system, shining bright harmony everywhere from society at large to university campuses. Katherine Levine Einstein is certainly an apostle of

this view. The College of Arts & Sciences assistant professor of political science studies racially segregated areas and finds that separation polarizes and paralyzes those places' politics. But Boston's commuter rail system shakes her faith. In addition to the Harvard research, two Northwestern University studies fuel Einstein's pessimism. One found that as whites learned that they will become a minority, they grew more conservative and Republican-leaning. The other reported that whites who were aware of their future minority status became more negative towards nonwhites and preferred hanging out with their own race. That study's researchers had this to say: "These results suggest that rather than ushering in a more tolerant future, the increasing diversity of the nation may instead yield intergroup hostility." Einstein is persuaded by the Northwestern work. "You can replicate these kinds of psychological studies across different age groups....There's very strong psychological research that we do see these perceptions of threat" by whites. "So it's hard to imagine that we will ever be moving to a totally post-racial world, where a sense of racial threat doesn't exist."...The results are in line with "a huge line of scholarship" suggesting that "greater conflict emerges from greater interracial contact."[8]

When the ruling class says "Diversity is our strength," what they mean is diversity is *their* strength. "Diversity" is a powerful weapon in the ruling class's arsenal; its benefits to the bottom line work synergistically with mass media and the "virtual experience" of lives increasingly led online. As a vehicle of demoralization and atomization it is also devastatingly effective. As Michael Jonas reported in his 2007 article, "The Downside of Diversity":

It has become increasingly popular to speak of racial and ethnic diversity as a civic strength. From multicultural festivals to pronouncements from political leaders, the message is the same: our differences make us stronger. But a massive new study, based

8   Barlow, Rich, "BU scholars assess research suggesting whites fear minority status," September 25, 2014. *BU Today.* Boston University. Available at: http://www.bu.edu/articles/2014/does-diversity-breed-intolerance.

on detailed interviews of nearly 30,000 people across America, has concluded just the opposite. Harvard political scientist Robert Putnam...found that the greater the diversity in a community, the fewer people vote and the less they volunteer, the less they give to charity and work on community projects. In the most diverse communities, neighbors trust one another about half as much as they do in the most homogenous settings. The study, the largest ever on civic engagement in America, found that virtually all measures of civic health are lower in more diverse settings. Higher diversity meant lower social capital.[9]

These findings were echoed by economists Matthew Kahn of UCLA and Dora Costa of MIT, who reviewed fifteen studies, all of which linked diversity with lower levels of social capital. Greater racial and ethnic diversity was linked to lower school funding, census response rates, and general levels of trust. Kahn and Costa also conducted their own research, which found higher desertion rates in the Civil War among Union Army soldiers serving in companies whose soldiers varied more by age, occupation, and birthplace. Conrad Ziller's findings in Europe echo those in the United States:

The results show that across European regions, different aspects of immigration-related diversity are negatively related to social trust. In longitudinal perspective, an increase in immigration is related to a decrease in social trust. Tests of the conditional hypotheses reveal that regional economic growth and ethnic polarization as a cultural context moderate the relationship. Immigration growth is particularly strongly associated with a decrease in social trust in contexts of economic decline and high ethnic polarization.[10]

9　Jonas, Michael, "The Downside of Diversity," August 5, 2007. *The New York Times.* Available at: www.nytimes.com/2007/08/05/world/americas/05iht-diversity.1.6986248.html

10　Ziller, Conrad, "Ethnic Diversity, Economic and Cultural Contexts, and Social Trust: Cross-Sectional and Longitudinal Evidence from European Regions, 2002-2010," March 2015. *Social Forces*, Vol. 93, Issue 3. Available at: https://academic.oup.com/sf/article-abstract/93/3/1211/2332107.

Economic growth does have an ameliorative effect on in-migration's consequences, but it only masks them and is only to a point, as the current situation in the US clearly shows.

Despite Robert Putnam's optimistic claim that, "successful immigrant societies have overcome...fragmentation by creating new, cross-cutting forms of social solidarity and more encompassing identities," there is absolutely no evidence to support it, and plenty to refute it. In all of the cities and towns he studied, Robert Putnam found trust was lowest in Los Angeles, "the most diverse human habitation in human history." Peter Y. Hong recounted, "Those who live in more homogeneous places, such as New Hampshire, Montana or Lewiston, Maine, do more with friends and are more involved in community affairs or politics than residents of more cosmopolitan areas." Unfortunately, though these words were written less than two decades ago, they no longer apply to Lewiston, having been suitably "enriched" by Somali "refugees," gangs of whom have taken to marauding in and around Kennedy Park and savaging and killing locals. Considering Lewiston only averages around 1.5 homicides a year, this is no small matter; the Somalis have been responsible for virtually all of the lethal crime in the small Maine city since their arrival.

When Putnam's data were adjusted for class, income and other factors, they showed that the more people of different races lived in the same community, the greater the loss of trust. "They don't trust the local mayor, they don't trust the local paper, they don't trust other people and they don't trust institutions," said Putnam. "The only thing there's more of is protest marches and TV watching." And social media, porn, and e-commerce.

Clearly "diversity" has a corrosive effect on social capital. Julie Hotchkiss and Anil Rupasingha state that:

> Higher levels of in-migration lead to lower levels of community social capital. In-migration may increase a community's demographic heterogeneity, which Alesina and La Ferrara (2000) have found to diminish the community's level of social

capital. Additionally, communities with high migration rates may not bother to invest in social capital development (e.g., see Glaeser and Redlick 2009). And, since migrants are less likely to have close family ties in their new communities, high levels of in-migration may very well undermine feelings of trust (Kan 2007). While our findings are more in line with the studies cited here, they contradict findings by Lesage and Ha (2012) in which they report that in-migration has a positive effect on county-level social capital.[11]

Surely the one positive study on immigration and social capital will be shouted to the heavens, but with the overwhelming evidence to the contrary, as Steve Sailer writes:

Because policymakers almost certainly won't do what it would take to alleviate the harms caused by diversity – indeed, they won't even talk honestly about what would have to be done – it's crazy to exacerbate the problem through more mass immigration. As the issue of co-operation becomes ever more pressing, the quality of intellectual discourse on the topic declines – as Putnam's self-censorship revealed – precisely because of a lack of trust due to the mounting political power of "the diverse" to punish frank discussion.[12]

Yet another benefit of ethnic and racial diversity is that it hinders innovation! Wait, what? Yes, that's right: Bala Ramasamy and Matthew Yeung found in *Applied Economics Letters* that "ethnic diversity or fractionalization...has a negative effect on innovation. We find that countries that are ethnically homogenous but diverse in values orientation are the best innovators."[13] So exactly the opposite

---

11   Hotchkiss, Julie and Anil Rupasingha, "In-migration and Dilution of Social Capital," June 2018. Center for Economic Studies. Available at: www2.census. gov/ces/wp/2018/CES-WP-18-32.pdf.

12   Sailer, Steve, "Fragmented Future," January 15, 2007. *The American Conservative.* Available at: www.theamericanconservative.com/articles/fragmented-future/.

13   Ramasamy, Bala and Matthew CH Yeung, "Diversity and innovation,"

of everything that's being said and done. Westerners get to have everything stripped away from them to accommodate the enriching diversity – but not of thought, and certainly not anything white – that, as the Jewish Barbara Lerner Spectre said of Europe, "must occur." Dovetailing with the explosion in mass media and especially social media, a study of college students by University of Michigan researchers showed a 34% to 48% decline in empathy over an eight-year period. Say it with me: Freedom is slavery, and diversity is our strength. For Ricardo Duchesne:

> The most powerful moral assault on European pride and identity is the idea that Western civilisation achieved its greatness, industrial economic take-off in the eighteenth century, and subsequent mass affluence in the twentieth century, by exploiting and under-developing the rest of the world. This is one of the biggest lies inflicted on millions of European students in the last half century. The truth is that the diffusion of European technology has been the ultimate factor responsible for development outside the West…The question should never have been how Europe underdeveloped the Third World, but why did Westerners come to hold themselves morally culpable for the poverty of other nations when it should have been evidently obvious that without diffusion of their technologies no development would have been possible anywhere outside Europe.[14]

He is absolutely right, and it is that question we shall now answer.

February 12, 2016. *Applied Economics Letters*, Vol. 23, Issue 14. Available at: www.tandfonline.com/doi/abs/10.1080/13504851.2015.1130785.

14   Duchesne, Ricardo, "The Underdevelopment of European Pride," August 2016. *Salisbury Review*. Available at: www.researchgate.net/publication/311962969_The_Underdevelopment_of_European_Pride.

Chapter 3 - Outrage and Academia

"European man alone bears the spirit of civic republicanism, a tradition still largely alien to other races and peoples ...There is no shortage of evidence that the Changs, the Gonzales, and the Singhs still practice forms of ethnic nepotism strictly forbidden to Anglo-Protestants."- Andrew Fraser

The phrase "Demography is destiny" is an uncomfortable truth for many of us to accept, believing that all people cherish liberty and freedom. Unfortunately, this is simply not true. Consider the Democratic Party platform: it consists mostly of hand-outs, blaming, shaming, and the *restriction*, not expansion, of rights—unless of course you happen to belong to one of their privileged classes. The kind of America they are striving to create is one of strife and dysfunction, one where we can't trust each other, where we lock our doors and bar our windows, and retreat from public life and civic engagement to buying stuff on Amazon and binge-watching Netflix.

What happens next is classic divide-and-conquer for this isolated, disaffected, and easy-to-control population as suspicion and conflict become the order of the day. The Left is a civilization-destroying force that wants nothing more than not only to erase the people that built it, but their entire legacy. Their forward operating base has been the academy, starting all the way back in the 1920s with the institutionalization of the "Culture of Critique." Though many of the seminal Cultural Marxist figures were active prior to this time period, it was in the 1920s and 1930s that ideological pseudo-science began to co-opt academia and suffocate dissenting viewpoints particularly in the United States. Many had been expelled from Europe for their subversive ideas and activities. Especially relevant to our present discussion, quoting Andrew Joyce:

In a sense, the Frankfurt School, or Institute for Social Research, was the tip of the iceberg. The work of Horkheimer, Adorno, et al, both drew from, and enthused, a large and growing army of Jewish academics working in the field of public opinion and mass communications. This was a body of academics and activists keen to translate theories on "prejudice and the authoritarian personality" into action—to change the opinions and thinking of the host population. They would go on to develop forms of testing and analysis to further these goals, and their students would go on to take dominant positions in the fields of the mass media and mass communications. In many cases the academics speak openly of the need for control of the media and the mass dissemination of sophisticated propaganda (all of which could be tried and perfected at the expense of their universities in the name of "prejudice research").[1]

In-group favoritism and networking allowed for the rapid dissemination of their ideas, manufactured out of whole cloth with no empirical evidence to substantiate their claims, and in short order the old guard of the ivory tower had been supplanted by the new relativists.

What happened next, as Kevin MacDonald states, was "the assault on intergroup animosity was likened to the medical assault on deadly infectious diseases, and people with the disease were described by activists as 'infected' (Svonkin 1997, 30, 59)... Negative attitudes toward groups were viewed not as the result of competing group interests but rather as the result of individual psychopathology (Svonkin 1997, 75)." A plethora of academic studies—not to mention our real-world experiences—disconfirm the notion that opposition to demographic displacement/replacement is some kind of pathology or is born of "hate," but rather as Julie Hotchkiss and Anil Rupasingha report:

> Opposition to immigration can be shown to be rooted in economic competition, cultural prejudice, and redistributive financial pressures (Baerg, Hotchkiss, and Quispe-Agnoli 2018)...Loss in

---

1   Joyce, Andrew, "Modify the Standards of the In-Group," September 25, 2018. *Unz Review*. Available at: www.unz.com/article/modify-the-standards-of-the-in-group/.

community social capital may be yet another source of opposition to immigration.[2]

Of the four primary reasons for opposition to more immigration, only one could potentially be construed as a pathology, but whether it is or not, it occurs across all population groups, regardless of race, creed, or context. Dunbar's number, proposed by British anthropologist Robin Dunbar, holds that humans can comfortably maintain approximately 150 stable relationships. This is roughly equivalent to the outer limit of a tribe. It is only through empathy that one is able to emotionally project themselves past the hard limitations of tribe. Whites are genetically much more empathetic as a population than any other.

Additionally, the impulse or instinct to organize purely along racial lines and the prevalence of negative views of out-groups is *least* pronounced among whites, which may be pathological in its own right, but certainly not in the way the anti-white narrative has been constructed. The psychopathology claim also does not hold up when we consider postjudice – the views one forms *after* contact – nor does it account for the subconscious survival mechanisms we have adapted to identify danger and protect ourselves, in a word: instinct. Preferring the in-group is evolutionarily essential for long-term survival in genetic terms. What is pathological is the impulse to embrace the alien at the expense of one's own, especially in the face of overwhelming evidence that such actions are imperiling, not enriching.

Most population groups never progress beyond the limitations of tribe and kin, and it is only through the relative weakening of kinship ties that a society may advance into what we call civilization for it requires large-scale cooperation. As Edward Goldsmith notes, "Democracy, in the sense of self-government, only becomes possible once the people become bound by a common culture and once a strong public opinion develops to oppose any deviation from the established code of behaviour."

---

2   Hotchkiss, Julie and Anil Rupasingha, "In-migration and Dilution of Social Capital," June 2018. Center for Economic Studies. Available at: www2.census. gov/ces/wp/2018/CES-WP-18-32.pdf.

Our common culture and established code of behavior are at present unraveling in the form of social disintegration. The more isolated someone is, the fewer bonds they have, and the easier they are to control. The maintenance of the modern super-state depends on an ever-increasing crack-down on the truth, and a deliberate, coordinated effort to sever all communal, familial, and national ties via rigorous exposure to propaganda generated by the media, and state- and corporate-sponsored policies meant to atomize people. To again quote Goldsmith:

> If a society disintegrates beyond the clan or village level, it ceases to be a viable social unit. Such disintegration can qualify as pathological...The largest unit of organization is the family and above this, no effective co-operation is possible. According to [Edward] Banfield, such a society will display a number of related characteristics. For instance; "No-one will further the interest of the group or the community except as it is to his private advantage to do so. In other words, the hope of material gain in the short run will be the only motive for concern of public affairs...the law will be disregarded when there is no reason to fear punishment...an office holder will take bribes when he can...but whether he takes bribes or not, it will be assumed by society that he does." Clearly such a society will not be capable of running itself, i.e. of constituting a self-regulating system. Rather, it will require a bureaucracy and other external controls to keep it together. Similarly, a society in which the families themselves have disintegrated and in which the largest unit of effective organization is the individual or the incomplete, single-parent, family, is even more clearly pathological.[3]

Pathology, for the ruling class, is obviously a very good thing indeed. It is essential, in fact, for the implementation of their agenda. Questioning their now-established orthodoxy is a one-way ticket to being branded a "racist," "anti-Semite," or "phobe" of some kind (even if you never

---

3   Goldsmith, Edward, *Can Britain Survive?* Sphere Books: London. 1971. Accessed via: http://www.edwardgoldsmith.org/1074/social-disintegration-causes/.

mentioned race, religion, or orientation), which keeps most people in cowed silence in abject fear of such an accusation, and precludes any public deviation from the Cult-Marx line.

The self-contained epistemology of critical theory and Leftist historical revisionism, in addition to the re-definition of terminology to suit political purposes, has the net effect of closing certain avenues of inquiry which would undoubtedly refute their egregious fabrications. In a page straight out of the Saul Alinsky playbook, however, they are eager to paint any contradictory evidence as "discredited," "debunked," or "pseudo-scientific." This is one key aspect of how the transgender and climate change agendas have been so successful in recent years.

Critical theory has largely supplanted the Socratic method of inquiry not only on North American campuses, but in the United Kingdom and across much of the rest of the West. It has been so ensconced for so long that several generations of university-bound students have positively marinated in it. Little wonder, then, that society at large is beginning to resemble the seemingly-isolated episodes of screeching wokelets on campus that drew attention at places like Yale University, Evergreen State College, and Middlebury College in the middle of the last decade.

Any system predicated on totalitarianism wants – *needs* – control of your gray matter. If it's nothing but addled Cult-Marx soup with a purse or wallet, so much the better. As with so much else emanating from the academy and taking root in our hyper-restricted discourse – indeed, as much of the cause of this restricted discourse – the concept of speech-as-violence is derived from critical theory, giving the notion an intellectual patina of legitimacy in order to justify the suppression of non-ideologically-compliant speech and thought. It is, in essence, sophistry as censorship, guilt-as-immutable-characteristic, and on top of that, wouldn't you know it, collective violence is strongly correlated with social pluralism![4] Certainly no one saw that coming!

---

4   Rummel, Rudolph J., "Is Collective Violence Correlated with Social Pluralism?"

More Lenin than Lennon, these dogmatic ideologues find it appropriate to destroy your livelihood because you don't have the correct viewpoint, and even more galling, often cannot articulate why they believe you are wrong. Thought is secondary to emotion for them. We have entered the realm of extreme subjectivity and relativism. The Left has so thoroughly altered the linguistic and moral landscape, it's been rendered *terra incognita*. Duke University theology professor Paul Griffiths was forced to resign his post not long ago after issuing a response to an e-mail urging professors to attend "voluntary diversity training." Condemned as a "racist, sexist, and bigot" (naturally), Griffiths, who merely pointed out the exercise would be "intellectually flaccid...[with] bromides, clichés, and amen-corner rah-rahs in plenty," is just another victim in the ideological war being waged on reality.

Those who do not toe the party line and support the notion that enforced equity and racial parity is for the greater good, will be tarred, feathered, and made to walk the plank. The growing ranks of unemployed collegiate dissidents is growing at an alarming rate, replaced by ideologues and administrators. Contrast the words of Griffiths with those of Drexel University professor George Ciccariello-Maher's: "All I want for Christmas is white genocide." Ciccariello-Maher was not forced to resign because his comments evidently fell under the umbrella of "protected speech," while Griffiths and many like him, such as Nicholas and Erika Christakis at Yale and Susan Quade at Concordia University have been forced out of their positions for what range from legitimate critiques to simply figures of speech, as in Quade's case, but what campus higher-ups (and their Cultural Marxist students and professors) decry as "hate speech."

If, as James Frank Dobie once mused, "The average PhD thesis is nothing but the transference of bones from one graveyard to another," we can see the application of academy-aided Marxism transporting bones from a graveyard with an awful lot of plots to the new intersectional one being freshly prepared. It is vital here

May 1997. *Journal of Peace Research*, Vol. 34, No. 2. Available at: https://journals.sagepub.com/doi/10.1177/0022343397034002004.

to consider what Tomislav Sunic tabbed "the cavaderous Freudo-Marxian scholasticism that rots in the dank catacombs of postmodern academia." The Frankfurt School, synthesizing the terribly destructive philosophies of Marx, Gramsci, and others, set up shop on American college campuses in the 1930s and never left, mutually reinforced by the Boasian anthropologists and other Marxist apologists who had established a presence on campus even earlier, only growing stronger with time to the point where we now have almost total ideological conformity among the professoriat.

With alarming regularity, from moral panics to "anti-fascist" riots to professors with ties to ISIS (Julio Pino of Kent State University, who also allegedly attempted to recruit students to join; maybe he should call Anjem Choudary), it has been incident after incident illustrating how deeply corrupted academia has become. From the lunacy of a Vanderbilt University professor blaming 9/11 on racism, slavery, and the Navajo genocide to a Diablo Valley College professor smashing someone's head with a bike lock, the modern academy – with its Cult-Marx professoriate, bloated bureaucracies that ensure "compliance" with the ruthless efficiency of the NKVD, and "student-activists" – is no longer the bastion of open inquiry and debate it was intended to be. A university education looks ever-more like a combination of a Soviet re-education camp and a day-care. The student body seems to be regressing to a median age of about five, distortions spoon-fed to them by doughy professional axe-grinders, agitators, and grievance-mongers. If sticks and stones break their bones, then words are what *really* hurt.

The omnipresence of "hate" appears to be the main preoccupation of the professoriate and the administrative commissars, and is certainly one of the central fixtures of campus life. Trinity College professor Johnny Eric Williams took to his Twitter account to use the hashtag #LetThemFuckingDie in reference to white males. Texas A&M professor Tommy Curry advocated violence against whites as a corrective measure to perceived racism in a podcast interview back in 2012. Now-terminated Essex County College professor Lisa Durden taunted whites on *Tucker Carlson Tonight* when the host pressed her on her support for racially-exclusionary events: "Boo-hoo-hoo, you white people are just angry you couldn't use your white privilege card to get invited to the Black Lives Matter all-black Memorial Day celebration."

University of Delaware anthropology professor Kathy Dettwyler declared on Facebook that Otto Warmbier "got exactly what he deserved" because he was "typical of a mind-set of a lot of the young, white, rich, clueless males." According to Boston University professor Saida Grundy, "White masculinity isn't a problem for America's colleges, white masculinity is THE problem for America's colleges." John Griffin of the Art Institute of Washington believes that Republicans "should be lined up and shot. That's not hyperbole." Fresno State professor Randa Jarrar gloated over the death of Barbara Bush on Twitter (s*ic*):

> Barbara Bush was a generous and smart and amazing racist who, along with her husband, raised a war criminal. I'm happy the witch is dead. Can't wait for the rest of her family to fall to their demise the way 1.5 million Iraqis have.

Kevin Allred, formerly of Rutgers University, had the following to say on Twitter:

> "Will the Second Amendment be as cool when I buy a gun and start shooting at random white people or no …?"

Another Boston University professor, Kyna Hamill, published a paper condemning "Jingle Bells" for its "racist history" as a jingle in blackface. Sarah Bond of the University of Iowa lamented the fact that sculptures from the classical world are now primarily associated with white marble. Princeton University Keeanga-Yamahtta Taylor made the deeply revealing and insightful comments during her commencement address at Hampshire College that Donald Trump is a "racist, sexist megalomaniac."

As Middlebury College, Yale University, Evergreen State College, the University of California at Berkeley, and so many other institutions of what we used to call higher learning have shown, the students are just as eager to get in on the action. Lucía Martínez Valdivia, a "mixed-race queer" assistant professor of English at Reed College, had a lecture about Sappho disrupted by students protesting the college's mandatory humanities class as "white supremacist." Just when you think the Left cannot get any more preposterous, there you go – protesting a queer, mixed-race woman's lecture on a queer female poet. The protesters also indicted Aristotle and Plato for good measure. Martínez Valdivia states:

> Nuance and careful reasoning are not the tools of the oppressor, meant to deceive and gaslight and undermine and distract. On the contrary: These tools can help prove what those who use them think – or even what they feel – to be true. They make arguments more, not less, convincing, using objective evidence to make a point rather than relying on the persuasive power of a subjective feeling…Ultimately, this is a call for empathy, for stretching our imaginations to try to inhabit and understand positions that aren't ours and the points of view of people who aren't us. A grounding in the study of the humanities can help students encounter ideas with care and…realizing – and accepting – that no person, no text, no class, is without flaws. The things we study are, after all, products of human hands.[5]

She's absolutely correct, but the un-reasoning Left refuses to consider what is actually a very insightful commentary on the nature of creation so fundamental to the arts, and on the beauty and tragedy of a fatally-flawed humanity. This idea that empathy does not need to be divorced from logic and reason – that it is in fact inextricably intertwined and that rationality and critical thinking aren't "tools of white supremacy" but are instead universally applicable and vital to processing the world and the people in it in all their dimensionality – is increasingly becoming antithetical to the deeply sentimental worldview of the Left

---

5   Martínez Valdivia, Lucía, "Professors like me can't stay silent about this extremist movement on campuses," October 27, 2017. *The Washington Post.* Available at: www.washingtonpost.com/opinions/professors-like-me-cant-stay-silent-about-this-extremist-moment-on-campuses/2017/10/27/fd7aded2-b9b0-11e7-9e58-e6288544af98_story.html.

wing, where the Western *logos* itself has become the enemy of emotive, panicked hysteria masquerading as a coherent set of principles. In this infantile worldview of good-and-bad, "hate" becomes a sufficient explanation for people's motivations, and for anything that falls outside the ideological confines of Leftist "thought." Even more disturbing, however, is the idea that even this floating emotion of "hate" may not even be fully understood.

One thing is clear, though – dissent will not be tolerated. Will Creeley, an attorney for the Foundation for Individual Rights in Education (FIRE), expresses concern that, the "U.S. Supreme Court's stark warning in *Sweezy v. New Hampshire* will prove prophetic: 'Teachers and students must always remain free to inquire, to study and to evaluate, to gain new maturity and understanding; otherwise our civilization will stagnate and die.'" Everywhere is the push for safe spaces, the conflation of speech with violence, and the drive to dis-invite and de-platform speakers who run afoul of the egalitarians. Nevertheless, these poisonous ideas have seeped deep into the fabric of academia, where they are not only perpetuated and remain unchallenged, but spread into our society's daily discourse as a direct result of sustained attempts at indoctrination in the academy, and increasingly even earlier in K-12.

The reason things seem to be deteriorating on campus has everything to do with its closed environment, where dissenting opinions are discouraged and forced out, and mutually reinforcing viewpoints are encouraged and advanced. Essentially you then have an echo chamber environment where bad or at least faulty ideas are perpetuated and due to viewpoint uniformity (and hostility to different perspectives) the ideas and suppositions advanced in the academy are never challenged, and in the rare instances where dissenting evidence emerges from the university setting, the data is suppressed and the individual responsible is punished or marginalized in some way.

Political orientation is a pretty good proxy for worldview; for all of the talk of diversity, in this crucial area it is sorely lacking on campus. From a 2016 *Boston Magazine* survey, we see that liberal professors in New England outnumber conservatives 28-to-1, and from a study conducted by UCLA published in 2012, we can see the growing uniformity among the professoriate nation-wide is approaching a totality of the profession:[6]

	2010-11	2007-8
Far left	12.4%	8.8%
Liberal	50.3%	47.0%
Middle of the road	25.4%	28.4%
Conservative	11.5%	15.2%
Far right	0.4%	0.7%

By 2014, a mere 10% of professors identified as conservatives, largely confined to business and the hard sciences. In contrast, per a 2007 survey, a whopping 17.6% of social sciences professors openly identified as Marxist, with 24% stating that their beliefs were "radical" and 20.6% describing themselves as "activists." From this same survey conducted by Neil Gross and Solon Simmons entitled "The Social and Political Views of American Professors," 19% of humanities professors self-identified as "radical" and 26.2% described themselves as "activists." In a sample of fifty-one of the top sixty liberal arts colleges studied by the National Association of Scholars' Mitchell Langbert in 2018, 39% of faculties had *zero* Republicans, and out of a pool of nearly 8,700 professors, registered Democrats outnumbered registered Republicans ten-to-one.

As bad as this is, John Wilson, an editor of the AAUP's "Academe" blog, believes that it is the administrators who are really the problem as the architects and enforcers of the censorship and speech codes that are so prevalent on college campuses. As one example of the blood-engorged ticks that are collegiate bureaucracies/administrations, the University of Michigan has *ninety-three* full-time diversity and equity staff, twenty-six of whom earn six figures, while nationally almost half of college classes are taught by adjunct (part-time) professors

---

6   Jaschik, Scott, "Moving Further to the Left," October 24, 2012. *Inside Higher Ed.* Available at: www.insidehighered.com/news/2012/10/24/survey-finds-professors-already-liberal-have-moved-further-left.

with no semester-to-semester guarantee of classes and no benefits (to their credit Ann Arbor only has 17% of its classes taught by adjuncts). Jon Marcus from the New England Center for Investigative Reporting illuminates:

> The number of non-academic administrative and professional employees at U.S. colleges and universities has more than doubled in the last 25 years, vastly outpacing the growth in the number of students or faculty, according to an analysis of federal figures. The disproportionate increase in the number of university staffers who neither teach nor conduct research has continued unabated in more recent years. From 1987 until 2011-12...universities and colleges collectively added 517,636 administrators and professional employees, or an average of 87 every working day, according to the analysis of federal figures... "There's just a mind-boggling amount of money per student that's being spent on administration," said Andrew Gillen, a senior researcher at the institutes. "It raises a question of priorities." Universities have added these administrators and professional employees even as they've substantially shifted classroom teaching duties from full-time faculty to less-expensive part-time adjunct faculty and teaching assistants...Since 1987, universities have also started or expanded departments devoted to marketing, diversity, disability, sustainability, security, environmental health, recruiting, technology, and fundraising, and added new majors and graduate and athletics programs, satellite campuses, and conference centers... "It's almost Orwellian," said [economist Richard] Vedder. "They'll say, 'We'll save money if we centralize.' Then they hire a provost or associate provost or an assistant business manager in charge of shared services, and then that person hires an assistant, and you end up with more people than you started with."[7]

All of this should rightly beg the question of what purpose all of this

---

7   Marcus, Jon, "New Analysis Shows Problematic Boom In Higher Ed Administrations," February 6, 2014. *Huffington Post*. Available at: www.huffpost. com/entry/higher-ed-administrators-growth_n_4738584?guccounter=1.

administrative bloat serves. It certainly isn't to benefit the quality of the education students receive, and it only adds to the onerous costs of attaining a college degree. The aforementioned AAUP is responsible for the 1915 document that still stands as the gold standard for the mission statement of what a university's actual purpose should be:

1. To promote inquiry and advance the sum of human knowledge;

2. To provide general instruction to the students; and

3. To develop experts for various branches of the public service.

Nowhere is there an imperative to produce "professional activists" or to advocate for that most nebulous of terms: social justice. Public service in this context is to contribute to society in a productive and meaningful way, be it as an engineer, a rocket scientist, or a teacher. Instead, students learn the wonders of communism, whites learn to hate themselves, and everyone else learns to hate them.

A recent event at The College of William & Mary sponsored by the ACLU entitled "Students and the First Amendment" was shut down due to Black Lives Matter protesters, who exercised the "heckler's veto" and asserted, among the usual tripe, that "Liberalism is White Supremacy." Where else can you go from there? What common ground can there be when a significant segment of the Left is saying *its own professed values* of pluralism and tolerance are white supremacy?

In the oppressor/oppressed paradigm espoused by so many members of academia and various advocates for "social justice," the layering of colonialism-informed contexts – to whatever limited degree they're transmitted or received – with feminist critique (such as feminist standpoint theory and gender socialization), post-structuralism, and all types of post-modernism and critical theory informs what has the appearance of a new linguistic construct, but one that's existence can only be assured, paradoxically, by the existence of that which it seeks to critique and undermine. Without it, most of the Cultural Marxists and their ilk would also cease to exist as they are largely incapable of providing an alternative; they deconstruct to deconstruct, not to re-construct. They "sort through" pop culture's detritus or historical narratives with the purpose of pointing out inequality, to reveal the (real or imagined) disenfranchised voices on the margins of text and discourse; they situate themselves in the flow of several critical discourses with contemporary resonance and engage with them with the intent to launch an assault on the foundations of Western society. They have been wildly successful thus far. Consider the following synopsis of critical race theory from Harvard University's website:

Critical race theorists thus try to combine pragmatist and utopian visions...Critical race scholars identify and embrace a radical tradition of race-conscious mobilization as an empowerment strategy for African-Americans, Latinos, Asians, and other persons of color...They oppose apparently neutral rules, such as color-blindness, and one-person, one-vote... Several critical race theorists became mobilized in the 1980s by incidents of hate speech on college campuses and elsewhere. They developed analyses of the injuries experienced by students of color who were targets of such incidents and critiques of the prevailing First Amendment/freedom of speech approach taken by the campus administrators. Words do wound, they argued. They worked to articulate codes for regulating campus speech and defended those codes against First Amendment challenges offered by both theorists and plaintiffs in courts. Noting that freedom of speech is never given absolute protection, they argued that curbs on hate speech would have much in common with existing defamation and obscenity laws and the doctrines excluding fighting words and threats from First Amendment protection. They argued that law, and the First Amendment, could be interpreted to fight subordination. They also argued that the First Amendment's values of self-fulfillment, knowledge, and participation are undermined, not served, when hate speech gains legal protection. Although no court upheld hate speech codes against First Amendment challenges, the critical race theorists' effort altered the terms of the debate and taught many about the kinds of injuries tolerated in the name of the First Amendment.[8]

---

8   "Critical Race Theory." *The Bridge*. Harvard University. Available at: https://cyber.harvard.edu/bridge/CriticalTheory/critical4.htm.

Given the "injuriousness" permitted by the First Amendment, abridgement of said amendment is necessary in the form of "hate speech" laws and other legal protections rendering all protected groups beyond reproach and legally immune from criticism. If the United States is only a set of principles that anyone can adopt, this clearly betrays that notion. It explicitly acknowledges that American values are at odds with its recent imports. Critical race theory rejects colorblind merit, it rejects the *logos* and objectivity, and instead of "combating stereotypes" as its adherents initially claim, it is at its heart a project aimed at demonizing whites and forcing us into positions of subservience, if not ultimately eradicating us. It is fundamentally anti-intellectual, anti-Western, and anti-white. These shock troops tear the West down bit by bit, many totally unaware that they're just doing the leg-work for the Establishment to re-fashion their New Soviet Men (or Androgynes as the case may be).

Critical race theory is just one aspect of Cultural Marxist considerations of "identity" explained in the theory of intersectionality built on a decidedly un-academic or even provable foundation. As Bill Barlow writes:

> Critical Race theory not only directs how to structure the university, but also how to structure the relation of the individual to the state. Racially-based taxes, racially-based employment quotas, racially-based redistributions of wealth: none would be beyond the theoretical horizon of Critical Race theory. All are justified by an appeal to inadequate racial justice, an appeal that can neither be proved nor disproved, an appeal that can just as easily be used for naked racial subordination. All fall within a context where speech labeled as "hurtful" and "racist" could be punishable by law, and opponents of the racial regime would be silenced.[9]

The precepts of critical race theory, and critical theory in general, are

---

9   Barlow, Bill, "Racism Justified: A Look at Critical Race Theory," February 2016. *The Harvard Law Record*. Available at: http://hlrecord.org/2016/02/ racism-justified-a-critical-look-at-critical-race-theory/#_ftn22.

by definition authoritarian. The Leftist-enforced equivalences, being wholly unnatural, can only exist in a totalitarian state. Cheryl Harris decrees:

> Property rights will then be respected, but they will not be absolute; rather, they will be considered against a societal requirement for affirmative action...In essence this conception of affirmative action is moving towards reallocation of power.[10]

We can observe the natural end-point of this kind of "thinking" in action in the former Rhodesia and increasingly South Africa, and though we are not there yet, it is moving toward its advanced stages in the United States as well. The poisonousness of critical theory in general and critical race theory (often in tandem with post-colonialism) specifically is certainly not limited to the ethnic cleansings in Africa or the authoritarian bid for power by the "Coalition of the Fringes" in the United States. The first critical race theory seminar in the UK took place in November 2006 in Manchester, England, and the mind-rot has spread with frightening speed; concurrently, the neo-liberal Establishment has given prominent platforms to anti-white mouthpieces such as the half-Jewish, half-Ghanaian Afua Hirsch and Jewish "migration" advocate/historian Simon Schama. The anti-white rhetoric in the UK is often even harsher than that in the US, perhaps as per capita compensation. The state has certainly thrown its entire legal apparatus behind white dispossession, and in extremely heavy-handed fashion. Bolshevik/Cult-Marx control of Canadian media and academe has seen the perception of the Great White North shift to the Great Brown Melting-Pot in record time.

Intersectional grievance-mongering starts by proclaiming the moral imperative of equal representation as long as it isn't too strenuous or doesn't involve an increased risk of death in the workplace: jobs in marketing or as college diversity coordinators or non-profit desk-jockeying are the order of the day. The goal-posts then inevitably

---

10   Harris, Cheryl, ed. Kimberle Crenshaw, "Whiteness As Property." *Critical Race Theory: The Key Writings That Formed The Movement.* New York Press: New York. 1995.

move to where whites need to "step aside" from positions of power, and finally to nakedly genocidal rhetoric. Consider Sarah Jeong and the non-reaction (by the Left) to her stance on "Canceling Whiteness."

Race is, apparently, a social construct yet whites bear the genetic stain of the Mark of Cain. The Women's March has an "algorithm" for "marginalized peoples," where they speak strictly of identity in not only a categorical sense – trans, "indigenous folk" – but again in unyielding, fixed binaries, which is rather peculiar for an ideology obsessed with pan-sexuality, gender-fluidity, and the like. Instead we hear about "white women trying to make it all about themselves..." Speaking of indigenous folk, Europeans are the indigenous people of their continent, although the BBC reports otherwise, stating that the Sami people are "the only officially recognised indigenous people in the EU" in an obvious effort to de-legitimize ethno-national claims to the soil and in the endgame fully erase Europeans altogether. As with "diversity," "indigenous" in its present usage simply means "non-white." Never mind that for tens of thousands of years there has been an unbroken chain from those ancient Europeans to the modern ones, as modern Europeans all share some ancestry with those ancient hunter-gatherer peoples. Nothing would appreciably change apparently if Germany became Turkish or Spain Moroccan or Italy Eritrean – a person is a person is a person, unless...

Outside of the obvious incongruence of this school of "thought," what sticks out is the vilification of one race and one race only, and the use of that race as a scapegoat for everyone else's shortcomings. Yet despite the inherent evil of whites and Western civilization, it is apparently a human right to have access to us and the kinds of societies we build. Recalling the concept of property rights, Gloria J. Ladson-Billings of the University of Wisconsin-Madison School of Education states that:

Whiteness [is] the ultimate property which whites alone can possess. It is valuable and is property. The "property functions of whiteness" – rights to disposition, rights to use and enjoyment, reputation and status property, and the absolute right to exclude – make the American dream a more likely and attainable reality for whites as citizens. For a critical race theory critic, the white skin color that some Americans possess is like owning a piece of property. It grants privileges to the owner that a renter (or a person of color) would not be afforded.[11]

There's a lot to consider there, but let me start with this: many Ashkenazi Jews do in fact "rent whiteness" when it is beneficial to them; by Ladson-Billings's logic, when Ashkenazim "pass," this is theft. Racial identity and group affiliation are encouraged for non-whites, so long as they espouse the proper set of beliefs, but it is absolutely forbidden for *all* whites unless they are "speaking on behalf of" whites in order to denigrate or disempower said group. One common phenomenon in the era of social media often sees Ashkenazi Jews, usually in the media, posing as whites in order to condemn or "apologize for" whites as a group, and then dis-avowing their "whiteness" to avoid personal blow-back, colloquially called the "Dear Fellow White People" strategy.

Similarly, many mixed-race individuals such as the pop star Halsey "pass" when it is beneficial but use the race card to critique whiteness, such as her asinine criticism of hotel shampoos, when it serves to signal a different kind of status. To my way of thinking this is the ultimate privilege, especially when you not only make the rules, but change them whenever it becomes expedient. For instance, Martin Luther King, Jr.'s "I Have a Dream" speech used to be the litmus test for the future, post-color America, but when parity failed to be achieved, the critical race theorists rejected merit as a valid criterion.

Returning to Ladson-Billings's concept of "whiteness as property," such a lens makes sense in the context of a wholly materialistic Left that not only uncritically supports consumer culture and environmental degradation, but has a bizarre fixation on "black bodies" and believes one's sexuality is a legitimate marker of "identity." Their "truths" are so self-evident that the Swedish professor Germund Hesslow came under fire for simply stating that men and women are biologically

---

11 Ladson-Billings, Gloria J., eds. Donna Deyhle, Laurence Parker, Sofia Villenas, *Race Isn't Real: Critical Race Theory and Qualitative Studies in Education.* Westview Press: Boulder, CO. 1999.

different. Such statements are liable to get you a lifetime ban from Twitter and perhaps a knock on the door from some rainbow-uniformed policemen in Dear Old Blighty.

In Dave Rubin's "marketplace of ideas," there are more gays and transgenders at Yale and Harvard, for example, than there are conservatives. Curious for an ideology whose adherents claim to not only value diversity, but believe that it is a sufficient reason to detonate Europeans' ancestral homelands for its cuisine, the growth of GDP, and record-setting rapes and acid attacks. In another paradox, many Leftists signal their "easy virtue," while simultaneously engaging in the intrusive policing of others' sexuality and dating preferences. Their "free love" is reflected in the fact that Millennials have less sex than their parents but somehow have more STDs. Beauty is not in the eye of the beholder any longer, it is in the eye of the judicial branch, the cultural commissars, and whatever the media-entertainment complex decide it is. In fact, I recently saw a sticker that proclaimed "Love is Pride," meaning, apparently, that the only legitimate form of love is something from the LGBTQ-etc. acronym. The rest of us are just acting, I guess.

Returning to the idea of ownership in Ladson-Billings's "property functions of whiteness," this is highly "problematic," to use the Left's parlance, for it evokes images of slavery, the kind that apparently was only ever practiced by whites and for which we must surrender everything and just die already! Nevertheless, though we may "own" our skin, the other "rights" enumerated no longer apply to whites. As far as reputation and status, we are being vilified for every possible inequity under the sun, even if we had nothing to do with it. Rights to use and enjoyment? That would be for "people of color" to have unfettered access to our nations, our cultures, our ideas, and our money. The absolute right to exclude? We are not even allowed our own neighborhoods, let alone countries. Where are the libertarians on freedom of association? Dead quiet. It is clear, from a critical race theory perspective and as affirmed by Cheryl Harris that property rights are *not* respected, let alone absolute, especially when there is a "reallocation of power" to be had.

As just one recent example among a depressing litany, the University of Pennsylvania Graduate Students Union (GET-UP) generated a list of grievances based upon the claim that, wait for it… "Graduate student workers from marginalized backgrounds still experience structural inequalities throughout their time at the University of Pennsylvania, and these problems often go unnoticed, ignored, or silenced."

GET-UP hopes to accomplish the following: "[Making] diversity about more than just inclusion, multiculturalism, or celebrating our differences, but about building the collective power to transform the structural inequalities that so many students from marginalized backgrounds face on a daily basis." Here's how they believe they are going to accomplish this:

- Working with the administration to collect and make readily available data on diversity and discrimination on campus;

- Improvements to concrete material conditions such as higher stipends, summer funding, and healthcare for dependents;

- Increased funds for Counseling and Psychological Services (CAPS) to hire more staff, with a focus on increasing diversity and specifically addressing the experiences of marginalized students;

- Greater transparency about funding, degree requirements, teaching and research opportunities;

- A legal contract with provisions against discrimination;

- A formal, neutral, centralized, legally-backed grievance procedure for all cases of discrimination;

- Greater visibility of the issues that Master's students from marginalized backgrounds face, such as the difficulty of securing financial aid;

- Legal support for students from marginalized backgrounds;

- Trainings for faculty, staff, and graduate students about discrimination, microaggressions, and diversity;

- More effective teacher training for graduate student TAs that foregrounds the role of diversity, discrimination, and privilege in the classroom;

- Lobbying for graduate student workers to become more involved in hiring processes;

- Holding the university accountable to its commitment to diversity;

- Following precedents set at other universities, such as the University of Michigan, including a provision in the union contract that provides compensation to graduate students who work to address diversity and racial inequality on campus, rather than relying on their unpaid labor;

- Offering support to existing minority student groups on campus.[12]

This looks identical to the "students of color" at Dartmouth College's list of demands or that of so many others.[13] Besides the fact that the university already does most of this, *these are graduate students at a prestigious American university.* "Colored" (of color?) or not, they can count themselves among the most infinitesimally small percentage of privileged human beings in history. Oh but, "Students from lower-income backgrounds have said they don't receive the material support they need, like better healthcare, travel grants, summer funding, or adequate funding to complete their degrees." Most middle-class students do not have that, either. And the part where, "International students worry about visas, taxes, and the lack of funding opportunities for non-citizens"? About how, "Undocumented students across the university constantly wonder if the administration will actually defend them from deportation"? Stay home. Simple.

What this list translates to is, "We want equitable treatment for all colors, creeds, and sexualities, but we want preferential treatment for these particular ones!" If that weren't the case, why feel the need

---

12 Available at: http://getupgrads.org/issues/diversity/.

13 See: www.scribd.com/doc/200999679/Transcription-of-the-speech-given-at-the-steps-of-Hill-Auditorium-BBUM; www.counter-currents.com/2017/05/american-university-the-unwitting-microcosm-of-american-universities/; www.thedamnds.org; www.dartblog.com/Dartmouth_Freedom_Budget_Plan.pdf

to, "Foreground and make visible the experiences of students from marginalized backgrounds"? If they cannot win based on merit – and why would someone successful bother agitating for such a list? – they will endeavor to change the playing field. Judge Macklin Fleming's response to Yale University's 1969 decision to establish a racial quota for each incoming class proved remarkably prescient:

> The faculty can talk around the clock about disadvantaged background, and it can excuse inferior performance because of poverty, environment, inadequate cultural tradition, lack of educational opportunity, etc. The fact remains that black and white students will be exposed to each other under circumstances in which demonstrated intellectual superiority rests with the whites…No one can be expected to accept an inferior status willingly. The black students, unable to compete on even terms in the study of law, inevitably will seek other means to achieve recognition and self-expression. This is likely to take two forms. First, agitation to change the environment from one in which they are unable to compete to one in which they can. Demands will be made for elimination of competition, reduction in standards of performance, adoption of courses of study which do not require intensive legal analysis, and recognition for academic credit of sociological activities which have only an indirect relationship to legal training. Second, it seems probable that this group will seek personal satisfaction and public recognition by aggressive conduct, which, although ostensibly directed at external injustices and problems, will in fact be primarily motivated by the psychological needs of the members of the group to overcome feelings of inferiority caused by lack of success in their studies. Since the common denominator of the group of students with lower qualifications is one of race this aggressive expression will undoubtedly take the form of racial demands–the employment of faculty on the basis of race, a marking system based on race, the establishment of a black curriculum and a black law journal, an increase in black financial aid, and a rule against expulsion of black students who fail to satisfy minimum academic standards.[14]

---

14 Fleming, Macklin, "The black quota at Yale Law School," June 9, 1969. Letter

Of all the lies of equality, the intellectual disparities at the group level between racial and ethnic groups are perhaps the most painful to accept. But we cannot continue pretending that fish climb trees as well as squirrels; each is uniquely adapted to its particular environment. This is biological fact, but the present dogma precludes any rational discussion of the obvious biological differences that separate Senegalese from Swedes.

A study by Donald I. Templer and Hiroko Arikawa concludes that:

Persons in colder climates tend to have higher IQs than persons in warmer climates. We correlated mean IQ of 129 countries with per capita income, skin color, and winter and summer temperatures, conceptualizing skin color as a multigenerational reflection of climate. The highest correlations were 0.92 (rho =0.91) for skin color, 0.76 (rho =0.76) for mean high winter temperature, 0.66 (rho =0.68) for mean low winter temperature, and 0.63 (rho = 0.74) for real gross domestic product per capita. The correlations with population of country controlled for are almost identical. Our findings provide strong support for the observation of Lynn and of Rushton that persons in colder climates tend to have higher IQs.[15]

As pertains to disparities in the United States specifically, just 16% of blacks have IQs over 100, and a paltry 5% of blacks have IQs over 110. Whites have an average IQ of 100. This is a very uncomfortable truth for many to acknowledge, but it is the Occam's razor that explains the persistent "achievement gap." Thomas Sowell writes:

My own research was financed in part by a grant from a foundation that told me to remove any mention of IQ research from the

---

to Louis Pollak. Available at: www.nationalaffairs.com/storage/app/uploads/ public/58e/1a4/ae3/58e1a4ae36717528770103.pdf.

15 Templer, Donald I. and Hiroko Arikawa, "Temperature, skin color, per capita income, and IQ: An international perspective," November 28, 2005. *Intelligence* 34. Available at: http://emilkirkegaard.dk/en/wp-content/uploads/Donald-I.-Templer-Hiroko-Arikawa-Temperature-skin-color-per-capita-income-and-IQ-An-international-perspective.pdf.

activities listed in my project's application...Many schools and boards of education also did not want it on the record that they had cooperated by supplying data for any such research...A well-known black "social scientist" urged me not to do any such research...As it turned out, the research showed that the average IQ difference between black and white Americans – 15 points – was nothing unusual.[16]

Richard Lynn and Tatu Vanhanen found that there was a correlation of 0.733 between GDP and national IQ over the eighty-one nations they measured, and there is also a clear correlation between IQ and crime. That in addition to the fact that racial differences – from athletic ability to intelligence to predispositions to certain diseases – are scientifically uncontroversial people are capable of pattern recognition and are hard-wired to be wary of outsiders is, for the Left, only proof-positive that "harmful stereotypes" continue to persist in the modern world. And yet, says Lee Jussim:

The double standard of heavy criticism of criteria for accuracy but acceptance of the very same criteria when used to demonstrate phenomena seeming to provide insights into sources of inequality is not restricted to interpersonal expectations. The same pattern can be observed regarding research on stereotype threat. Stereotype threat was originally the idea that cultural stereotypes about intelligence (e.g., for African-Americans) or achievement in some domains (e.g., math for women) leads to anxiety or concern among members of those groups for confirming those stereotypes...Such anxiety then undermines their academic achievement (e.g., Steele 1997). Stereotype threat has gained widespread visibility and acceptance among social scientists...I find one aspect of such acceptance peculiarly ironic. Despite the frequent objections to IQ tests that periodically appear in social science, editorial, and intellectual outlets...I am aware of no social scientific criticism of the use of cognitive ability tests as criteria for establishing stereotype threat-related phenomena.

16   Sowell, Thomas, "Race, IQ, black crime, and facts liberals ignore," October 8, 2002. Available at: http://www.sullivan-county.com/id5/sowell.htm.

If cognitive ability tests are invalid, then research identifying conditions under which some people score higher or lower on an invalid, meaningless test would not seem to be particularly informative. Why, then, have cognitive ability tests been the target of so much criticism as measures of intelligence or achievement, but not as criteria with which to establish stereotype threat?[17]

Because stereotype threat is yet another whole-cloth creation meant to obscure the real population-level differences between groups. These are very obviously not ironclad, but they are real and they are manifested in different ways.

Just as a point of reference, let's look at IQ break-down between sexes. Among whites, men are 1.438 times more likely to have an IQ over 120 than women and 2.525 times more likely to have an IQ over 140; women, however, are far less likely to have lower-end IQs than men. In general, men are more task-oriented and score higher in spatial reasoning involving "things" ("systematizing"), whereas women prefer people ("empathizing") and aesthetics. Men also have lower levels of neuroticism and have a greater propensity to work more hours, seek advancement as a sign of status in order to find a mate, et cetera. Among the black population, however, the sex IQ break-down at the high end is reversed and the disparity is actually more extreme; Thomas Sowell informs:

Studies had shown that females predominated among high-IQ blacks. One study of blacks whose IQs were 140 and up found that there were more than five times as many females as males at these levels. This is hard to explain by either heredity or environment...white males and white females have the same average IQs, with slightly more males at both the highest and lowest IQs.[18]

---

17 Jussim, Lee, *Social Perception and Social Reality: Why Accuracy Dominates Bias and Self-Fulfilling Prophecy*, 2012. Oxford University Press. p. 179.

18 Sowell, Thomas, "Race, IQ, black crime, and facts liberals ignore," October 8, 2002. Available at: http://www.sullivan-county.com/id5/sowell.htm.

This is not a measure of testing biases, either, as none other than the American Psychological Association states, "Large differences do exist between the average IQ scores of Blacks and Whites, and that these differences cannot be attributed to biases in test construction." IQ testing is actually one of the most reliable and accurate metrics we have for determining "g," or general intelligence. Per *The Journal of Blacks in Higher Education:*

> For black and white students from families with incomes of more than $200,000 in 2008, there still remains a huge 149-point gap in SAT scores. Even more startling is the fact that in 2008 black students from families with incomes of more than $200,000 scored lower on the SAT test than did students from white families with incomes between $20,000 and $40,000 dollars.[19]

So much for the "economic disadvantage" argument regarding black under-performance. For the 2009 SAT scores, whites with household incomes of less than $20,000 scored 12 points higher (out of 1600) than blacks from household incomes between $160,000-$200,000. For the 2005 test, again from *The Journal of Blacks in Higher Education*:

> In the entire country 244 blacks scored 750 or above on the math SAT and 363 black students scored 750 or above on the verbal portion of the test. Nationwide, 33,841 students scored at least 750 on the math test and 30,479 scored at least 750 on the verbal SAT. Therefore, black students made up 0.7% of the test takers who scored 750 or above on the math test and 1.2% of all test takers who scored 750 or above on the verbal section.[20]

Blacks, mind you, were 10.4% of the test-taking population measured. Given every chance for a leg up with greater government spending

---

19 "Family Income Differences Explain Only a Small Part of the SAT Racial Scoring Gap," 2009. *The Journal of Blacks in Higher Education*. Available at: http://www.jbhe.com/latest/index012209_p.html.

20 "The Widening Racial Scoring Gap on the SAT College Admissions Test," 2005. *The Journal of Blacks in Higher Education*. Available at: http://www.jbhe.com/features/49_college_admissions-test.html.

and additional programs and incentives to advance black student performance, the last thirty years has actually seen an increased gap in SAT scores between white and black students, by fifteen points to be exact. From the College Board's 2005 data on the SAT:

• Whites from families with incomes of less than $10,000 had a mean SAT score of 993. This is 129 points higher than the national mean for all blacks.

• Whites from families with incomes below $10,000 had a mean SAT test score that was 61 points higher than blacks whose families had incomes of between $80,000 and $100,000.

• Blacks from families with incomes of more than $100,000 had a mean SAT score that was 85 points below the mean score for whites from all income levels, 139 points below the mean score of whites from families at the same income level, and 10 points below the average score of white students from families whose income was less than $10,000.[21]

From the College Board's 2015 data, we learn that 48,000 whites and 52,800 Asians scored at least a 700 on the math, as opposed to 2,200 blacks and 4,900 Hispanics; 16,000 whites and 29,570 Asians scored above a 750, compared to 2,400 Hispanics and less than 1,000 blacks.[22] For 2015:

The data shows that the average score for Blacks on the reading section of the test was 431. This was significantly below the average score for Whites which stood at 529. The SAT is scored on a scale of 200 to 800 points. On the mathematics portion of the test, a slightly larger racial gap exists. Blacks had an average score of 428, compared to an average score for Whites of 534. On

21 "Tables and Related Items," 2005. College Board. Available at: https://research. collegeboard.org/programs/sat/data/archived/cb-seniors-2005/tables.

22 "2015 College Bound Seniors Total Group Profile Report," 2015. College Board. Available at: https://secure-media.collegeboard.org/digitalServices/pdf/sat/total-group-2015.pdf.

the writing section of the test, Blacks had an average score of 418. Whites scored an average of 513. The average combined score for Blacks of 1277 is 299 points below the average combined score for Whites.[23]

There is much liberal consternation about the annual National Assessment of Educational Progress (NAEP) scores released by the US Department of Education, where a number of public school systems perform very poorly on their math and reading proficiency tests. It is only through this "race blind" imperative/lens that the distress makes any sense. For those with an understanding of the biological differences between the races, it is all perfectly natural and exactly what you would expect. Some liberals might decry the "lack of funding," but many public school systems spend *more* than the national average. New York City spends twice the national average on its public schools, and Baltimore City Schools spends the fourth-highest amount per pupil in the country behind New York City, Boston, and Washington, DC. According to the National Center on Education and the Economy (NCEE), the average student in Singapore is 3.5 years ahead of their US counterpart in math, 1.5 years ahead in reading, and 2.5 in science. Children in Canada, China, Estonia, Germany, Finland, the Netherlands, New Zealand, and Singapore consistently outrank their US counterparts on the basics of education. How could this be? Some of this underachievement must no doubt be laid at the feet of the teachers' unions that actively shield awful teachers from being fired, as well as the socio-cultural pervasiveness of the self-perpetuating cycles of under-achievement and poverty in the black and brown communities.

Nevertheless, most of the dysfunction is biologically-derived, and the intractability of biology is an out-sized square peg for the egalitarians' little round hole; no amount of spending or hand-wringing or virtue-signaling is ever going to close the achievement gap.

The NAEP tests revealed that in 2017, in the Cleveland public schools,

23   Ibid.

only 11% of eight graders were proficient or better in math and only 10% were proficient or better in reading. Cleveland public schools' student racial/ethnic break-down is as follows: Black, Non-Hispanic: 64.5%; Hispanic: 15.8%; White, Non-Hispanic: 15.7%; Multiracial: 2.6%; Asian or Pacific Islander: 1.3%; American Indian or Alaskan Native: 0.2%. Cleveland public schools are 84.3% non-white.

In the Houston public schools, only 24% were proficient or better in math and only 18% were proficient or better in reading. Houston public schools are 62.1% Hispanic and 23.9% black; Houston's public school system is in total 91.3% non-white. In the Dallas public schools, only 20% were proficient or better in math and only 15% were proficient or better in reading. With Hispanics at 70.3% and blacks at 22.3%, Dallas public schools are less than 5% white.

In the Shelby County (which includes Memphis) public schools, only 12% were proficient or better in math and only 17% were proficient or better in reading. Shelby County public schools are around 60% black. In the Fresno public schools, only 11% were proficient or better in math and only 14% were proficient or better in reading. Fresno's public school system is 67.2% Hispanic and 89.7% non-white. In the Baltimore public schools, only 11% were proficient or better in math and only 13% were proficient or better in reading. At 80.1% black and 10.4% Hispanic/Latino, Baltimore public schools are 91.3% non-white.

In the Milwaukee public schools, only 12% were proficient or better in math and only 15% were proficient or better in reading. Milwaukee public schools are 55% black, 26% Hispanic, and 88% non-white. Only 5% of Detroit public-school eighth graders were proficient or better in math and only 7% were proficient or better in reading. Detroit's public school system is 82.3% black and 13.2% Hispanic; it is 97.6% non-white.

It is not my intention here to be gratuitous or to use the data as a means to prove anything beyond the simple fact that population groups do vary dramatically; no one complains about the NBA being 75% black or the NFL being 70% black but a 75% white college campus is cause for much consternation. A Google workforce of 32% Asian and 2% black is un-remarked upon. Isn't that something?

The advancement of individuals beyond their capability has severe consequences, not just for those who should rightfully occupy a spot in a university or job but are passed over due to onerous federal legislation, but for those who are themselves advanced beyond their capability. There is a twenty-point IQ gap, on average, between blacks and whites in professional positions, meaning blacks are at *even more* of a disadvantage relative to the general population (fifteen point IQ gap between American blacks and whites) after being "aided" by affirmative action than they would have been otherwise. This professional aid follows collegiate aid and, quite possibly, high school aid. Thus, for the better part of a decade, particular groups are often advanced well beyond their capabilities, as well as sheltered from the possibility of failure, and when they reach a situation where merit becomes the sole or primary determinate of their value, they suddenly find themselves severely – and genuinely – disadvantaged.

Why do you think colleges have become such breeding-grounds for therapeutic demands, for increasing race and ethnic studies departments, and for ever-expanding speech codes that wall off entire areas of inquiry? It's because we have broadened the collegiate base of students, and, coupled with racial acceptance quotas that put certain population groups in universities way over their ability level, they agitate for their surroundings to become more congenial. Hence, the various identities can spend four years talking about their "lived experience" in one of the grievance studies departments, learning nothing and not being challenged, and emerge with a degree no more prepared for the real world than when they entered, probably less so in fact.

The increasingly anti-Western, anti-white bilge pumps from these reeducation camps like waste from a broken sewer pipe, and the more students who have their loans under-written by the federal government to enter into the camps, the more who are exposed to this toxic worldview, which finds strongest purchase among the most vulnerable mentally and capability-wise who would probably not be in the university system in the first place but for the present climate and set of circumstances. As just one example of what has become standard practice on university campuses these days, Evergreen State College has decided to continue its long and illustrious tradition of the Day of Absence:

> "In addition to POC centered events there will be antiracist workshops for white folks and people who do not identify as POC. Please bring a dish or your own packed lunch and dishes! Potluck-style. No one who's intentions are to cause harm are allowed (sic)."

They apparently no longer teach the basics of grammar up there in Olympia, WA, and that is not (just) a "snappy" aside, it is genuinely part of the problem. Instead of the daily tempest-in-a-teapot for ideologically-distorted "issues of race," maybe they ought to be learning real subjects. I'm more than sure the biological causes of these much-kvetched-about racial disparities won't come up, as that would be perceived to be "causing harm." Chalk it up to "systemic racism and oppression," then.

Returning specifically to the collegiate setting, per Inside Higher Ed, white and Asian students completed their programs at similar rates – 62% and 63.2%, respectively – while Hispanic and black students graduated at rates of 45.8% and 38%, respectively.[24] Additionally, Hispanic and black women are twice as likely as their male counter-parts to graduate from college. The impact on the fabric, mission, and purpose of the university – frankly its very construction – has been radical. Setting the Cult-Marx takeover of academia aside for a moment, Hispanics and American blacks (a 2004 study indicated that most of the black alumni of Harvard were from either the West Indies or Africa, or were the children of West Indian or African immigrants) have begun to agitate for the university to alter

---

24 Tate, Emily, "Graduation Rates and Race," April 26, 2017. *Inside Higher Ed.* Available at: www.insidehighered.com/news/2017/04/26/college-completion-rates-vary-race-and-ethnicity-report-finds.

its rigorousness, or else provide different, less challenging avenues (such as ethnic and gender studies) where the students may be more successful. The manifesto of simmering discontent by the privileged Penn graduate students "of color" is saturated in Cult-Marx jargon – we don't have to guess where it was learned. As described by critical race theorist Richard Delgado, "[Critical Race theorists] are suspicious of another liberal mainstay, namely rights....Rights are...alienating." As you can see, there is no respect of any of the fundamental organizing principles of Western society, namely property rights, human rights, merit, the rule of law, freedom of speech, and even the much-vaunted democracy.

What we're witnessing is the criminalization of reality. There are specific patterns and basic truths that govern our existence. It is only because of the privilege of power that these Leftists can delight in their virtue, congratulating each other, often on television, for their nonsensical beliefs of how the world works. Their vision, put into practice, doesn't. Invariably, the truer something is, the more triggered the Left will get. If we're born *tabula rasa*, as so many on the Left believe, then you're nothing but a hunk of flesh, infinitely malleable, no agency, governed only by your basest impulses, needing to be shepherded and controlled for your own good. Incidentally, that is precisely how they view the darker-complexioned peoples they fawn over but refuse to live next to.

The Establishment's out-facing ideologues cannot be reasoned with; we know empirically and incontrovertibly that diversity is a destroyer yet we must have *more* of it. Too much, of anything, save self-respect and restraint, is never enough.

It is tempting to think of such high-minded concepts as duty, dignity, honor, and posterity to be antiquated notions no longer applicable in our more "enlightened era" – but if there's one thing that is abundantly clear, it is that despite all of our gadgets and toys, we are far from enlightened. Nevertheless, too many Westerners have deluded themselves into thinking that voluntarily abasing themselves and their culture will somehow lead to unity, especially as they themselves accept the mantle of cultural and racial whipping-posts. For Mark Point:

> What's obvious is that when mainstream media personalities like Don Lemon or *New York Times* employees like Sarah Jeong freely spew textbook anti-white racism the world takes notice, the Overton window shifts and the temperature rises in the frog-pot. Over in Canada, in Europe and Australia whites are under attack. Due to unprecedented immigration and fatalist progressive experiments, there is no country where anti-white cultural currents are not rising. It wasn't supposed to be this way, weakness, wealth transfers, preferential treatment, open borders and accommodation were supposed to invite warm feelings, equal outcomes and racial blindness...The "Diversity" program has unmasked itself–hopefully too soon. Diversity is no transcendental virtue it's a political program with one denominator "less white." No champion of Diversity is decrying China for being too Chinese, Sudan for being too black or that Detroit's backwards for a lack of whites. "Person of Color" is the latest newspeak cynically designed to isolate white people. There is a cultural force that has hit critical mass and it needs to be confronted head-on.[25]

This cannot happen, however, because to do so would be to admit that not just the policies of the Left (and that weak-kneed "conservatives" acquiesce to) are getting people raped, maimed, traumatized, and killed, *but that their entire worldview has been invalidated.* It's why for the Outer Party censorship will always be their answer to the truth, and that reality, alongside their avariciousness, cowardice, and spitefulness, makes them *very* dangerous.

For those behind the curtain, the Inner Party, they certainly do not believe these outrageous fictions of equality, but find them useful to further their own agenda. Whether it be the #MeToo hysteria and

25 Point, Mark, "Racism on the Rise," November 6, 2018. *American Thinker.* Available at: www.americanthinker.com/articles/2018/11/racism_on_the_rise. html#ixzz5X9kXgrJU.

feminism's "impossible burden" of proof – a burden shared by all Cultural Marxist schools of "thought" – or cries of police wantonly gunning-down inner-city blacks (the same blacks who are four-and-a-half times more likely to kill a police officer than is a white person), these narratives do not need to be factually-based to be effective. In fact, the more divorced from reality, the better. Empiricism and the *logos* itself are anathema to the Left for both purposes of consolidating power and for the cult-like zealotry of many of its "true believers."

Aristotle divided the means of persuasion into three categories: *logos* (logic and reason), *ethos* (ethics, morality, and credibility), and *pathos* (emotion). The *logos* has come to define Western civilization and its quest for objective truth. For the ancient Greeks, *ethos* was at least as important as *logos* (Socrates was willing to die to avoid sophistry). *Logos* and *ethos* are inextricable: one's worldview or moral code should be logically coherent and consistent, each syllogism sound and testable, like a mathematical proof. Furthermore, *ethos* is not "just" an appeal to the audience's sense of ethics or morals, but also involves the established credibility of the sources one uses in one's argument and, of foremost importance for the ancient Greeks, of the credibility and character of the very individual making the argument. One does not establish credibility of character or of an argument through deception and sophistry; one does so through forthrightness, and in terms of argumentation, through empirical evidence, objective truths, and, where relevant, through a clear delineation of one's logically-substantiated ethical code.

Instead, the youth are indoctrinated in critical theory and all kinds of moral and cultural relativism. Relativism excuses the individual from having to make difficult choices, from having to stand for something; it excuses the individual from having to work out internal contradictions and potentially worldview-altering cognitive dissonance. We'll pull down the statues of any historical figure we deem "problematic," and so we'll never have to stop and think about the fact that there's good and bad in all of us. Thomas Jefferson was evil because he owned slaves, but…wait…his work on…*never mind that*! It allows for complexity of character and motive and asks that we understand this human being on a three-dimensional plane in historical context. Whatever doesn't fit the new (if you'll pardon the pun) white-washed historical narrative must be expunged, erased. *Get on the right side of history, you Neanderthal!* Strange, isn't it, the preeny moral narcissism of people who espouse moral relativism?

The Left feels the urgent need to politicize everything, to infuse even the most banal of activities with their narrative. For the Left, narrative will always trump fact, and if there isn't sufficient evidence for a claim, they'll *invent* evidence for the claim. I hesitate to even bring it up because it's so hackneyed and frankly boring at this point, but this incessant refrain of "Punch Nazis" by the Left suffers from a severe lack of supply, so they have to go to great lengths to create Nazis – even going so far as to fabricate hate crimes. The mainstream media, of course, only sensationalizes the "discovery" of vandalism, poop swastikas, graffiti, et cetera, but they conveniently never cover the inevitable revealing of it as a hoax.

If the Left cannot literally level the playing field, they can, as in the case of ESPN for example, at least charge the spectacle of sport with its narrative. Anchors that have targeted entire metropoles as "racist" (see: Hill, Jemele, City of Boston, not to mention her condemnation of the "white supremacist" Donald Trump) remain; *Baseball Tonight* is effectively gone. The vast majority of hockey coverage has been axed (noticing a trend?), but columns by racial apologist Tim Wise writing about how "woke" the Wisconsin basketball program is on ESPN imprint The Undefeated remain. The Undefeated also ran another piece entitled: "Belichick, Brady, and Kraft's Relationship with Trump is Complicated for Patriots Fans of Color." Scan some headlines from the main ESPN website and try not to have your eyes roll into the back of your head: "Stories of Activism in the NBA," "James Blake's Pursuit of Social Justice," "NFL GMs Will Hide behind Their Hypocrisy about Kaepernick," "Who is Dolores Huerta? How the Chicana Activist Changed the World," and the list goes on.

Facts are not racist. It is in the interpretation of information that we often fall into the trap of, if you'll pardon the pun, coloring for our biases. It is absolutely vital to be able to take a step back and see if we can evaluate issues dispassionately. As human beings, we are inherently emotional creatures, and it is only with the greatest of care that we are able to dispense with our pathologies and biases and engage with the facts as they are. For example, there are real, quantifiable differences between the races and sexes. Mentioning this publicly, or even under the ostensible protection of company feedback in the case of ex-Google software engineer James Damore, is tantamount to white supremacy.

Mr. Damore, we hardly knew ye. It turns out writing a benign, well-reasoned, fact-based intra-company memorandum with all of the necessary qualifiers, questioning Google's practices regarding "diversity and inclusion," is beyond the pale. Who knew? Simply pointing out that, "At Google, we talk so much about unconscious bias as it applies to race and gender, but we rarely discuss our moral biases" and that, "Google has several biases and honest discussion about these biases is being silenced by the dominant ideology," which creates an echo chamber and an environment hostile to different views and opinions, is cause for Google doing exactly what Damore feared: "Our shaming culture [creates] the possibility of being fired." This possibility was realized swiftly and resolutely by the company, with Damore axed more or less instantaneously once his identity was publicly revealed.

The reactions to Damore's memo spoke volumes about where we are as a society. The memo has been called "inflammatory" and "sexist" and "anti-diversity." It was labeled a "screed." I would be willing to venture the vast majority of those, including those in the company, reacting to the memo either hadn't read it, or have lost the plot so badly that the mere *suggestion* of chromosomal or other biological differences sends them into a fit. The guy was obviously well-intentioned and he clearly cared about the company he worked for, enough that he was willing to put his job on the line as it turned out to share his views on why there might be discrepancies within the company; he also offered a number of solutions to help rectify said disparities, particularly between the sexes, beyond the blatantly discriminatory programs and policies the company currently practices, with proactive measures that would emphasize women's relative strengths, including more collaborative and more "out-facing," customer relations-based work.

It wasn't good enough. It never is. The relentlessly virtue-signaling eunuchs rushed to the defense of these women who are so empowered they need...men to come to their aid? A paternal overlord to intervene on their behalf? *Need the day off from work for being emotionally traumatized?* Vice President of Diversity, Integrity & Governance (yes, evidently that's a real position), Danielle Brown, informed her triggered colleagues that, *of course* Google is committed to, "Building an open, inclusive environment [which] means fostering a culture in which those with alternative views, including different political views, feel safe sharing their opinions."

Wilfrid Laurier University Professor Nathan Rambukkana certainly understands Brown's "positionality." Wilfrid Laurier Graduate Teaching Assistant in Communications Lindsay Shepherd ran afoul of Leftist dogma for showing a short clip of the gendered pronoun usage debate between University of Toronto professors Nicholas Matte and Jordan Peterson, among others, on *The Agenda with Steve Paikin*, an extremely fair, moderate television program that does a great job of providing different viewpoints. Paikin is a terrific moderator, one of the best in fact, and the debate in question, which I've viewed several times, is handled professionally by Peterson, though Matte resorts to *ad hominem* attacks and accuses Professor Peterson of abusing his students by refusing to use the Cult-Marx pronouns. The only thing you could claim is controversial about the episode and clip in question from my point of view is how abominably Matte conducts himself.

For the Leftist functionaries at Laurier, however, it is that Peterson will not acquiesce to using what are obviously invented pronouns and will not sacrifice the distinction between singular and plural with respect to the use of "they" and "their." *The Agenda* is aired on public access television, so the program is not of "dubious origin." Assuming Shepherd's use of the clip was pedagogically sound – and all indications are that it was – then the only issue can be the objections voiced by Peterson.

Apparently one of Shepherd's students is students is a Stasi informant and filed a complaint against her for violating the school's Gendered and Sexual Violence policy for showing the clip. Shepherd was summoned to a secret meeting with two professors and a mid-level functionary from Gendered Violence and Prevention Support who probably makes more than the professors. Sensing a trap, Shepherd had the prescience to record the meeting on her laptop. Shepherd's inquisition Troika was helmed by Grand Poohbah Nathan Rambukkana. You can tell this guy's just been marinating in Cult-Marx jargon for the best part of twenty years, to the point where it's virtually impossible for him to string a coherent sentence together, which is hilarious considering he's meant to be a Professor of Communications.

His arguments are deeply flawed and contradictory, and at one point he goes so far as to say that Shepherd showing the clip is violating the Canadian Human Rights Code, Bill C-16, which would be a legal issue. Shepherd makes clear in the recording that she doesn't even agree with Peterson's viewpoints, but she presented the video neutrally "in the spirit of debate," so the only possible offense would be exposing the students to Peterson's position, not even espousing it herself, which Rambukkana equates with the Alt-Right and, "Hitler and Milo Yiannopoulos."

The other professor, Herbert Pimlott, throws Richard Spencer in the mix, because why not, right after saying, "I would find it problematic if my tutorial leaders were representing positions that didn't have any substantial academic credibility to that evidence." Pimlott is effectively saying that grammatical rules and humans' sexual dimorphism are *not* credible or backed by evidence. Only their created-whole-cloth self-referential word-soup is legitimate scholarship, and its scientific basis is informed exclusively by their own specific views on morality. Grammatical convention and biology can *both* take a hike. Rambukkana is recorded as saying:

> Okay, so, I understand the position that you're coming from, and your positionality, but the reality is that it has created a toxic climate for some of the students...one or multiple students who

have come forward, saying that this is something that they were concerned about, and that it made them uncomfortable. You are perfectly welcome to your own opinions, but when you're bringing it into the context of the classroom, that can become problematic, and that can become something that is – that creates an unsafe learning environment for students.[26]

The only danger here from Rambukkana's positionality is that they might actually learn something for a change.

26 Camp, Frank, "University TA 'Censured' After Playing A Clip From A Debate About Transgender Pronouns," November 20, 2017. *The Daily Wire*. Available at: www.dailywire.com/news/university-ta-censured-after-playing-clip-debate-frank-camp#.

Chapter 4 - Liberal Censorship

"In the face of the tectonic changes sweeping over Europe, keeping a low profile and a high bank account is no longer an option. The endgame has started for real and the Enemy is there to get us all." -Tom Sunic

As multi-culturalism increasingly becomes the reality in so many Western countries, identity politics for all but whites, academia-fueled Cultural Marxism, and the race grievance industry all contribute to the toxic atmosphere of public discourse and make it extraordinarily difficult to engage in productive dialogue exploring complex issues – and this is all before considering the iron fist of censorship backed by the very real threat of imprisonment. Nearly 3,400 people were arrested and detained for violating Section 127 of the Communications Act in the UK in 2016 alone;[1] essentially, these people had done nothing but voice their opinions on social media. For that, they are guilty of "hate speech." The punishments for the heresies of empiricism grow more severe by the day. As Andrew Joyce writes:

[In the UK] for every pork-inspired teenage prank, there were probably a couple of Muslim rapes being carried out at the same time. I know which crime I view most seriously. Even looking at the picture from a racial rather than religious viewpoint, the figures of the Crown Prosecution Service show that Whites are under-represented in rape convictions relative to their proportion in the population, whereas Blacks, 'Asians' (the label most often applied to Pakistanis, etc.), and those of mixed ethnicity all far exceeded their proportion of the population. So the media prefers

1   Parker, Charlie, "Police arresting nine people a day in fight against web trolls," October 12, 2017. *The Times*. Available at: www.thetimes.co.uk/article/police-arresting-nine-people-a-day-in-fight-against-web-trolls-b8nkpgp2d.

the false alarm over hate crime to the real alarm which needs to be sounded over the ethnic rape epidemic.[2]

A recent proposal was floated to attach a six-year prison sentence to a conviction for "online blasphemy." Meanwhile, *Quilliam* found that 84% of those convicted of mass rape and grooming of underage British girls are of "Asian" origin; seven-in-ten of those convicted are believed to be Pakistani-Muslim. "Asians," by the way, only make up about 7% of the UK's population. Even in the face of such stark evidence that there's clearly something going on here, repeating these facts will likely find one accused of "racism" or "Islamophobia" at best, thrown in jail, losing your livelihood, and/or being ganged up on and killed increasingly more likely. You could ask Kevin Crehan about that – or not, since he's now dead after being found unresponsive in his jail cell following a conviction for putting bacon on the doorstep of a mosque and tying an English flag to a railing.

Whether or not your ideological sympathies lie with National Action, the simple fact that they each face at least half-a-decade of prison time simply for membership in the group while Anjem Choudary (not to mention potentially thousands of known terrorist suspects) walks free in Britain today – Choudary at a cost to taxpayers of two million pounds for police protection per annum – should tell you what the current state of affairs is. Choudary served less than half of his five-and-a-half year sentence for inviting support for ISIS; he also led a network banned under terrorism laws and linked to the murder of Lee Rigby, the London Bridge attack, and the 7/7 London bombing. Many have fought for al-Qaeda, the Taliban, and ISIS abroad. The September 2017 Parsons Green bucket bomber explicitly told officials in an asylum interview in January 2016 that he had been trained by ISIS and that he blamed the UK for his father's death in Iraq – but he was allowed to stay and was placed with a foster family who were given no indication of his background.

2   Joyce, Andrew, "On Muslim Crime, Genetics and the Rape of Europe," 2015. Available at: https://gazetawarszawska.net/judaizm-islam/1184-rape-of-europe.

Once in the West, these asylum-seekers drain the host country's resources while terrorizing the native populace, which is perfect for the consumer economy and for keeping people cowed and demoralized. In Germany, these "migrants" have crime rates well in excess of native Germans. Asylum-seekers have a crime rate 7.3 times that of native Germans. Foreigners are approximately 4.8 times more likely to commit murder than native Germans and asylum seekers in particular are 10.6 times more likely. In the case of violent crime, foreigners are five times more likely than native Germans and asylum seekers are over fifteen times more likely to commit such crimes. Foreigners are about 5.2 times more likely than native Germans and asylum seekers are about 15.2 times more likely to commit sexual assault and rape, and gang-rapes are 10.3 times more likely to be committed by foreigners and 42.7 times more likely to be committed by asylum seekers![3]

As of 2018, 54.7% of the prison population of Austria was of foreign origin. 44.2% of those incarcerated in Belgium's prison system were foreigners; in Liechtenstein it was 75%, in Luxembourg the number was 74.7% (for 2019), in Andorra it was 88.5%, and in Monaco it was 100%! For the latter four, this probably has more to do with size and other unique factors than anything else, though. Similar dramatic overrepresentations of foreign offenders can be seen elsewhere, however, such as in Greece (52.7% of the prison population in 2018 consisted of foreigners), Cyprus (41.1%), Estonia (35.5%), Norway (30.9%), Denmark (28.6%), Iceland (26.7%), and Finland (17.1%). Foreigners were 21.7% of France's prison population in 2014, 19.7% of the Netherlands' in 2015, 22.1% of Sweden's in 2016, 71.5% of Switzerland's and 24% of Germany's in 2017, and 41.4% of Malta's, 32.7% of Italy's, 29.8% of Slovenia's, 28% of Spain's, and 15.5% of Portugal's in 2019.[4] 17.1% of Australia's prison population in

---

3   Lemoine, Philippe, "A quick look at immigration and crime in Germany," July 25, 2017. Available at: https://necpluribusimpar.net/quick-look-immigration-crime-germany/; figures from: www.epochtimes.de/politik/welt/ines-laufer-die-fluechtlings-kriminalitaet-zwischen-fakten-und-medienluegen-a2132375.html.

4   Available at: www.prisonstudies.org/map/europe.

2019 was born outside the country.[5] According to Ministry of Justice figures, 16% of the prison population of England and Wales in 2020 was Muslim – an astounding overrepresentation compared to their share of the population and the fact that the police seem so unwilling to arrest them in the first place. The number of Muslims in high security facilities was even higher, at one-in-five.

The European security apparatus basically does not exist: 90% of all Muslim terrorist attackers were known to authorities beforehand. There are, at a conservative estimate, 5,000 active jihadis in the European Union right now, and at a more liberal estimate that number is 50,000. The UK has an enormous 30,000 individuals on its terror watch-list, but the concern is less on these terror suspects and grooming gangs and more on arresting people for social media posts and attending Pride parades. When their control of the information supply begins to loosen, when their narrative begins to show serious cracks, the "liberal democracies" must resort to more draconian measures, such as imprisoning political dissidents, but in the most gutless and cowardly manner possible, without coming out and calling them dissidents. Their censorship follows along the same lines, and the very ruined society they have created does, too.

And yet, in the span of just a few months from late 2018 to early 2019 alone we witnessed: James Fields sentenced to 419 years in prison for a crime he did not commit; the Chemnitz Seven in Germany arrested on terrorism charges simply for objecting to the Germans' population replacement; the aforementioned National Action Six's sentencing; the arrest of three Spanish "Neo-Nazi" writers through a coordinated effort between Spanish and Swiss police and Europol; the arrest of Yellow Vest organizer James Goddard; and a New York teenager arrested and charged with a hate crime for hanging posters on a college campus, not to mention the attempts to destroy the lives and livelihoods of Tucker Carlson (whose home was also visited by an Antifa mob), Virginia paramedic Alex McNabb, and Columbia University student Julian Von Abele. A Maryland man was literally

---

5   Available at: www.prisonstudies.org/country/australia.

executed by police for lawfully exercising his Second Amendment rights. Oh, and don't forget the French government considering the use of chemical agents on its own people in order to quell the Yellow Vest protests when it lets imported peoples torch Citroens for days on end with scarcely an official peep (Jean Raspail could scarcely have better imagined it). The post-modern anti-reality is such that the British police don't have the resources or will to stop industrial-scale grooming and rape of underage girls, but they can somehow spare the resources to investigate people like Posie Parker and Caroline Farrow for their supposed "transphobic hate speech."

Despite all the evidence to the contrary, the diversity project has been an abject failure by any rational metric – for all but the very few, that is. But even for so many of those being harmed, that's just it – we're no longer within the confines of the rational, our grotesque sentimentality ruthlessly exploited by the multi-national corporations endlessly in search of ever-cheaper labor, the power brokers to exploit them, and by the vessels of our compassion, greedily sucking down our largesse while they stab us in the gut, laughing. The profane now sacred, we are not simply a civilization in decline, but rather an anti-civilization rapidly becoming an exact negative of what it was.

There's something really sick about watching whites continue to debase themselves on behalf of the diversity time bomb. I'm thinking of the family of Maria Ladenburger, the nineteen-year-old German medical student raped and killed by an Afghan "migrant" (who was curiously classed as an "unaccompanied minor" as a thirty-three-year-old man), who asked well-wishers to donate on her behalf to an NGO that actively obstructs the deportation of said "migrants" from the European Union. Or Amanda Kijera, the activist who blamed her rape in Haiti by a black man on white colonialism (she also mentioned that she was "grateful for the experience"). Or Amy Biehl, the white activist who went to South Africa to "show solidarity" with the blacks and was savagely murdered by a mob screaming anti-white epithets. The South African government pardoned the killers, claiming the violence had been "politically motivated," and during the trial, recounts Rex van Schalkwyk, "Supporters of the...men accused of murdering [Biehl]... burst out laughing in the public gallery of the Supreme Court...when a witness told how the battered woman groaned in pain." After the acquittal, Biehl's father shook hands with the killers and ended up employing several of them through a foundation Biehl's parents set up in her name to advocate on behalf of "township youths." Or the Norwegian man, Karsten Nordal Hauken, who said he felt guilty after the Somali man who raped him was deported. Or...well, you get the idea.

It's basically unheard-of for a "migrant" in Europe to *actually* be deported no matter how bad the crime committed or whether they even have any legitimate business being in the country in the first place, though. More likely the authorities will turn a blind eye; the offender might get probation or, at worst, a couple years in prison for raping or killing someone, or leading a terrorist cell. It's all a "cultural misunderstanding," you see. And yet, the results of a recent YouGov poll were released, and nine of the eleven nations surveyed – Italy, Sweden, Germany, Lithuania, Finland, Greece, Denmark, France, and the UK – listed "immigration" as their top concern (Spain and Poland listed it as second), and eight voiced "terrorism" as their second concern (Poland had it first); unsurprisingly, unemployment weighed heavily on the Italians, Greeks, and Spanish – with 84% of Greeks, 80% of Italians, and 77% of Spanish respondents saying they felt insecure about employment opportunities in their area. Over half of Brits, French, Italians, and Greeks, and almost half of the Swedes polled, felt "totally pessimistic" about the future of the European Union. 69% of Greeks, 63% of Lithuanians, and 60% of Swedes felt insecure about their country's ability to combat terrorism, and other than the Danes and Finns, who were close to half, over a majority of the respondents had reservations that their country could effectively combat crime. Those are clearly very legitimate reservations, and that's putting it all rather nicely.

Deportations in the US increasingly resemble the man in a sinking boat bailing water with a small pail. There is something seriously pathological about the manner in which the West conducts itself and the depths it will go to protect the very same people who want to rape and pillage it. And that's precisely what they're doing, with Western governments as tacit and often explicit accomplices. As Viktor Orbán stated in a recent speech, "The liberal democracies are neither liberal nor democracies." Orwellian to be sure. For Orbán:

> The argument we can provide to support our assertion that there is an absence of democracy is that in Western Europe censorship and restrictions on freedom of speech have become general phenomena. Working together, political leaders and technology giants filter news items that are uncomfortable for the liberal elite. If you don't believe this, just visit these websites, visit social media sites, and you'll see the ingenious and cunning means by which they restrict access to negative news reports on migrants, immigrants and related topics, and how they prevent European citizens from facing reality. The liberal concept of freedom of opinion has gone so far that liberals see diversity of opinion as important up until the point that they realize, to their shock, that there are opinions which are different from theirs. Liberals' vision of press freedom reminds us of the old Soviet joke: "However I try to assemble parts from the bicycle factory, I end up with a machine gun." However I try to assemble the parts of this liberal press freedom, the result is censorship and political correctness.[6]

Thus we see the result of a subverted media, fulfilling its duties: focusing on non-issues, manipulating the people, and discrediting any dissenters. The oligopoly gradually squeezes out all conflicting points of view until all one hears are the same voices screeching about "privilege" and "undocumented persons" or, if they don't identify as people, anthropoid bi-peds, in unison. The desired end result for the subverter, as related by ex-KGB agent and Soviet defector Yuri Bezmenov: uninformed myopia. Double standards, reality upside down. A culture focused on false idols, consumption, fads, mass taste,

---

6   Orbán, Viktor, "Prime Minister Viktor Orbán's speech at the 29th Balvanyos Summer Open University and Student Camp," July 28, 2018. Available at: www.kormany.hu/en/the-prime-minister/the-prime-minister-s-speeches/prime-minister-viktor-orban-s-speech-at-the-29th-balvanyos-summer-open-university-and-student-camp.

addiction, hedonism, and nihilistic excess. We are alienated by and do not see ourselves in this horrid modernity because it is not a product of our people; to quote Revilo P. Oliver:

> The underlying thought is simply not that of Western man. It has nothing in common with the logic of Aristotle or Descartes, and if it is, as it appears to be, systematic, the system is that of a world in which, for aught we know to the contrary, the radius of a triangle may be equal to the cosine of its Electra complex. We feel ourselves confronted by the incomprehensible purposes of an alien race, and shuddering we wonder whether Martians or Neptunians, inwardly more weird than any imagined by H. G. Wells or Clark Ashton Smith, may not have already invaded our luckless planet.[7]

Certainly, the levelling ideology of Bolshevism has been chained to our civilization like a lead weight, a la "Harrison Bergeron." How long before people are literally weighted down or otherwise handicapped? The people's brains are already badly addled. Just as in "Harrison Bergeron" as well, beauty and objectivity have been cast aside in favor of all that is profane, idiotic, and hideous.

In this deranged anti-reality, where the state religion of egalitarianism preaches "equality with exemptions," where all cultures are equal except our own, freighted as it is with Original Sin, the European is the last among equals, a reversed King Arthur weighed down with the baggage of guilt for centuries of colonialism and (often fictitious) genocide. As penance, we are told that European and European-settled nations must don sackcloth and ashes and, contrary to one line of Leftist propaganda that "Diversity Is Our Strength," allow our homelands to be flooded with often-hostile aliens from cultures utterly unlike our own who impose a terrible price on us, a price that must be paid not just with the loss of our homelands but our very existence. As Douglas Murray explains:

---

7   Oliver, Revilo P. *America's Decline.* Historical Review Press: Sussex. 2006 (re-print). p. 155.

And so the policies that had already made the native British a minority in their own capital city ineluctably sped up a change in the demographics of the entire continent. The 'dark specialism' of the French turned out to be the dark discovery of Europe. Promised throughout their lifetimes that the changes were temporary, that the changes were not real, or that the changes did not signify anything, Europeans discovered that in the lifespan of people now alive they would become minorities in their own countries...What is more, it had all been done on the laughable presumption that while all cultures are equal, European cultures are less equal than others.[8]

The migrants, then, are not a cause but a symptom of artificially-induced guilt and Western ennui, affluence, and apathy. The politicians who allowed this to happen have betrayed us, but it would seem that despite the continued resistance by the native populations to accelerated immigration, and many governments' indiscriminate granting of asylum, many others have simply given up. They have stopped having children, they have internalized the postmodern guilt complex, and they have turned away from the foundational greatness of their civilization. They have sought satisfaction in fleeting pleasures and set their aspirations no higher than waist-level. To again quote Murray:

Today, if you walk through a gallery like Tate Modern in London the only thing more striking than the lack of technical skill is the lack of ambition. The bolder works may claim to tell us about death, suffering, cruelty or pain, but few have anything actually to say about these subjects other than pointing to the fact that they exist. Certainly they provide no answers to the problem they present.[9]

The only "solution" has been to seek oblivion through hedonism, to "escape" the harshness and tragedy of life through material

---

8   Murray, Douglas, *The Strange Death of Europe: Immigration, Identity, Islam.* Bloomsbury: London. 2017. p. 312.
9   Ibid. p. 272.

comforts and superficialities. Better not to interrogate the essence of existence – the act of which imbued the forebears of Western civilization with the Faustian spirit that now leaves Modern Man, as Douglas Murray describes him, splayed out and badly injured, like Icarus surviving the fall. Will he recover or will he expire, the dark discovery of Europe an eternal darkness?

The illusion of democracy has faded and the hideous Gollum-like creature jealously clutching his precious gold ring slouches finally revealed. Cravenness and greed rule the day. In light of the fact that a number of Senate and House seats and governor's mansions were stolen after the 2018 mid-term election in the US in egregious and blatant voter fraud, in light of the fact that the objections of the people to mass immigration are drowned out in a tsunami of endless Third World invaders, and in light of the fact that dissidents *are*, in fact, being hunted down and prosecuted (and persecuted) for their beliefs, there can be no other conclusion than that the entire system is designed to work against the very people it was originally designed to serve.

As Ann Coulter quipped, "Would that our borders are policed as well as our speech." The German government sentenced a man to prison for three years for selling rubber bullet-firing pistols in order to arm citizens in self-defense against rampant "migrant" crime. God forbid you try to defend yourself, or object to your replacement: German police regularly raid people's homes for online "hate posting." Nine people are arrested every day for "hateful comments" on social media in the United Kingdom. The West is a massive Panopticon whose governments will use the full force of their power to crush dissidents, but this tells only part of the story. With big tech happy to help, we have already been in Orwell's dystopia for quite a while and it's only going to get worse. A lot worse. There is no democratic solution to this problem because the game is rigged. Access to power is restricted and information control is increasingly becoming the exclusive province of the Establishment. Even in the time-span it took to write this book, a number of potential sources, especially of the first-hand variety, were purged from the internet.

The modern Western condition is one of increasing centralization of power on an institutional level, but de-centralization of access to anyone of positional authority. Think about the last time you called a customer service line for a large company and the experience you likely had – passed off from one customer service representative to the next, strung out over hours or days, somehow never managing to speak to a manager despite the fact that about every mid-level functionary has "manager" somewhere in their title.

Western discourse has become about avoidance, of not calling something by its actual name. Celia Dugger of *The New York Times* insists we refer to female genital mutilation as "genital cutting" because the former term is too "culturally loaded." You'll certainly be familiar with the litany of other terms meant to code, confuse, or obscure: migrants, undocumented persons, alternative beauty standards, positive body image, gender-neutral pronouns, "on a spectrum"…and on and on it goes. The ideology is so self-referential and ties itself into such dense linguistic knots it is an extremely tall order to even begin to untangle them. That said, the tension between overly-simplified solutions and linguistic gymnastics may well be bound to unravel of its own accord. Barack Obama can mouth his platitudes – "Kindness covers all of my political beliefs" – but that is simply not good enough. Empty vessels like Justin Trudeau and Angela Merkel mouth clichés about immigration and diversity and open borders as inherently positive, but why is that the default? And at what cost does this mindless compassion come?

In 2017, 34.4% of Swedish women from ages 16-24 were subjected to sexual offenses[10] largely at the hands of the "new Swedes." Sweden saw over 100 bombings in 2019, an unthinkable phenomenon in a Sweden that is uniformly Swedish; the government, though, is committed to suppressing anything that contradicts their kumbaya narrative. The Swedes have become second-class citizens in their own nation. Perhaps you believe there's something inherently insidious about the Swedes, and that the land of ABBA and Ace of Base should

---

10   Available at: www.bra.se/statistik/statistiska-undersokningar/nationella-trygghetsundersokningen.html.

be erased by the coming throngs of Afghanis and Somalis and Turks. At the present rate, they'll be a minority in their homeland soon enough, perhaps within a couple of decades. Their only home stripped from them, justice will have been served. But the question is: what have they done to deserve this?

Their Scandic brethren in Minnesota recently spent five million dollars to contain a measles outbreak from its unvaccinated Somali population. Disease and crime rise in direct proportion to the concentration of Third World immigration in a given community. Illegal aliens rape schoolchildren throughout the United States and major news outlets cover it up. Muslim migrants make whole European cities borderline uninhabitable and rape European women and children in staggering numbers. Unconstitutional speech codes proliferate on American college campuses and hate speech laws like C-16 and M-103 in Canada, dealing with "transphobia" and "Islamophobia" respectively, are sponsored by many Western governments. The peace, love, and harmony so lauded by Leftists is at direct odds with every single actuality. They pretend to care about every kind of diversity, but that is obviously not true. "Diversity" requires "un-packing," but when you can only feel and no longer think you're reduced to the likes of these college student sloganeers shouting down free speech or fundamentalists gunning down *Charlie Hebdo* cartoonists.

It is in this environment of advanced decay and grotesque contradiction that a block away from a police station whose force's only concerns are "diversity" and fighting "online hate" in between prancing about festooned in rainbow garb at various Pride parades, a sex-segregated mosque encourages female genital mutilation, polygyny, incest, and violent jihad with impunity. The contradictions are legion and, far from proving the un-doing of the "liberal" ideology, have the paradoxical effect of reinforcing it. It is a truly hysterical, demented age, a perpetual Year Zero, which demands unthinking compliance to the dictates that seem to change by the hour.

Our common culture and established code of behavior are at present unraveling in the form of social disintegration. The more isolated someone is, the fewer bonds they have, and the easier they are to control. The maintenance of the modern super-state depends on an ever-increasing crack-down on the truth, and a deliberate, coordinated effort to sever all communal, familial, and nationalistic ties via rigorous exposure to propaganda generated by the media, and state-sponsored policies meant to atomize people. This super-state is run by and for corporations and financial institutions along the private equity model; the notion of "citizenship" thus becomes, at best, a quaint anachronism. It is an obstacle to a more pliant population of consumers and a cheap, ready labor force who will do the bidding of their overlords without questioning "why?"

When a population becomes sentimentalized, it becomes much easier to shroud totalitarianism in emotional terms. The idea of "hate" hinges on the notion that the legislator or judge or commissar can determine your motive. This is legal machinery built upon a logical fallacy, but the populace is so inured to the absence of logic that they accept the need for hate speech laws in order to protect the perpetrators, not victims, of crimes. Emotion is subjective and should not, in a properly-functioning society, form the basis for any kind of law-making, let alone things as vaguely- or poorly-defined as the universe of multitudinous genders or "Islamophobia." Even these terms – transphobia, Islamophobia, homophobia, xenophobia – are meant to paint the accused into a corner of ignorance as possessed by an irrational fear of the subject in question. It is meant to short-circuit any reasonable objections to, say, transformative immigration. As shocking as this may seem, there's nothing irrational to the objection of seeing your homeland engulfed by aliens, dissolved in what Jim Goad calls "a cleansing wave of softly genocidal immigration."

A genocide by any other name, however, is still a genocide. Cheaper consumer goods do not constitute "progress" and suicidal delusions of "equality" do not bring them any closer to reality. When an organism is threatened, it does not reproduce. Fecundity relies on stability and safety, or else imperviousness to danger and future planning, a decidedly dysgenic characteristic. Since we have both working in tandem, it is little wonder the bottom is dropping out.

No rational or functional society would *increase* immigration or welcome untold and unvetted millions en masse from countries and cultures that are avowedly trying to kill them. It is one thing to have mass migration forced upon you from above and/or without, but it's quite another to have a good-sized chunk of your population calling for its own destruction and erasure. This happens as a matter of course when a population has been sufficiently subverted along these lines, when the natural defense mechanisms have been disabled, and when a people has stopped understanding the true essence of who they are. As the Czech writer Milan Kundera, no stranger to totalitarianism, wrote, "The first step in liquidating a people is to erase its memory. Destroy its books, its culture, its history. Then have somebody write new books, manufacture a new culture, invent a new history. Before long that nation will begin to forget what it is and what it was."

It is a dark irony that, as Bertolt Brecht sardonically noted in his poem "The Solution," the ruling class has simply elected to elect a new people. The reasons are actually very simple: profit, power, and racial- and class-based animus. Despite the lip-service paid to democracy, the engine of neo-liberalism remains geared toward the oligarchy winning and the untold billions losing. Not that the ruling class is held accountable to their own standards or rhetoric, of course. That's simply for you to adhere to. Nor, despite their professed love of "our democracy" and "our values," do they respect any outcome that does not favor increased wealth, power, and control for their increasingly-exclusive circle. If diversity is what they want, diversity is what you'll get!

The very idea of democracy itself has been corrupted, its definition expanded to a ludicrous degree of "inclusivity," while containing several self-negating contradictions. A democracy, at its core, cannot be racially or even ethnically pluralistic. Before we go any further, it is vital first to understand the etymology of the word "democracy," and what, exactly, an actual democracy was intended to look like and function as. Christopher W. Blackwell illuminates:

> For the Athenians, "democracy" (*demokratia*) gave Rule (*kratos*) to the Demos. Demos (pronounced "day-moss") has several

meanings, all of them important for Athenian democracy. Demos is the Greek work for "village" or, as it is often translated, "deme." The deme was the smallest administrative unit of the Athenian state, like a voting precinct or school district. Young men, who were 18 years old presented themselves to officials of their deme and, having proven that they were not slaves, that their parents were Athenian, and that they were 18 years old, were enrolled in the "Assembly List" (the *pinax ekklesiastikos*). Another meaning of Demos, to the Athenians, was "People," as in the People of Athens, the body of citizens collectively. So a young man was enrolled in his "demos" (deme), and thus became a member of the Demos (the People). As a member of the Demos, this young man could participate in the Assembly of Citizens that was the central institution of the democracy. The Greek word for "Assembly" is *ekklesia*, but the Athenians generally referred to it as the "Demos." Decrees of the Assembly began with the phrase "It seemed best to the Demos...," very much like the phrase "We the People..." that introduces the Constitution of the United States. In this context, "Demos" was used to make a distinction between the Assembly of all citizens and the Council of 500 citizens, another institution of the democracy.[11]

In order to have democracy one must have *demos* – a polity, a people, a culture, and a hierarchical structure roughly in keeping with the natural order. Even in the Athenian democracy, there were significant restrictions regarding the franchise and clear delineations of authority. The *polis* was the defining political and territorial unit of Grecian classical antiquity – it was the city-state and its surrounding countryside. That said, it is indisputable that despite the fractious nature of what we now know as the nation-state of Greece, the various city-states of Sparta, Athens, Corinth, Thebes, et cetera (and the Kingdom of Macedonia to the north) were all permutations of Hellenistic culture

---

11 Blackwell, Christopher W., "Athenian Democracy: a brief overview," in "Athenian Law in its Democratic Context," Adriaan Lanni, ed., Center for Hellenic Studies On-line Discussion Series, February 28, 2003. Available at: http://www.stoa.org/demos/article_democracy_overview@ page=3&greekEncoding=UnicodeC.html.

and were all ethnically Greek. The notion of a Nubian Athenian was – and is – preposterous. We understand who Greeks are and what they look like. Simply being born within a nation's confines does not make someone *of* that nation.

But what is a nation? The *Stanford Encyclopedia of Philosophy* first differentiates between a nation and a state – "whereas a nation often consists of an ethnic or cultural community, a state is a political entity with a high degree of sovereignty" – before elaborating that nationalism, "Centrally encompasses two phenomena... (1) the attitude that the members of a nation have when they care about their identity as members of that nation and (2) the actions that the members of a nation take in seeking to achieve (or sustain) some form of political sovereignty." The word "nation" is derived from the Latin *natio*, which is translated as: "native place," birth, people, race, and class. This is an extraordinarily dense word, one with so many connotations it is little wonder its essence has remained contentious to this day.

Understanding what, exactly, a nation – our nation – is, however, is absolutely vital to framing essentially all of the existential debates surrounding its purpose, its function, and its very existence. Montserrat Guibernau defines the nation as, "A human group conscious of forming a community, sharing a common culture, attached to a clearly demarcated territory, having a common past and a common project for the future and claiming the right to rule itself."[12] The nation, then, is as much a reflection of its people as it is a parcel of land – much more so, in fact. We can consider the nation to be a living organism, much like the human body, where something as seemingly minor as the changing composition of gut bacteria can have significant effects on the body's health and well-being, and even psychological state. Anthony Smith characterizes the nation as:

"A form of culture – an ideology, a language, mythology, symbolism, and consciousness" with four goals: (1) turning a

---

12   Guibernau, Montserrat, *Nationalisms: the Nation-State and Nationalism in the Twentieth Century*. Polity Press. 1996. p. 47.

passive ethnic category or group into an active ethnopolitical community, a "subject of history," (2) organizing the community's culture and creating a standard, official, and "high" culture if one is absent, (3) forming the community into a "culturally homogeneous 'organic' nation," and (4) obtaining a home territory or even a state for the nation.[13]

I would go further and state that the ethnic consistency of the nation must be homogeneous or near-homogeneous; with certain select outliers, small numbers of ethnically- or racially-distinct peoples may find themselves woven into the fabric of the nation, but this is a very complicated process that presupposes an ethnic super-majority, a strong sense of civic duty *and* both civic and familial obligations, communal ties, a vibrant high culture, and the synchronicity of the spirit of the person(s) in question with the host culture. For Revilo P. Oliver:

"Populists" must remember, first of all, that Jeffersonian democracy was not intended for Timbuktoo, Fiji, or Erewhon. It was designed for the thirteen colonies that had just won their independence for a specific people in an historically unique situation. Those colonies came close to being a nation in the primary sense of that word, a nation...formed of persons related by ancestry and birth, ie-a racially homogeneous people.[14]

Europe may be racially homogeneous, but given historical, cultural, genetic, and other contextual realities, even they have grappled with major consequences with what appear from the outside to be minute differences (Northern Ireland comes to mind, but even Switzerland has had its complications and has had to make accommodations); racial rather than ethnic coherence has been to some extent possible in the United States, making it an extreme outlier in human history, but

---

13   Eller, Jack David, "Ethnicity, Culture, and 'The Past,'" Fall 1997. *Michigan Quarterly Review*, Vol. 36, Issue 4. Available at: https://quod.lib.umich.edu/cgi/t/text/text-idx?cc=mqr;c=mqr;c=mqrarchive;idno=act2080.0036.411;view=text;rgn=main;xc=1;g=mqrg.

14   Oliver, Revilo P., "Who's for Democracy?" from "Populism and Elitism," 1982.

just because the US has been largely adept at enfolding genetically similar (all things considered) peoples from one continent, however, does not mean that it can accept anyone and everyone, especially in importing wildly divergent races and cultural dispositions whose people are told *not* to assimilate into American culture – and, what's more, when American culture itself is being de-legitimized *and* the country's industry is being simultaneously strip-mined while its people's life expectancies are in decline. That would be called "a recipe for disaster," and speaking of recipes, since "the food" is about the only concrete benefit from diversity anyone in power ever comes up with, well…we have the recipes. They can be found on this thing called "the internet." We don't need to import millions of people to learn how to prepare cuisine from other cultures. If you'd like to taste it firsthand, that's part of why people travel.

The nation-state is a much more complex entity than the city-state for obvious reasons, but it reflects the ideal for a people's self-determination with both ethnic unity and the ability to marshal force to protect its sovereignty, whereas the city-state is too weak and results in unnecessary fractiousness. The nation-state need not be purely democratic – should not be, in fact, given its volatility and impracticality – but it should reflect the best interests of the people even if those decisions are not always popular. For Peter Alter:

> [Nationalism] is both an ideology and a political movement which holds the nation and the sovereign nation-state to be crucial indwelling values, and which manages to mobilize the political will of a people or a large section of a population; it exists primarily whenever individuals feel they belong primarily to the nation, and whenever affective attachment and loyalty to that nation override all other attachments and loyalties.[15]

This is clearly distinct from a country, which is merely a designation

---

15 Eller, Jack David, "Ethnicity, Culture, and 'The Past,'" Fall, 1997. *Michigan Quarterly Review*, Vol. 36, Issue 4. Available at: https://quod.lib.umich.edu/cgi/t/text/text-idx?cc=mqr;c=mqr;c=mqrarchive;idno=act2080.0036.411;view=text;rgn=main;xc=1;g=mqrg.

for a political unit governing a given territory. Nigeria would be one such example, for it has multitudinous tribes and ethnicities within its borders with varying degrees of power and autonomy. This also leads to instability and often violence; as evidenced by the horrors in Biafra in the 1960s or on the other side of the continent in Rwanda in the 1990s, that violence can quickly turn genocidal. This volatility manifests itself in fractious, typically multi-ethnic, multi-racial, and/or multi-cultural countries and in the post-colonial world is often preceded by "identity politics" via democracy. As Jack David Eller writes:

> Paradoxically, efforts toward some degree of democracy – either in the late stages of colonialism or with independence – have often if not usually had the effect of intensifying group competition and identification; under the practice of "communal representation," which was viewed in some colonies at some times as the best way to represent all the people and to balance the interests of the constituent groups, group differences were reified, institutionalized, and politicized in unprecedented ways to assure groups a share of power as groups. Post-independence democracy continued the group rivalry but removed the foreign obstacles to competition and conflict; the potential for friction, even conflict and war, is immanent when numbers and population count toward power. Groups – ethnic, nationalist, class, caste, race, or what have you – are voting blocs or potential voting blocs, and mobilizing voters on the basis of ethnicity or identity, while "natural" in a certain sense, is also a powerful enticement to candidates and would-be leaders.[16]

These kinds of societies need not always be post-colonial, either, although the doomed-to-fail nature of these former colonies is by design in order to keep them reliant on the globalist system, be it through loans or the deadly military-industrial complex. The perpetual conflict also enables the creation of a never-ending wave of "displaced persons" who can be shoveled into the West in huge numbers.

---

16   Ibid.

The nation stands in stark contrast with multi-culturalism, which allows for essentially parallel sub-societies within one larger one, where broad agreement on who we are as a people is lost to tribal self-interest. Voting becomes its own kind of internecine warfare, and each group feels that by necessity they must keep their knives sharpened in order to cut out their slice of the pie and defend themselves and their interests as they endeavor to do so. This has not been a problem Iceland, for example, has had to struggle with because Iceland is a harmonious and homogeneous nation…for now.

Constant mass immigration only compounds the existing problems with more gasoline to the fire – the same immigration we are told is at once enriching and a punishment. Strange claim, that. Douglas Murray makes a great point:

> For even if you believe…that some immigration is a good thing and makes a country a more interesting place, it does not follow that the more immigration the better. Nor does it mean – however many upsides there are – that there are not downsides which should be easy to state without accusations of malice. For mass immigration does not continue bringing the same level of benefits to a society the more people who come in.[17]

The globalist super-structure and its vassals have unilaterally decided Europe and its progeny must continue importing huge numbers of people who, to be charitable, have little to offer their new countries, and are often downright hostile to their new environs. There's a strange paradox in all of this; Western leaders are squeamish about any troop casualties abroad, but seem perfectly willing to let an indefinite number of civilians be raped, maimed, or killed by alien, antagonistic populations. Our rulers have consciously adopted what I call the "Longshanks Strategy" toward their own populations (English King Edward the Longshanks from *Braveheart* referring to his policy of Scottish conquest: "If we can't get them out, we'll breed them

---

17   Murray, Douglas, *The Strange Death of Europe: Immigration, Identity, Islam*, Bloomsbury: London. 2017. p. 28.

out"). On the one hand, the ruling class facilitates mass immigration of alien peoples and on the other, the alien peoples themselves view the exercise as a conquest.

Turkish dictator Recep Erdogan is publicly urging all Muslims engaged in the *hijrah* in Europe to have at least five children, echoing Norway-based imam Mullah Krekar's sentiment that the key to victory lies in the wombs of Muslim women, and that the Mohammedans must "breed like mosquitoes."

Make no mistake, these teeming millions of "migrants" are treating this as an invasion, albeit the likes of which we've never experienced before. Victor Leman reports that, "The Turkish AKP government sells passports and birth certificates at affordable prices. Many migrants have no passport, no ID, and refuse to give fingerprints." The majority-Muslim "migrants" are taking full advantage of Europe's pathological altruism to bleed her dry. "British" imam Anjem Choudary (Wikipedia calls him a "social activist") advocated that Muslims use the British welfare state as a way to, colloquially speaking, milk the host country dry, a kind of economic warfare waged by abusing the bloated entitlement system dispensed from the even more bloated state apparatus.

In 1990, Muslims in Spain numbered 100,000. By 2010, the number had increased to 1.5 million. In 2017, the number was nearly two million, a growth of 1,900% in 27 years. Today there are 1,400 mosques in Spain which, according to the Observatory of Religious Pluralism, represents 21% of all places of worship in the country. The Islamization project was confirmed in November 2000 in the paper "The Strategy for Islamic Cultural Action Outside the Islamic World":

The demographic constituents of Western countries…will change and become subject to restructuring into a multi-ethnic and multi-cultural society. Thereby, Western countries will no longer remain that harmonious and monolithic society constituted on the basis of a specific historical, economic, social and cultural lineage…Sensing the importance of Islamic communities and minorities in the West...immunize the second, third and even fourth generations of those communities, who settled outside the Islamic world, against cultural assimilation and loss of their Islamic identity.[18]

And we scratch our heads as to why the children, grandchildren, and even great-grandchildren of the "migrants" are more radical than their forebears. These enclaves are cancerous tumors of anti-Western resentment, acting out on the people of the West while its governments stand by and not just allow it to happen, but enable it. In fact, resisting migrant predations may well see you prosecuted: not long ago a 17-year-old Danish girl used pepper spray to protect herself near a migrant asylum center and was herself prosecuted for carrying a weapon.

In the Zero Migration projection by Pew Research, the Muslim population on the continent will have grown 39% by 2050 with a 10% decline in the continent's non-Muslim population, a scenario which would have profound ramifications on the life and culture of the continent as we know it – *and this is assuming not a single more "migrant" set foot on the continent.* We all know that is not going to happen. In the Medium Migration scenario from Pew Research, the Muslim share of the population would grow 125%, and in the High Migration scenario, 193%.

Even if the majority of these "migrants" do not become jihadis and instead become "just" deracinated hyper-consumers in the *homo globicus* mold, this is still a huge problem. Though the Islamic conflict with Europe and Christianity is most pronounced in this context for a variety of reasons, transformative immigration from the equatorial regions more broadly is a major concern, existential in fact. Since 2010, Syria has witnessed a 536% explosion in emigration; South Sudan is at 334%, the Central African Republic 204%, Sao Tome

---

18   "The Strategy for Islamic Cultural Action outside the Islamic World," November 2000. Adopted by the 9th Islamic Summit Conference (Doha-State of Qatar). Available at: culturalanalysis.net/wp-content/uploads/2018/04/Strategy-for-Islamic-Cultural-Action-ISECO.pdf.

and Principle 167%, Eritrea 119%, Namibia 90%, Rwanda 73%, Botswana 70%, Sudan 63%, and Burundi 55%. In 2017, about 5.2 million North African immigrants lived in the EU countries, Norway, and Switzerland. The total number of emigrants worldwide from all sub-Saharan African countries combined grew by 31% between 2010 and 2017; the Middle East-North Africa region saw a larger increase (39%) of people living outside of their birth country during the same span. The scariest part is that all of this has simply been a drop in the bucket in terms of the global Third World population explosion.

Of the top forty countries with the highest birth-rates, only three – Iraq, Afghanistan, and East Timor – are *not* in sub-Saharan Africa, and most of the rest of the high birth rate populations are either in Latin America or the Muslim world. Here are just some of the countries whose populations are set to triple or quadruple by the end of the century: Niger (leading the charge at 7.3 live births per woman), Somalia, Chad, Mali, Angola, the Democratic Republic of the Congo, Nigeria, Mozambique, Tanzania, Malawi, and many more. By contrast, most of the nations with the lowest birth-rates are located in Europe or East Asia. The average person's age in some of these countries bears significant attention:

- Niger: 15.3 years of age
- Uganda: 15.7 years of age
- Mali: 16.2 years of age
- Malawi: 16.5 years of age
- Zambia: 16.7 years of age
- Burundi: 17
- South Sudan: 17.1
- Burkina Faso: 17.2
- Chad: 17.6
- Tanzania: 17.6
- Ethiopia: 17.8
- Somalia: 17.9

Contrast this with the developed world:

- Japan: 46.9 years of age
- Germany: 46.8 years of age
- Italy: 45.1 years of age
- Spain: 42.3 years of age
- Canada: 42 years of age
- South Korea: 41.2
- France: 41.2
- The United Kingdom: 40.5
- Taiwan: 40.2
- Australia: 38.6
- The United States of America: 37.9
- New Zealand: 37.8

The situation in contemporary Europe is particularly dire. In February 2018, Silvio Berlusconi declared that if his party proved victorious in the next month's elections, the homogeneous Mediterranean island nation of Malta "will have to share in the burden" of accepting migrants again – an ongoing point of serious contention between Malta and Italy to the north – presumably because a nation that is 95% Maltese is an intolerable injustice in this multi-cultural era.

At Europe's other extremity, the Icelandic government has used the excuse of a "labor shortage" to upset the country's fragile demographic balance; at 91% Icelandic, the indigenous share of the population, at the present rate, is expected to decline another six percentage points by 2030. These are not nations with large populations; at 450,000 and 350,000, respectively, Maltese and Icelandic society could be dramatically transformed by a relatively small number of migrants. No man is an island and no island is safe.

Professor John O'Hagan of Trinity College Dublin is unconcerned with wholesale demographic transformation, stating emphatically, "Clearly [Ireland] could accommodate say a twofold increase in population." This would be to the order of about five million immigrants arriving in the Emerald Isle. To the south, politician Luigi Arru wants to flood the Italian island of Sardinia with migrants in order to "re-populate" it, despite stiff local opposition to expanding the Algeria-to-Sardinia pipeline. Both men share "concern" for their graying populations, though why exactly a managed decrease in population or much better incentivizing your own people's fecundity is so abhorrent as opposed to turning Sardinia into Algeria or Bute in Scotland into Syria is never articulated. Lampedusa, Lesbos, Kos – all are becoming unrecognizable, a product of governmental and supra-governmental re-settlement, open-borders NGOs, opportunistic human traffickers, and major corporations and financial institutions endeavoring to jam as much bio-mass as possible into the space available. Does no one ever stop to ask *why*?

It seems even having the benefit of geographic separation cannot protect a nation from the contagion of multi-culturalism. Europe stood by while Turkey took over the northern part of Cyprus and razed all of its churches, and it now does the same as ever-increasing numbers of migrants flood its shores and Turkey maintains its territorial aggression. Foreign Minister Ioannis Kasoulides condemned the United Nations as "Pontius Pilate" in response to their lack of response to the Turkish blockade, and singled out Britain in particular for their inaction. Meanwhile, as European Parliament member Eleni Theocharous sounds the alarm about the economic and social fallout of the "dramatic increase" of migrants swamping the island, the EU leadership's ears remain deaf.

Perhaps Iceland would be willing to take some of the influx off of the Cypriots' hands. Multi-culturalism is as much a thought contagion as anything. In defiance of all empirical evidence that large-scale immigration is transformative, which should already be axiomatic, the resultant dysfunction, discord, and damage doesn't seem to dampen the positive attitudes of the many European and Euro-Diaspora nations that remain very warm to the prospect of population replacement. According to a 2017 Gallup poll, out of the 138 countries surveyed, Iceland was the world's most immigrant-friendly using the Migrant Acceptance Index with a score of 8.26 out of 9, narrowly "beating" New Zealand's 8.25. Other Western nations in the top ten were Australia with a 7.98 score, Sweden with 7.92, and Ireland with 7.74. The least-welcoming, which is encouraging from the perspective of preserving their existence, included Macedonia, Montenegro, Hungary, Slovakia, Serbia, Latvia, the Czech Republic, Estonia, and Croatia.

The European Union will be damned if its member states don't start accepting migrant quotas, however; the Visegrad Group (Poland, Czech Republic, Slovakia, and Hungary) have been threatened with legal action and economic sanctions for refusing their "fair share" of migrants. The Court of Justice has described its quotas as "necessary," whereas the V4 correctly recognize that to capitulate to these quotas is both to surrender their right to self-determination and national sovereignty and would jeopardize the safety of their citizens, not to mention cause the inevitable erosion of the unique cultural and social fabric of their nations. *New York Times* writers Steven Erlanger and Marc Santora, however, clutch their pearls at the notion that a European nation has a right to pursue its own interests without inviting in the entire Third World, especially if that nation is explicitly Christian (if it were Israel the narrative would surely be a little different): "Poland's Nationalism Threatens Europe's Values, and Cohesion." A nation seeking to preserve its cohesion and values threatens Europe's cohesion and values. Right.

According to Redouane Ahrouch, the leader of Belgium's Partij Islam ("Islam Party"), by 2030 Belgium will be a majority-Islamic country. In 2017, Belgium had an infusion of at least 13,000 *documented* asylum applicants, with the largest share being from Syria, followed by Afghanistan and Palestine. First of all, genuine refugees are, according to international law, supposed to claim asylum in the first safe point-of-entry, and there are quite a few between Syria, Afghanistan, Palestine, and Belgium. Granted a nation need not – should not – follow "international law" if it isn't in their best interest to do so, but the point here is that if these individuals were in real fear for their lives, they would take safe haven wherever they could find it. Color me just a little bit skeptical.

By sheer force of numbers, between the importation of mass numbers of "migrants" and their very high birthrates (the Muslims of Europe average around 3.5 children per woman, and many marriages are polygamous), coupled with a Belgian birthrate of about half that, Ahrouch may well be right that Belgium will be majority Islamic by 2030. The situation is just as grim elsewhere.

Greece, with its abysmal birthrate, "welcomed" 16,345 Syrian (or people who claim to be Syrian), 8,350 Pakistani, 7,875 Iraqi, 7,485 Afghani, and 17,000 other asylum applicants in 2017. Again, this is before considering both legal and illegal immigration. What's more, Maria Polizoidou informs us, "Greece's Syriza coalition appears to be adopting a strategy of garnering votes from immigrants by expediting their naturalization process. It will be easier to obtain Greek citizenship than a fishing license. A total of 800,000 immigrants – almost one-tenth of the native Greek population – will soon become citizens. Transposed to the United States, that would be the equivalent of 32 million new voters."[19] Italy and its bottomed-out birthrate received 126,550 asylum applicants in 2017 alone and has almost half a million illegal aliens within its borders; Spain and its bottomed-out birthrate received 30,485 and Germany and its extremely low birthrate received 198,255. You get the idea. The "migrant crisis" is far from over. In fact, it's just begun. The wholesale demographic and cultural transformation of Europe continues unabated and it is our duty to both our ancestors and to posterity to resist it with everything we've got, because once it's gone, it's gone forever.

The Hungarians understand this, and "Stop Soros" legislation aimed at shutting down open-borders and foreign-funded NGOs, as well as those deemed a national security risk, has been introduced in the country's parliament; government spokesman Zoltan Kovacs says, "These organizations (the NGOs) definitely don't have a democratic mandate because they have never been voted for, nobody elected them." According to Hungarian Prime Minister Viktor Orbán, Soros's goal is to "sweep away governments which represent national interests, including ours." Contrast this with the state of nearby Germany, where journalist Anabel Schunke opines, "The question is no longer: How do

---

19 Polizoidou, Maria, "Flooding the Voter Rolls in US and Greece," April 30, 2018. Gatestone Institute. Available at: www.gatestoneinstitute.org/12227/voter-rolls-greece.

we want to live here as Germans in the future and defend our position in the world, but how can we make it as comfortable as possible for Muslims in the name of tolerance?"

Far healthier is the attitude of the V4 and many other Eastern European nations resisting the tyranny of the EU and the nation-destroying NGOs, open borders advocates, and globalists doing everything in their power to dispossess native Europeans of their homelands via these throngs of unassimilable and violent migrants. Michaela Paulenova, spokeswoman for the Slovak Ministry of Interior, said: "We will not accept any refugees based on the agreement between the EU and Turkey that has so far been agreed," and Czech President Milos Zeman has identified Europe's self-induced "migrant crisis" as an Islamic invasion. Says Orbán, "What we did not tolerate from the Soviet Empire, we shall not tolerate from the Soros Empire. We shall defend our borders, we shall stop the Soros plan, and eventually we shall win."

The Polish Health Ministry released a video in 2017 to encourage its citizens to start "breeding like rabbits." Poland has one of the lowest birth rates in Europe, and coupled with large-scale emigration, it is resulting in severe population decline. In 2015 the rate was at 1.32 children per woman, with only Portugal having a lower figure among EU countries, while Spain and Greece were almost the same. A Danish travel agency put out an ad asking would-be grandparents to pay for a holiday for their children so that they are more likely to get grandchildren, which was credited for the births of an extra 1,200 babies, but a similar effort in Italy by a government ad campaign for a "fertility day," was predictably denounced by the usual suspects as sexist and racist. In Russia, the decline in population has been an acute concern since the breakup of the Soviet Union. Between 1992 and 2009, the country lost about six million people, or 4% of its population. In an attempt to combat this, Vladimir Putin introduced schemes to give extra cash to people who have second and third children, and if you have seven or more children you get invited to the Kremlin to receive a medal!

Two-thirds of Belarusian couples have just one child, and like its neighbors, Belarus is rapidly losing population due to a confluence of low birth rates and high emigration; additionally, there is a decade-wide gap between the life expectancies of men (67 years) and women (77 years). In 2030, the population is expected to be a full million less than it is now, a loss of one person every thirty-seven minutes. Russia and the Ukraine have similar issues, with women outliving men by an average of ten years; this is such an extreme disparity in Russia in particular that there are 10.5 million more women than men. Additionally, both countries have higher death rates than birth rates, and once again factoring in emigration, Russia has a net loss of one person every twenty-six minutes, and the Ukraine has a staggering net loss of one person *every two minutes.*

Romania experiences a net population decrease of one person every five minutes, and Bulgaria experiences a net population decrease of one person every eleven minutes. Romania currently has 19.4 million people but is projected to have just 15.3 million in 2060. Bulgaria had a population of nine million in 1986, and now has less than six. Along with Latvia, it is the only country in the world with a lower population now than it had in 1950. Aldis Austers, Chairman of the European Latvians' Association, said, "We have a joke that in 2030 the last Latvians can switch off the lights at the Riga airport." The Baltic region has lost one-fifth of its population since the fall of the Soviet Union, making it one of the most rapidly de-populating areas of the world. Latvia loses about 30,000 people a year, mostly the young to emigration, and coupled with the disparity of births versus deaths equates to the net loss of one person every half hour. Estonia's population was so devastated by World War II and the Soviet occupation that it just recently reached its pre-war population of ethnic Estonians; the total population has been in decline since the fall of the USSR, and is expected to decline from a little over 1.3 million at present to 1.1 million in 2030 to 860,000 in 2060. Lithuania's population has gone from 3.7 million in 1992 to 2.9 million today to a projected 2.5 million in 2060. According to World Population Review, Serbia:

Has been in demographic crisis since the early 1990's with a death rate that still exceeds its birth rate. Serbia, along with Bulgaria, has one of the most negative population growth rates in the world, with one of the lowest fertility rates (just 1.44 children per woman). 1/5th of all households consist of just one person and Serbia has among the ten oldest populations in the world. Serbia had the largest refugee population in Europe just twenty years ago, accounting for 7.5% of its population. 300,000 people left the country in the '90s, one-fifth of which had a higher education... Serbia has been struggling to overcome its population decline, even turning to singles nights, generous maternity leave and cash bonuses for new parents in some towns. Despite its best efforts, Serbia has been unable to reverse this trend, and its population is expected to continue its downward movement for many years.[20]

In Croatia, the death rate has exceeded its birth rate since 1991, and its population has fallen from 4.7 million in that year to 4.1 million, and is expected to be 3.1 million by 2050. Moldova's current population of just over four million is expected to be under three million by 2060; estimates range from a fifth to a quarter of Moldova's population currently living abroad and, like most of the rest of Europe, its live births are outpaced by deaths and emigration. Slovakia's population is due to decline by about half a million by mid-century, and a similar fate awaits Bosnia and Herzegovina, which already has 800,000 fewer people than in 1991.

Despite the entirety of Europe having sub-replacement-level birthrates, the ideal remains at least two children; for example, every country polled by the OECD – Italy, Estonia, Finland, Ireland, Latvia, Denmark, Cyprus, Sweden, Greece, Lithuania, Slovenia, France, Poland, Belgium, Luxembourg, the UK, the Netherlands, Hungary, Slovakia, Spain, Germany, Austria, Portugal, Malta, Romania, Bulgaria, and the Czech Republic – had an ideal family size of at least two children. Over 50% of Estonians polled and 46% of Finns had an ideal family

---

20   "Serbia," World Population Review. Available at: http://worldpopulationreview. com/countries/serbia-population/.

size of three children. There is obviously something preventing people from having more children. 40% of Swiss and German women with at least a college degree are currently childless, and the current child-bearing age of Austrians is on pace to numerically reduce itself by 70%. The results, coupled with mass immigration, would be nothing short of catastrophic.

Even worse, the populations ear-marked for replacement are financing their own dispossession and attempted destruction. In the US for FY 2011-FY 2015, "refugees" 25-plus averaged just 8.7 years of education before arrival, and 56% of "refugees" over this time span collected food stamps. For Middle Eastern refugees specifically, 84% in 2009 and 91.4% in 2013 were on food stamps. Roughly one-third have no insurance. Steven A. Camarota goes further:

> In 2012, 51% of households headed by an immigrant (legal or illegal) reported that they used at least one welfare program during the year, compared to 30% of native households...Welfare use is high for both new arrivals and well-established immigrants. Of households headed by immigrants who have been in the country for more than two decades, 48% access welfare...Welfare use varies among immigrant groups. Households headed by immigrants from Central America and Mexico (73 percent), the Caribbean (51 percent), and Africa (48 percent) have the highest overall welfare use. Those from East Asia (32 percent), Europe (26 percent), and South Asia (17 percent) have the lowest.[21]

So that's how the government is using the "safety net" that is welfare—treating your country and your labor as the world's largest charity *against your will*. Except it's not charity, it's a wealth re-distribution scheme on an unprecedented scale.

Even if nations' only considerations were economic, which belies the very idea of a nation, the economic arguments for immigration,

---

21 Camarota, Steven A., "Welfare Use by Immigrant and Native Households," September 10, 2015. Center for Immigration Studies. Available at: https://cis. org/Report/Welfare-Use-Immigrant-and-Native-Households.

especially of the kind currently being forced on host populations in Europe and across the West, are unconvincing at best. Japan has the third-largest economy on the planet with minimal-to-nonexistent immigration. The Polish economy is growing at a whopping 4% – with minimal-to-nonexistent immigration. The United States' economy in the 1950s grew at 4% as well, with low immigration following decades of restriction.

Even if we needed more warm bodies for labor (keep in mind the staggering youth unemployment rates, especially in the Mediterranean countries), why not incentivize your own people to have more children by making it less expensive? Why not incentivize marriage and reproductive efforts with large tax breaks, especially since there exists a gap between the number of children Western women are actually having versus the number they really desire? A recent Eurobarometer poll found that immigration is the main concern of 40% of European Union residents, with another 20% naming terrorism as their primary concern – so basically the same thing. In other words, 60% of EU residents will admit to immigration and its consequences as their primary concern, and given that not all residents are Europeans and that many respondents were likely bashful about admitting their legitimate concerns, the percentage is surely higher.

It doesn't have to be this way. After the completion of their wall, Hungary witnessed the number of migrants illegally crossing into the country fall from over six thousand to twenty-nine *in one week*. Bulgaria built at least 91 miles of fence on its Turkish border to discourage migrants from entering a country that's no stranger to Islamic machinations within its borders, to say nothing of the centuries-long Ottoman/Turkish occupation. As Hungarian Prime Minister Viktor Orbán rightly stated, "Hungary does not need a single migrant for the economy to work, or the population to sustain itself, or for the country to have a future." Orbán has banned seditious NGOs from his nation, and pledged to combat Cultural Marxism in education. Indeed, the nations that continue this suicidal practice of welcoming whoever washes up on shore – or is ferried across the Mediterranean by these subversive NGOs – and allows their nations to be subverted from within will not have a future. There is precious little separating Europe from an African continent where the United Nations 2017 world population prospects predicts 2.5 billion inhabitants by 2050, with many countries' populations tripling or quadrupling by the end of the century, to say nothing of the five hundred million-plus potential migrants from the Middle East.

We have now before us a choice: bury our heads in the sand as demographic sea-change, censorship, violence, and corruption transforms our precious countries into neo-liberal dystopias, which may well ultimately result in our oblivion, or reassert not just our right to exist but to flourish.

The right-to-rule is neatly summed up by Pliny the Younger: "If he is to rule over all, he must be chosen from all." All isn't the whole planet – it is from the people of the *polis* the leaders derive their right to rule, and it is those same people who may revoke that right. "Nobody cares about what Donna Brazile has said in [her] book [about the rigging of the Democratic Primary and the cult-like Clinton campaign]. Nobody," says former Virginia Governor Terry "93 Million Americans Die Every Single Day from Gun Violence" McAuliffe. On his side – the Uni-Party – he's right. They don't care about the Constitution, they don't care about due process, and they certainly don't care about this country. Their publicly-expressed faux-compassion seemingly knows no bounds *unless* it is the ravaged white working and middle classes, in which case, no amount of scorn is too much for the beleaguered bedrock of America, or any other Western nation.

The fundamental struggle of our time is neo-liberalism and globalism versus nationalism, localism, and particularism. Much as throughout the previous 8,000 years or so tensions existed between empires and their various constituent tribal or ethnic parts – always dominated by one ruling group, and often a relatively small minority at that – so, too, did the cataclysms of the first half of the twentieth century usher in the era of the "invisible," or supra-national empire. There is obviously significant over-lap here, and empires that are both financial and traditionally territorially-acquisitive such as China remain in existence, but I am speaking of the predominant mode of power expression and how power organizes and perpetuates itself. The nature of empire has changed somewhat over time, but its essence remains the same – the top-down imposition of social mores and economic conditions by a ruling minority.

Now there must always be a minority in charge for optimal governance, but here are two crucial distinctions: we are talking about the difference between an empire and a nation, firstly, and a minority of individuals derived from the indigenous population governing on behalf of the indigenous population based on merit (optimal) versus an alien minority dictating to the indigenous population (sub-optimal and immoral), secondly. That latter minority, or "elite," may still come at least in part from the indigenous majority, but as Greg Johnson explicates:

> Every society is ruled by elites. The only question is whether they rule in the interests of all, or in their own interests. Currently, white nations are ruled by the wealthiest, most powerful, and most diabolically evil elite in human history. When Plato and Aristotle compiled their catalogs of bad forms of government, neither of them imagined a regime so evil that it was dedicated to the replacement of its own population with foreigners.[22]

What we're witnessing is the conscious re-engineering of the social contract and even more fundamentally the population base of the West. The present authoritarianism initially manifested itself under the auspices of a kind of state-managed liberalism in Europe (and most European-majority countries), which has yielded to a pan-continental bureaucratic order and tyranny. The European Union is a supra-national governing body that has become a globalist monstrosity, consciously subverting the will of the people and implementing policies, particularly as they pertain to immigration, that undermine the sovereignty of the individual nations.

---

22   Johnson, Greg, "A Winning Ethos," August 2018. Counter-Currents. Available at: www.counter-currents.com/2018/08/a-winning-ethos/.

Corporations and financial institutions have taken the lead in the United States, though their role remains central elsewhere, just more covert. Clearly the bureaucratic functionaries and multi-national string-pullers have decided to take Bertolt Brecht seriously and elect a new citizenry. If a government will not protect its people – indeed, goes out of its way to harm and even *replace* its own people – then it's lost all legitimacy and should be replaced with one that will.

Chapter 5 - Cultural Corruption

"Jesus, I thought. We've raised a generation of stone desperate cripples...The importance of Liking Yourself is a notion that fell heavily out of favor during the coptic, anti-ego frenzy of the Acid Era – but nobody guessed, back then, that the experiment might churn up this kind of hangover: a whole subculture of frightened illiterates with no faith in anything."-Hunter S. Thompson

Suicides in the US have risen 30% since 1999, and will continue to do so; as liberalism expands its gentle caress, numbers like the 45,000 American suicides in 2016 will only increase, as it is those who most strongly experience progressive hedonism who take their own lives to experience *la petite mort*, or death-as-orgasm/orgasm-as-death in the final orgiastic release as they go to join the jihadis and their thousand-year orgasms on the next plane of sensuousness and delights. For all life – and death – is only so much Epicureanism: novelty, sensation, play. On earth as it is in heaven, pleasure and righteousness are inextricable, or at least they are in the rose-colored fantasies of the privileged Left. To quote Pat Buchanan, "We are an unserious nation, engaged in trivial pursuits, in a deadly serious world."

Freedom is slavery and all people are equal, just as "climate change" né global warming is "settled science" but the sexual dimorphism of human beings is not. The idea of sex as gender, which is itself wholly a social construct, is ludicrous, just as "race is a social construct." It's not that there aren't socially-reinforced expectations for men and women, for example, but these expectations are themselves reflections of biological predisposition, as culture is inextricable from biology. Every culture ever didn't arbitrarily decide men made better warriors due to their superior strength and higher levels of aggression. We now know women have, on average, just 50% of the upper body strength of men and 67% of the lower body strength. Our ancestors didn't know the exact numbers but they had eyes and they could practice deductive reasoning. They were not, as is today the iron law of the land, forbidden from practicing pattern recognition. They understood the unique dispositional traits that make women more nurturing and men more rational. They understood that different peoples and races were fundamentally different. They knew that these different peoples probably did not have your best interests at heart. Only the poisonous influence of Cultural Marxism in our society has made such fundamental and obvious truths "problematic." So the feminists will continue to try and castrate Western men while throngs of Third World men run roughshod over their countries.

They'll be experiencing *dhimmitude* before they realize it, the Gloria Steinem's of the world pushing the only civilization that was obviously dumb enough to cater to their whims right off a cliff. Then they'll have seen their standing in society regress about 2,000 years in the blink of an eye. Only Europeans, East Asians, and the Igbo have monogamy and high-investment parenting as civilizational fixtures, and only European societies traditionally elevated women to almost angelic figures and certainly as invaluable ones. Though they may have had fewer rights as we understand them today, this was based on an understanding of women's dispositional differences, chiefly an inclination to the sentimental, which precluded them from voting and holding office. In Rome, for example, women more or less had the same status as civilians in Robert Heinlein's *Starship Troopers*. This strongly suggests that Western culture has always been more egalitarian, generally speaking, than other cultures, and should it be extinguished, these women will have lost far more than most can presently comprehend.

The gorgeous 16th century Renaissance church Chiesa San Paolo Converso in Milan has been deconsecrated and transformed into an indoor tennis court by the "Qatari-American" Asad Raza and is being billed as an "interactive art piece" named *Untitled (Plot for Dialogue)*. That alone is a most poignant image of where we are as a civilization, the mix of frivolity, irreverence, and ignorance a perfect metaphor for the civilizational ennui that's engulfed us and the willingness to capitulate and sacrifice that which is our most sacred, from our monuments to the few children we are willing to have.

Coupled with the extension of citizenship to all free men of the Roman Empire by Caracalla in 212 AD (the historical record seems to indicate that this was done to increase tax revenue – sounds familiar) and the founding Roman families dying off, not to mention the increasing permeability of the border, the Western Roman Empire began to fall apart, and it is little wonder. As Dio (Cassius, not Ronnie James) recounts Augustus's speech to an assembly of Roman patricians, anticipating the trajectory of Rome:

We liberate slaves chiefly for the purpose of making out of them as many citizens as possible. We give our allies a share in the government that our numbers may increase; yet you, Romans of the original stock, including Quintii, Valerii, Iulii, are eager that your families and names at once shall perish with you.

Populations that remain stuck at sub-replacement-level typically bottom-out and almost never recover. They either die out or are swallowed up by other population groups. Wholesale importation of foreign peoples is very clearly not the solution if one wants to preserve their nation. As Polybius wrote in his *Histories*, cataloguing the cratering birthrates as a result of the frivolity and excess that had gripped his society:

In our time all Greece was visited by a dearth of children and generally a decay of population, owing to which the cities were denuded of inhabitants, and a failure of productiveness resulted, though there were no long-continued wars or serious pestilences among us...For this evil grew upon us rapidly, and without attracting attention, by our men becoming perverted to a passion for show and money and the pleasures of an idle life, and accordingly either not marrying at all, or, if they did marry, refusing to rear the children that were born, or at most one or two out of a great number, for the sake of leaving them well off or bringing them up in extravagant luxury.

Frivolity and excess, or at least base materialism, is a major component of the dearth of fecundity in the modern Western world, though it is not the exclusive cause; demoralization, competition for resources, economics, environmental factors, and ideologies like feminism also contribute to and compound the problem. In short: the putrid package of neo-liberalism. To quote Max Weber, "If one says 'the future of socialism' or 'international peace,' instead of native city or 'fatherland' (which at present may be a dubious value to some), then you face the problem as it stands now."

It's not difficult to see where this is heading, nor will I be the first to point it out. Failed states, abominable living conditions, and the allure of the West and its bountiful entitlements…this is going to get ugly very quickly. It's not exactly my idea of progress to be subjected to cultures where they sever the limbs of albinos to sell on the black market for witchcraft and other assorted spell-casting; in Mozambique, there's been a rash of murders as bald men specifically, rumored to have gold in their heads, are having their skulls cracked open to find the hidden wealth. Talk about cultural enrichment!

As was the case in the late Roman Empire or in the modern Western countries, as an evolving stance on what constitutes belonging, the set of values or characteristics an individual needs to possess to belong to the dominant discourse are subject to change. In classist cases this becomes a question of sub-sets within a society, but when faced with barbarian incursions, as an example, the ruling class needed to also foster a variable sense of nationalism across their territories – what Caspar Hirschi calls "the reception of Roman law as a vehicle of patriotism." In short, an ancient version of civic nationalism. It clearly did not work.

There is a stunning cathedral in the center of York, England, called the York Minster that offers a perfect metaphor. Originally a Roman fortress, in 627 AD a wooden church was hurriedly constructed to be able to baptize King Edwin of Northumbria. A more permanent, but still humble, church was eventually erected, but it burned down in 741; a much more ambitious church with thirty altars was constructed on the site, and lasted until its severe damage in 1069 during William the Conqueror's harrying of the North and its ultimate destruction in 1075 by a Danish Viking raid. From 1080 another church was built in the Norman style. The present structure, which took over two hundred years to construct (1230-1472), is Gothic in style and sits on the Roman, Anglo-Saxon, and Norman foundations that came before. Given its size, intricacy, centrality, and importance, the cathedral requires consistent maintenance and renovation in order to preserve it in all its grandeur, but the expense is more than worth it to honor the region's history and to be able to awe oneself in the presence of the cathedral's stained glass, opulent ornamentation, magnificent architecture, and tombs of seminal religious and political figures. Visiting the Minster, you can time travel the two thousand years below the cathedral through the previous foundations and their artifacts, and climb the central tower to see the still-intact medieval walls of York and the medieval Clifford's Tower that still stands on the thousand-year-old site on its outskirts. The diligence, respect, patience, talent, faith, and cooperation it takes to create and maintain such a house of worship across many lifetimes is really a testament to civilizational pride and religious devotion, a true labor of love, and it speaks to something deep and profound in the Western psyche.

The role of giving, cooperation, and altruism also forms an important cornerstone in the development of the West. The evidence for altruism having a strong biological component is mounting, and its occurrence varies across different races. Whites seem to have the highest levels of altruism, and are unique among the races for their de-emphasis on kinship and re-orientation of society to a more person-to-person "contractual" system, whereby cooperation between non-familial societal sub-groups and individuals takes on extra importance. To be sure, familial ties remain central to the organization of white societies, but beyond the immediate family, the ties, generally speaking, rapidly diminish. In *Infidel*, Ayaan Hirsi Ali wrote about the kin system in Somalia, where everyone was expected to know their lineage ten or twenty generations in the past as a form of social organization and hierarchy, which could certainly be a source of strength and function both as a "networking tool" and as its own kind of welfare system in times of need, but could also in times of instability, such as the Somali civil war, turn into a tribal nightmare. The kin system is not conducive to building a modern nation-state.

Kin selection is just one mechanism in the evolution of cooperation, which also involves three different kinds of reciprocity, a "guardian function," and group selection, which with the de-emphasis of kinship in Western societies allowed for voluntary association and hence a much greater degree of cooperation, which in turn allowed for the development of more complex social, political, and economic systems. Coupled with the genetic impulse among whites to be more altruistic than other groups – perhaps owing to climatic factors, but more research needs to be done here – the ready embrace of Christianity conjoined with the unique and varying local pagan customs, rituals, and spirituality, helped facilitate an extreme emphasis on the individual relative to other cultures.

Western civilization surged ahead of its competitors after the Black Death as the works of luminaries such as Chaucer, Boccaccio, Dante, and Petrarch writing in the vernacular in the High Middle Ages melded with the Renaissance of classical antiquity's intellectual and artistic traditions, and were widely dispersed following the invention of the moveable-type printing press. This double fusion – first of Christianity with local paganism, then with a re-discovery and advancement of the ideas and ideals of classical antiquity – imbued Europe with tremendous energy and brought it to the doorstep of modernity, for better or, increasingly, worse. Near about the Enlightenment, the altruistic cooperation that was once so central to the development of Western civilization became a weird distortion, and several things happened simultaneously: Western Man "rationalized" himself out of belief in anything truly transcendent, the Church was subverted, and Christianity began reverting to its original emphasis on universalism with an abandonment of the Indo-European essence that was infused into what is essentially an alien faith of slaves and outcasts. Christianity focuses on the weak and downtrodden, and while it is noble to help those most vulnerable among us, it is not to say we should neglect the noblest aspects of man to forever put the needs of others before our own. It is, as was well-understood in classical antiquity and the Renaissance, a balance. Western Man also became more materialist and concerned with trade and money, which, all things taken into account, opened the doors to the subversion and perversion of banking and finance on the one hand and the religious institutions on the other. The Occident's immune system was down. To quote Barbara A. Oakley:

> For cooperative behavior to continue in complex biological or sociological entities, that is, for entities not to fall prey to ever-present, ever-evolving defectors, some form of evolving active guardian function must be present that detects when debilitating or destructive advantage is being taken of cooperative or altruistic behavior. The guardian system must not only detect but also disable such noncooperative behavior or render the entity immune to the pernicious effects. Without such detection and mitigation mechanisms, we see modeled evolutionary entities that are wiped out by defectors.[1]

These mechanisms are no longer present, and the defectors are eating away at the Western organism. These are the "enlightened free-loaders," and we are the guilt-ridden "pathological altruists" who enable them. Metapedia defines pathological altruism as: "Sincere attempts to help others that instead harms others or oneself and where this harm could have been reasonably anticipated. It is often caused by cognitive and/or emotional biases that blind people to the potentially harmful consequences of their actions." Our immune system is down and the carrion of our civilization is up for grabs. In fact, we'll help you strip the carcass bare! As Mark Steyn says, "You don't extinguish prudence for utopian delusions," but that's precisely what we've done.

The Left has positioned itself as "The Resistance," diametrically opposed to all that Western civilization stands for and represents – from the race that built it, to the centrality of the *logos* and the quest for

1   Oakley, Barbara A., "Concepts and implications of altruism bias and pathological altruism," June 18, 2013. *Psychological and Cognitive Sciences*, 110 (Suppl 2), Proceedings of the National Academy of Sciences of the United States of America. Available at: www.ncbi.nlm.nih.gov/pmc/articles/PMC3690610/.

truth as its primary organizing feature. It is inevitable that when *logos* and *pathos* find themselves in opposition, as they must in the present paradigm, *logos* for the Left must yield, even become criminalized, for the survival of the *logos* means the survival Western civilization. Simply making some superficial changes to the culture is not the order of the day; our adversaries want to build on this particular site, and nothing less than a complete demolition will do.

The demolition takes many forms; superficially, what at first glance appears to be an over-emphasis on compassion, both real and (in most cases) manufactured, has become a kind of status marker – a cache of "moral rectitude" which signals one's belonging to an exclusive and superior group. Cultural "cues" are crucial to consider as we are social creatures; when one group has an "elite" hostile to its own people, or more accurately in the West the people whom the elite rule over, this helps explain some of the incentives for self-dispossession and dis-incentives for fashioning a racially- or ethnically-oriented basis for in-groups versus out-groups. As Kevin MacDonald explicates, the elites are cultivating:

> Feelings of moral rectitude resulting from subscribing to the moral dictates of the society as defined by media and academic elites. Since these elites unanimously regard the traditional people and culture of the West as uniquely immoral, dissenting from these views results in shame and guilt, whereas going with the flow results in very positive feelings that one is a member in good standing of the mainstream society...Without elite control, there is no infrastructure that makes displays of guilt and abasement profitable. Social learning only becomes a weapon against Whites after the forces opposed to Whites control the elite media and the academic world; the same can be said for the creation of moral ingroups.[2]

This is designed to short-circuit any discussion, no matter how rational

2   MacDonald, Kevin, "Psychological Mechanisms of White Dispossession," March 24, 2013. *The Occidental Observer*. Available at: www.theoccidentalobserver. net/2013/03/24/psychological-mechanisms-of-white-dispossession/.

and *factual*, through its rejection of *logos* in favor of a by-definition irrational *pathos*. It also results in the warping of *ethos*, both in the sense of establishing credibility, and in the criteria for what constitutes credibility, as well as in the perversion of our code of ethics, which is (in a properly functioning society) also the province of reason to a large degree. In such an environment of relentless virtue-signaling and status-marking, many well-intentioned people will be unconsciously pathologized into accepting not only false doctrines of equality, but even the moral imperative of their own dispossession. What would otherwise appear monstrous now takes on the patina of virtue.

White liberals believe themselves to be given the duty of "global uplift" – "The White Savior Industrial Complex" – and the "White Man's Burden" has long been a trope in Western ventures foreign and domestic. Combined with maladaptive ethno-non-centrism/racial consciousness (or worse, an ethno-masochistic pathology, as the term was first coined by Alain de Benoist, or "white submissives" as Spencer Quinn calls them) and an Orientalizing of the Other (xenophilia), racial White Knighting has founded itself on a perversion of a natural biological impulse; an increasingly dumbed-down discourse saturated in saccharine platitudes of "compassion" also funnels white women's "motherly instincts" into the Third World instead of the babies these women refuse to have. High maternal/parental investment is one of the factors in whites developing the way they do; nuke the family and the entire civilizational apparatus breaks down.

This hyper-individualism wears the mask of caring, nurturing compassion but it is instead a sensualistic narcissism which, imbued as it is with puritanical moralizing, renders the barren Western womb, devoid of any true femininity, nothing but a childless prude in epicureans' clothing. This is the archetypal "cat lady," who, incidentally, makes for both a ruthlessly effective cultural commissar *and* a tremendous consumer in her own right. An additional factor to consider is the recently introduced and researched concept of "superhumanization bias," where whites "preferentially attribute superhuman capabilities to blacks versus whites."

One of the most powerful weapons in the ruling class's arsenal is guilt transference, whereby the guilty party or parties transfer the guilt of what they themselves are doing or have done on to others, creating often totally innocent scapegoats while they behave with impunity. Donald L. Carveth states that, "The single word 'guilt' can refer both to the ontological state of *being* or being judged to *be* guilty and the psychological or experiential state of *feeling* guilty. Someone who does not *feel* guilty may be judged by his own or another's superego to *be* guilty."

White guilt and its cousin white privilege are probably the most readily apparent examples, where wealthy and powerful "progressives" such as those found in Silicon Valley who are primarily responsible for the conditions of the country today can blame any and all of their misdeeds on the beleaguered out-of-work coal miners in West Virginia simply because of their skin color, their "antiquated" beliefs, and the fact that they have no way to counter these accusations in any appreciable way. They become the blank slate for which the population can project their grievances on to, the guilt receptacles as it were. The truly guilty can go on with their agenda with the population none the wiser, having directed their fury elsewhere. This predisposition to feelings of guilt dovetails with elevated levels of affective empathy, particularly in Northwestern Europeans. Quoting Peter Frost, this population exhibits:

A greater capacity for affective empathy [which] seems to reflect an environment of relatively high individualism, relatively weak kinship, and relatively frequent interactions with nonkin. This environment has prevailed west of the Hajnal Line since at least the 12th century, as shown by the longstanding characteristics of the Western European Marriage Pattern: late age of marriage for both sexes; high rate of celibacy; strong tendency of children to form new households; and high circulation of non-kin among families. This zone of weaker kinship, with greater reliance on internal means of behavior control, may also explain why Northwest Europeans are more predisposed to guilt than to shame, whereas the reverse is generally the case elsewhere in the world.[3]

3   Frost, Peter, "We are not equally empathetic," November 15, 2014. Evo and

This helps explain why the Northwest Europeans especially have proven so susceptible to subversion. There is also a greater tendency to complementary projection, in which "people believe that more people share their beliefs and values than actually do. We 'project' our beliefs and values onto other people and overestimate the extent to which other people also have them." There are fundamental reasons why the developed parts of the Orient have been able to resist demographic replacement and its terrible costs while much of the Occident has not. One aspect in which the developed Northeast Asian nations in particular differ greatly from ours is in their cultural and biological predispositions to conformity/uniformity. Additionally, their cultural policing as it were is predicated on shame rather than guilt.

While it is tempting to cite culture as the lone culprit, culture is at its heart the product of biology – a culture is comprised of its people. So even though an alien anti-morality is being pressed upon us, if we were not receptive or at least susceptible to it, then I would not have needed to write this book, quite frankly. That said, the propaganda of the "elite" and their control over all of the major institutions has been, in every sense of the word, transformative, and it has weaponized our predispositions to altruism and reciprocity against us.

The biologically-driven cultural differences between races are embedded deep in our neural wiring, and though there is clear evidence that all races are neuro-chemically wired to feel greater empathy toward their in-group, this response seems to be weakest among whites. Additionally, whites, unique among races, appear to have an elevated empathetic response, and it is not just limited to human beings. We know that, "Race results suggested a comparative lack of interest in, and concern and affection for animals among nonwhites."[4] Edinburgh Castle, for example, has a graveyard, complete with headstones, for the castle's former watchdogs, and the

---

Proud. Available at: http://evoandproud.blogspot.com/2014/11/we-are-not-equally-empathic.html.

4   Kellert, S.R., "American attitudes toward and knowledge of animals: An update." In M.W. Fox & L.D. Mickley (eds.), *Advances in animal welfare science* 1984/85. The Humane Society of the United States: Washington, DC. p. 189.

Romans often wrote inscriptions in honor of their deceased pets. This is very unusual in most other cultures.

Could the weak racial consciousness of whites in the presence of more racially-conscious groups be one reason for the cratering birthrates across the West? After all, as E. Raymond Hall, Professor of Biology at the University of Kansas states, "It is biological law that two subspecies of the same species do not occur in the same geographic area...To imagine one subspecies of man living together on equal terms for long with another subspecies is but wishful thinking and leads only to disaster and oblivion for one or the other."[5] Only Ashkenazi Jews have evidenced the ability to not just survive but thrive in the presence of other, to use Hall's term, "subspecies of man." It has proven to be an essential group evolutionary strategy, in fact. As Eva Ritvo informs us, "The altruism center of the brain is considered a 'deep brain structure,' part of the primitive brain." Our brain's ability to process emotional influences is directly tied to our genes; according to lead author Rebecca Todd of a recently-conducted study by the University of British Columbia, "People really do see the world differently...For people with this gene variation, the emotionally relevant things in the world stand out much more":

The gene in question is ADRA2b, which influences the neurotransmitter norepinephrine...Carriers of the gene variation showed significantly more activity in a region of the brain responsible for regulating emotions and evaluating both pleasure and threat...The ADRA2b deletion variant appears in varying degrees across different ethnicities. Although roughly 50 per cent of the Caucasian population studied by these researchers in Canada carry the genetic variation, it has been found to be prevalent in other ethnicities. For example, one study found that just 10 per cent of Rwandans carried the ADRA2b gene variant.[6]

---

5   Hall, E. Raymond, "Zoological Subspecies of Man at the Peace Table," November 25, 1946. *Journal of Mammology*, Vol. 27, Issue 4. Available at: https://academic.oup.com/jmammal/article-abstract/27/4/358/1251712?redirect edFrom=fulltext.

6   Todd, Rebecca et al., "Neurogenetic Variations in Norepinephrine Availability

Another Danish study conducted on children found that non-Westerners were significantly less empathetic than their white counterparts.[7] Two other studies found the gene at an incidence of 50% in Swiss participants[8] and an incidence of 56% in Dutch participants.[9] Blacks have consistently been found to have the fewest carriers of the ADRA2b gene variant; two American studies found a higher incidence in whites at 31% and 37%, respectively, versus that of blacks at 12% and 21%, respectively.[10,11]

There are other measurables as well; for example, blacks give less than all other races in gratuities. According to a study conducted by Lisa Leslie at the University of Minnesota, women donate more to charity than men, and minorities donate less to charity than whites. Even in death blacks are less charitable, seldom listing themselves as organ donors – apparently because, according to Patia Braithwaite writing for *Vice*, "It's hard to make a case for altruism in organ donation when our medical system has historically not been altruistic to us." This is a pathetic "justification" that actually has its basis in biology, not whatever they're teaching in the race grievance studies departments at the local university. Empathy is vital to be able to imagine things

Enhance Perceptual Vividness," April 22, 2015. *The Journal of Neuroscience*, 35 (16). Available at: https://archive.md/Pqueg.

7 "Report," August 24, 2016. Information. Available at: www.information.dk/indland/2016/08/rapport-ikkevestlige-boern-mindre-empatiske-danske.

8 de Quervain, D.J. et al., "A deletion variant of the alpha2b-adrenoceptor is related to emotional memory in Europeans and Africans," 2007. *Nature Neuroscience* 10 (9). Available at: www.ncbi.nlm.nih.gov/pubmed/17660814.

9 Cousijn, Helena et al., "Acute stress modulates genotype effects on amygdala processing in humans," May 25, 2010. *PNAS*, Vol. 107, No. 21. Available at: www.pnas.org/content/pnas/107/21/9867.full.pdf.

10 Small, Kersten M. and Stephen B. Liggett, "Identification and functional characterization of α_2-adrenoceptor polymorphisms," September 2001. *Trends in Pharmacological Sciences*, Vol. 22, Issue 9. Available at: www.sciencedirect.com/science/article/abs/pii/S0165614700017582.

11 Belfer, Inna et al., "Haplotype-based analysis of alpha 2A, 2B, and 2C adrenergic receptor genes captures information on common functional loci at each gene," February 2005. *Journal of Human Genetics*, 50 (1). Available at: www.researchgate.net/publication/8134892_Haplotype-based_analysis_of_alpha_2A_2B_and_2C_adrenergic_receptor_genes_captures_information_on_common_functional_loci_at_each_gene.

from others' perspectives – which might well explain why high-empathy whites are overrepresented in classic works of literature, strong as they are at crafting narratives, especially ones that do not revolve specifically around their race. Another study found low levels of affective empathy in Pacific Islanders,[12] and the Chinese [13] seem less likely to distinguish between cognitive empathy and affective empathy.

While ADRA2b is not necessarily the be-all end-all to understanding affective empathy, the consequences of these findings are extremely significant in understanding not just how Western civilization developed but how it has proven susceptible to the pathologizing of altruism, which seems to be the root of these maladaptive psychological mechanisms. Charitable giving feels good – it floods our neural pathways with dopamine from the "reward circuit" in our brains, causing a "helper's high."

There's additional evidence that oxytocin may also be released; oxytocin is associated with an elevated mood, and in the presence of higher oxytocin, dopamine and serotonin levels also rise. This has the effect of creating a positive feedback loop, whereby the neural circuitry rewards us for "doing good" and thus being rewarded emotionally. This loop can be self-perpetuating as the promise of the "helper's high" leads one to continuously seek that "hit." The loop may even be self-elevating as well, for the greater the levels of oxytocin, the more altruistic and "giving" one feels. Even if the "helping" is deeply harmful, these behaviors are positively reinforced by every social mechanism and in every institution from the media to academia. As Barbara A. Oakley elucidates:

---

12 Lepowsky, M., "The boundaries of personhood, the problem of empathy, and 'the native's point of view' in the outer islands," in D.W. Hollan, C. J. Throop (eds). *The Anthropology of Empathy: Experiencing the Lives of Others in Pacific Societies*, Berghahn. 2011.

13 Siu, Andrew M.H. and Daniel T.L. Shek, "Validation of the Interpersonal Reactivity Index in a Chinese Context," March 1, 2005. *Research on Social Work Practice*. Available at: https://journals.sagepub.com/doi/abs/10.1177/1049731504270384.

Our empathic feelings for others, coupled with a desire to be liked, parochial feelings for our in-group, emotional contagion, motivated reasoning, selective exposure, confirmation bias, discounting, allegiance bias, the Einstellung ("set") effect, and even an egocentric belief that we know what is best for others, can lead us into powerful and often irrational illusions of helping. In other words, people's own good intentions, coupled with a variety of cognitive biases, can sometimes blind them to the deleterious consequences of their actions...[There is] potential harm from cognitive blindness that arises whenever groups treat a concept as sacred.[14]

The aforementioned oxytocin also lowers one's suspicion of strangers and outsiders; in a particularly insidious iteration, one recent study conducted by American and German researchers on German subjects recommended that the German people be dosed-up on oxytocin to make them more amenable to their population replacement at the hands of Angela Merkel's decision, with the backing of the European Union, the financial institutions, the multi-nationals, and the Barbara Lerner Spectre set to "elect a new people," suggesting, "*Oxytocin-enforced norm compliance* reduces xenophobic outgroup rejection,"[15] which has profoundly disturbing implications for what the ruling class is willing to do in the future to ensure the "acceptance" of their agenda.

For now, though, pathological altruism and rampant white guilt under the manipulative guise of "liberalism" have proven to be exceptionally powerful instruments in the dismantling of the Occident. With Christianity increasingly the gospel of Social Justice – and Social Justice the repudiation of Christianity – we are at once spiritually devoid of the animating energies of the uniquely European version

---

14 Oakley, Barbara A., "Concepts and implications of altruism bias and pathological altruism," June 18, 2013. *Psychological and Cognitive Sciences*, 110 (Suppl 2), Proceedings of the National Academy of Sciences of the United States of America. Available at: www.ncbi.nlm.nih.gov/pmc/articles/PMC3690610/.

15 Marsh, Nina et al.," Oxytocin-enforced norm compliance reduces xenophobic outgroup rejection," August 29, 2017. *PNAS*, 114 (35). Available at: www.pnas.org/content/114/35/9314.

of Christianity from our "middle age" while at the same time, for those seeking guidance in Christianity's doctrines, the ancient/modern form encourages, paradoxically, the radical and the defective while simultaneously belonging to the masses.

We have these competing-yet-intertwined models of universalism and individualism, pride in the herd and the sanctity of the collective but racial denialism for whites only. The entire orientation of Western civilization has become centered on its own self-destruction as a uniquely evil force in the world – a mindset diametrically opposed to the actual truth of the matter. Through a devastating combination of fear, guilt, apathy, nihilism, narcissism, affluence, cultural amnesia, pathological altruism, incentives to virtue-signal, irreligiosity and Christian meekness, the transference of the religious impulse, psycho-pharmacology, a disabled guardian function, the scars from and the loss of two generations from the two World Wars, and plenty of internal subversion, the synergistic effect of these afflictions has created the perfect storm of "privilege-abdicating," civilization-dismantling whites.

When our natural reaction of shock and disgust to all of this is condemned as "bigotry," there can be no other conclusion than that the very fabric of our societies is disintegrating. By essentially recriminating our hard-wired response to these alien mores, gross bodily violations, and violations of societal taboos, we are being asked to partake in an inversion of not just our culture and moral code in favor of the alien Other, but to deny our basic human instincts that *this is wrong*. Roger Giner-Sorolla and Pascale S. Russell make the useful distinction that:

> With the recent upswing in research interest on the moral implications of disgust, there has been uncertainty about what kind of situations elicit moral disgust and whether disgust is a rational or irrational player in moral decision making. We first outline the benefits of distinguishing between bodily violations (e.g., sexual taboos, such as pedophilia and incest) and nonbodily violations (e.g., deception or betrayal) when examining moral

disgust. We review findings from our lab and others' showing that, although many existing studies do not control for anger when studying disgust, disgust at nonbodily violations is often associated with anger and hard to separate from it, while bodily violations more consistently predict disgust independently of anger. Building on this distinction, we present further empirical evidence that moral disgust, in the context of bodily violations, is a relatively primitively appraised moral emotion compared to others such as anger, and also that it is less flexible and less prone to external justifications.[16]

The infantile notions of "hate" and xenophobia predicated on the idea that those opposed to wholesale demographic change are somehow small-minded and ignorant, and are irrationally raging against "progress," is itself a simple-minded and ignorant reduction of something much more complex into a playground sense of morality. Art Markman states:

Studies suggest that there is a tight relationship between our sense of moral purity and the emotion of disgust. Violations of our sense of moral purity lead us to feel the emotion of disgust. When we experience the emotion of disgust, we also change our judgments of the moral purity of others... This view of disgust suggests that the emotion of disgust is strongly connected to our sense of morality. That is, when we feel disgust, we should also express feelings of moral outrage. And to counteract those emotions, we should increase our concern with purity.[17]

If we perceive ourselves to have been wronged, or worse, violated, and our desire for redress is ignored if not outright condemned, the

16 Giner-Sorolla, Roger and Pascale S. Russell, "Bodily moral disgust: what it is, how it is different from anger, and why it is an unreasoned emotion," March 2013. *Psychological Bulletin* 139 (2). Available at: www.researchgate. net/publication/235785781_Bodily_Moral_Disgust_What_It_Is_How_It_Is_ Different_From_Anger_and_Why_It_Is_an_Unreasoned_Emotion.

17 Markman, Art, "Disgust and morality," December 8, 2009. *Psychology Today.* Available at: www.psychologytoday.com/us/blog/ulterior-motives/200912/ disgust-and-morality.

mechanisms of disgust and outrage – real outrage – will rightly find themselves in the embrace of righteous anger. If left unchecked, this increase in concern for purity can have momentous consequences. What starts as a very legitimate desire to maintain both purity and sanctity, if not properly channeled, can lead to the most extreme cases of violence and even genocide. I've no doubt many people on the Left are simply viewing both historical and contemporary events through an opposite prism, that is, essentially, "they know not what they do" (though clearly many of the so-called "elites" have a particular agenda), but the accelerating polarization between Left and Right, and the Left's unwillingness to engage in dialogue, is producing rhetoric that is, and I mean this literally, genocidal. This is not emanating from the Right, the supposed home of the "Nazis," but on the Left, where the global extermination of whites is viewed as the highest moral calling.

Of course I believe that it is right to want to not only preserve that which we hold dear and most sacred – family, nation, tradition, religion for some – but that we are morally justified in fighting back to reverse these trends of dissolution and dispossession. The collision course is set because I truly believe that the radical Left has passed the point where they no longer view us as equals but as both corrupted and de-humanized obstacles to attaining utopia. Our extermination, as buck-toothed, in-bred hillbillies or backwards fossils of another era is morally justified in their view. Purity on the Right involves far "cleaner" distinctions such as male-female, right-wrong as opposed to relativism, or ethno-cultural-derived demarcations between nations; for the Left, it is moral purity that is of the utmost concern, and for us, their morality is alien and ugly. It luxuriates in its impurity, and that disgusts us. The problem with the Right is that it's paralyzed by fear of being labeled a "phobe" of some kind and it's been hijacked by the GDP Mafia.

People have always been divided, both in real, fundamental terms like race and sex, and in more socially-constructed terms such as taboos, dietary restrictions, and cultural customs. Tribalism is ingrained in our very nature, and we are being compelled to deny our nature by the Cult-Marx globalist utopians. Even that which is a product of culture is informed by biology, though there is in this current age the inclination to dismiss tradition as somehow antiquated, and thus of no use to us in the present day. As the Jewish social psychologist Jonathan Haidt writes:

> If morality is about how we treat each other, then why did so many ancient texts devote so much space to rules about menstruation, who can eat what, and who can have sex with whom? There is no rational or health-related way to explain these laws. (Why are grasshoppers kosher but most locusts are not?) The emotion of disgust seemed to me like a more promising explanatory principle. The book of Leviticus makes a lot more sense when you think of ancient lawgivers first sorting everything into two categories: "disgusts me" (gay male sex, menstruation, pigs, swarming insects) and "disgusts me less" (gay female sex, urination, cows, grasshoppers).[18]

Many of these religious prohibitions look absurd to us today, especially through the prisms of modern scientific knowledge and atheism, but Haidt is wrong – there were perfectly legitimate reasons for these decrees, even if they seem a bit obscure or strange. First, they helped define who the in-group was versus the out-group through specific practices that could be held in relief against surrounding tribes or societies; second, with an incomplete understanding of viruses, germs, and pathogens, ancient peoples could still make observations and practice deductive reasoning, and might rightly conclude certain foods and/or activities had a propensity to produce illness; and third, outsiders may well bring foreign pathogens with them that could decimate the tribal unit or local settlement that didn't have a specific immunity.

In any case, we know, for example, that sodomy does carry an increased risk of certain STDs as opposed to vaginal intercourse, particularly due to both the exposure to fecal matter and the sensitivity

---

18 Haidt, Jonathan, "What Makes People Vote Republican?" September 8, 2008. *Edge.* Available at: www.edge.org/conversation/jonathan_haidt-what-makes-people-vote-republican.

of the anus to micro-tears, and given that most STDs are contracted from bodily fluid transmission, especially as it pertains to blood and semen, this makes a lot of sense; menstruation, though obviously not an illness, is often accompanied by mood changes, nausea, cramps, and dizziness, and so, coupled with the discharge of blood, might give ancient peoples the impression that there was something to this monthly occurrence that was either harmful or at least significant in ways they may not fully have understood.

Returning to Haidt's list, there are many bacterial infections people may contract from swine, especially with limited knowledge of hygiene and none of bacteria. Per the South African Pork Producers' Organisation, "If all the causes of foodborne disease are analysed, pigs and pork could theoretically be implicated in over 40% of cases. In 2003, the CDC found that in America, Salmonella caused 26% of all food poisoning cases." Salmonella is commonly found in the intestine of pigs. "The other causes of foodborne disease that pigs might carry… are *Clostridium perfringens* (4%), E. coli (6%) and Campylobacter (4%)." These last three are also common in the intestine of pigs. Finally, pertaining to swarming insects, locusts (technically a kind of grasshopper) are notorious for wiping out crops and thus, in a far less technologically-advanced age and with no bug-resistant pesticides and GMOs, the ancients would be right to regard swarming insects with apprehension as locusts often were harbingers of famine. As noted by the Food and Agriculture Organization (FAO):

A swarm the size of Niamey (Niger) or Bamako (Mali) eats the same amount of food in one day as half the respective country. A swarm the size of Paris eats the same amount of food in one day as the half population of France; the size of New York City eats in one day the same as everyone in New York, Pennsylvania and New Jersey; the same size of San Francisco eats the same as half of California, the size of Sidney (Australia) eats the same amount of food in one day as Australia eats in 1.5 hours…There are 10 species of locusts but the Desert Locust is the most destructive. Found in Africa, the Middle East, and Asia, they inhabit some 60 countries and can cover one-fifth of Earth's land surface. Desert locust plagues may threaten the economic livelihood of one-tenth of the world's humans.[19]

Conversely, other grasshoppers can make for a decent snack, and though I know they are not the same thing, their crepuscular cricket cousins can be ground into a type of flour for baking. We need to be very careful of trying to impress our modern understanding and morality on to the past. That said, there are certain dangers in clinging too tightly to tradition, ranging from cultural ossification and the inability to adapt, evolve, or innovate, to lashing out in the most extraordinary violence at a world changing too quickly to be understood. This change, as we shall see, is not always, or even usually, positive and much of this violence is also being turned inward by people against themselves. Why? Because modernity is largely unnatural, an exercise in trying to jam square pegs and other things that don't belong into round holes. Mark Point asks:

> So where have three decades of feverish placation and encouraging our sons and daughters to take a backseat landed us? Statue toppling, knock out games, self-segregated graduations, implicit this, privilege that, people being fired for thought-crimes, higher taxes on struggling families to subsidized race-based transfers, racialized comic book warriors, real historical heroes defaced with graffiti, suppressed speech, our national anthem undermined, and an endless torrent of millions of new immigrants adding more complexity to a difficult situation... Your daughter's daffy feminism, the lionization of increasingly bizarre sexual anomalies, undying dream of economic collectivism and Christophobia are all skirmishes that need managing but America is becoming dangerously anti-white at a time when with the world's only white-majority societies are becoming white minority.[20]

---

19   "The Differences between Grasshoppers and Locusts," Act For Libraries. Available at: http://www.actforlibraries.org/the-differences-between-grasshoppers-and-locusts/.

20   Point, Mark, "Racism on the Rise," November 6, 2018. *American Thinker.* Available at: www.americanthinker.com/articles/2018/11/racism_on_the_rise.

The "elites" prime the population for replacement with ceaseless propaganda, and they dis-arm peoples' counter-arguments with "nation of immigrants" pap; this ploy relies on ignorance, but it's obviously working. In the universities, whites are trained to despise themselves and their heritage with all of the vitriol of any good champagne socialist – and they get to pay for the privilege – while non-whites are charged with the same hatred of their white "oppressors." The minds of impressionable youths are being shaped to demand their own imprisonment at the hands of a heavy-handed and intrusive bureaucracy and to find being a cog in the corporate machine "empowering." Meanwhile, the high school and college years, and increasingly the following decade or two, are spent in a drunken stupor racking up as many sexual partners as possible.

The youth has plenty to feel aggrieved about, but none of it can be given voice. Control the language, control the thoughts. Thus the rage festers and remains inchoate. "Righteous in their loathing of anything and everything that smacked of present-day Western society, and boundless in their love of whatever might destroy it," to quote Jean Raspail, the Left remains feverishly committed to flooding the West with as much of Emma Lazarus's "wretched refuse" as it takes to drown our civilization: "Everywhere, rivers of sperm. Streaming over bodies, oozing between breasts, and buttocks, and thighs, and lips, and fingers . . . a welter of dung and debauch," as Raspail described in *The Camp of the Saints*. The degree to which Rome, New York, or London increasingly resemble Abuja, Monrovia, or Freetown is a product of the fact that, to quote Evelyn Waugh, "Civilization has no force of its own beyond what is given it from within. It is under constant assault and it takes most of the energies of civilized man to keep it going at all." When these energies are displaced in favor of displacement, the process can only accelerate. For William Gayley Simpson:

> We have allowed our religious superstition and our sentimental humanitarianism almost completely to frustrate the operation of natural selection. Blinded by the fact that human life is of very

unequal worth, we actually sacrifice the more valuable to the less valuable. In our folly, we burden the sound and the capable among us with the support of a colossal load of human wreckage. ... The cost of carrying all this load is prodigious, and it is growing. If we do not soon reverse the present process the land will at last be possessed by those unable even to take care of themselves. We are following the path of national and racial suicide.[21]

These are hardly the conditions of ideal governance, let alone a nation's basic functionality or even survival. As Polybius wrote in his *Histories*, "There are two things fundamental to every state in virtue of which its powers and constitution become desirable or objectionable. These are customs and laws. Of these the desirable are those which make men's private lives holy and pure, and the public character of the state civilized and just." Following the at-minimum century-long impoverishment of the Occident through moral degradation, civilizational ennui, two suicidal world wars, an infatuation with destructive and de-humanizing ideologies such as communism and unbridled capitalism, and transformative mass Third World immigration, the United States and many of its kin in the West are scarcely countries anymore, let alone nations. Their very existence is imperiled.

Concepts like truth and purity are central to the human condition, and in the media and in the modern academy, the constant push to "problematize" is often at direct odds with the strange moral purity exhibited by the Left. The Mouth of Truth ("La Bocca della Verita") is a carved marble face fabled in Roman lore to bite off the hand of anyone who told a lie – scholars today believe it to have been a common, *vulgar* sewer-covering, and as such it literally "talks shit." Elitist and classist attitudes regard the intersection of the "vulgar" with the "refined" as cause for unease, and in a modern context this is commonly portrayed as "cow shit on the Grecian urn."

---

21   Simpson, William Gayley, *Which Way Western Man?* National Vanguard. 2003 (2nd edition). p. 76.

In another very recent inversion, however, the modern "patricians" seem invested in promulgating the "vulgar," even though they themselves generally continue to practice bourgeois values. I will quickly note here, however, that in the Renaissance, public spaces were specifically designed to be beautiful and open, and the wealthy and poor co-mingled here with great frequency. Yes, the wealthy could retreat behind their walls, but this co-mingling virtually *never* happens in modernity. The physical distance between "elites" and "plebes" has never been greater. Furthermore, and paradoxically, though high and low culture were once very rigidly differentiated (except where rare talents like William Shakespeare could elevate the vulgar not by denigration but by gift, and make the "high" comprehensible and enjoyable for all segments of the population), they still are, but the high has been brought low and the vulgar elevated. As Lothrop Stoddard wrote in *The Revolt Against Civilization*, this kind of impulse:

> Is instinctively hostile to intelligence. It pins its faith to instinct – that "deeper knowledge" of the undifferentiated human mass; that proletarian quantity so much more precious than individualistic quality. Both the intellectual elite and their works must make room for the "proletarian culture" of the morrow. Intellectuals are [according to Georges Sorel] a "useless, privileged class"; art is "a mere residuum bequeathed to us by an aristocratic society." Science is likewise condemned.[22]

Paradoxically, for an ideology that luxuriates in temporal pleasures, indeed, has gone so far as to sanctify the profane, the body is decidedly *not* a temple. For William Gayley Simpson:

> On our bodies is built our whole superstructure of character, intellect, spirit, and culture: when that goes, everything goes with it...I cannot believe that you can get great wisdom and enduring culture, or even plain healthy judgement about the values of life, from a people as shot through with disease as we are...The warning should be kept before the eyes of the entire nation: Any organism

---

22 Stoddard, Lothrop, *The Revolt Against Civilization*, 1922. p. 174.

that fails to excrete its waste products, dies.[23]

Simpson means "diseased" in both a literal and figurative sense. Sexually transmitted diseases are on the rise, previously eradicated and obscure exotic diseases are cropping up across the West's major metropoles; and drug overdoses, alcoholism, obesity-related complications, and other deaths-by-despair claim many Occidental lives each year.

This is a civilizational crisis, the genesis of which intellectually and spiritually extends well before the First World War, itself a grisly eruption of Western Man's suicidal and nihilistic impulses. Nietzsche first presaged the death of God in *The Gay Science* and *Thus Spoke Zarathustra* in the 1880s; the disillusionment of the failed Revolutions of 1848 may serve an even earlier starting point; and Kierkegaard augured the day when the ease of existence in the form of technological advancements and the like would prove corrosive as early as 1846: "You must do something, but inasmuch as with your limited capacities it will be impossible to make anything easier than it has become, you must ... undertake to make something harder."

When economics supersede everything else, the will of the people is more easily subverted with soft comforts and comfortable lies. Excessive comfort is as corrosive as anything yet encountered by man. It robs us of our very agency and makes us, in the ultimate irony, obsolete, for we are too irrational and flawed to match the speed and computational power of artificial intelligence, too weak and lazy to do the work of machines, and too stunted and numbed to be fully human. This is a living death too terrible to contemplate.

The prevalence of (post-) modern malaise and ennui presaged by Kierkegaard and Nietzsche, respectively, had to have been present in their time, or else they would not have been able to perceive it. When, precisely, Western Man fell ill will remain an open question, but perhaps it was the French Revolution and its proto-Bolshevist blood-letting

---

23   Simpson, William Gayley, *Which Way Western Man?* National Vanguard. 2003
      (2nd edition). p. 75-76.

in the name of *"liberté, égalité, fraternité"* that represented the first violent convulsion in the name of "equality." Whereas the American Revolution marked the high point of Enlightenment thought and the institutionalization of self-government, the French Revolution provided us with the first glimpse into the communistic killing fields of the future. Unfortunately, the American Experiment was doomed from the outset due to the irreconcilable tensions between republicanism and empire, and between its secularist "materialist legalism" as Solzhenitsyn called it and its messianic pretensions. Both Revolutions, in fact, were done in by promising temporal utopianism of a sort rather than synchronicity with the natural order.

The Bolshevist spirit manifested in the French Revolution, which we would call Leftism or Cultural Marxism today, necessitates purity but only in terms of ideological purity; that is the only arena not subjected to corruption, pollution, and "de-construction." Leftism is logically self-negating in its fluid morass of relativism, selling utopian visions while trafficking purely in the temporal; the most extreme narcissism and self-gratification is celebrated while at the same time the focus remains on the collective, but the collective in what Simpson characterizes as the "colossal load of human wreckage."

With no guardian function to purge deleterious persons and concepts, and no discernable in-group identity, whites find themselves adrift in a sea of anti-white animus – much of it genocidal – and excessive, nihilistic hedonism. Is it any wonder that ugliness is such a fixture of our daily lives now? As William Gayley Simpson wrote, "Nietzsche assigned [significance] to physical beauty as an index of desirability in a mate and of health and well-constitutedness in a people. Their sense of the beautiful and of the ugly was a deposit of their 'most fundamental self-preservation values." Whites, taken as a whole, currently have no values of self-preservation; there is only veneration of the mass of humanity, quantity over quality. Quantity and excess may take the form of the increasingly grotesque corpulent bodies we see waddling down the high street, or it may be the lifting up of the mass of humanity *over and above* those who are capable, beautiful, or otherwise of significant value to their people.

This is the communization of democracy, or the democratization of communism, both of which, in the end, venerate the undifferentiated mass over the individual and yet, paradoxically, we are given strong messaging that the individual is paramount. One recent television advertisement made the claim that, "There is no American Dream – there are 330 million of them," yet we hear incessantly from politicians about "our values." What, exactly, those are is never specified, but they seem to involve anal sex and student loan debt. We have a negative definition – we know who we're not – and that is intolerant and able to think for ourselves. "Bigotry has no place here"… unless it's directed at whites of course. Neo-liberalism is fraught with contradiction. It decries "racism" yet singles out whites for blood libel. It celebrates democracy but undermines pro-nationalist elected officials, manipulates elections, ignores results, and even sanctions the invasion of sovereign nations and the toppling of regimes if the results are not to the ruling class's satisfaction. It advocates for minority rights – unless those minorities happen to be whites in former African colonies or beleaguered Christians in places like Egypt and Syria. If Hispanics happen to be mass shooters such as the Jewish-Hispanic Nikolas Cruz, then they are dubbed by the media "white Hispanic," a term that entered the lexicon with George Zimmerman. The term's purpose is clear in much the same way that Hispanics are classed as white in criminal statistics as perpetrators but often treated as non-white when they are victims; similarly, they find themselves classed as non-white in affirmative action and college admissions processes.

Other examples abound: it's perfectly natural for a young boy to play with dolls but should he opt for army men, that's *toxic*. Believe all women so long as the accusations are politically expedient. Despite our sexual dimorphism, there are multitudinous genders, whilst race remains at once a "social construct" and totally fixed. Tolerate the intolerable, make endless war, call rapacious capitalism "social justice," *ad infinitum*. While you are harangued, attacked, and everything else up to and including being driven to extinction, you are simultaneously subject to pleas of compassion and tolerance, and vagaries referencing "our values."

The "elites" are intent on replacing dynamic and healthy populations with dumbed-down and (politically) docile ones. It's really quite brilliant in its own psychotic way, at least in the short-term. All pyramid schemes eventually come crashing down, though, but hey, if the world is going to end in twelve years due to "climate change" as Alexandria Ocasio-Cortez believes, you might as well send your consumption into overdrive and buy, buy, buy! – but only if your consumer purchases have rainbow packaging and are "sustainably sourced" from sweatshops in Sri Lanka, that is, in which case you've done a great service to mankind by helping the globalist establishment wipe out all individuality and avert a crisis that wasn't real to begin with, at least not the one they manufactured. There *is* a crisis, however, and it is existential and all-encompassing. As R.R. Reno writes:

> To a great extent, our progressive culture strips ordinary people of almost all settled roles, other than economic ones. This heightens the existential pain of the already harsh economic realities of our globalized economy, which can be very punitive to the poorly educated. Two generations ago, a working class man was often poor or nearly poor, but he could be respected in his neighborhood as a provider for his family, father to his children, law-abiding citizen, coach of a Little League team, and usher in church. The culture that made such a life possible has disintegrated, partly due to large-scale trends in our post-industrial society, but also because of a sustained and ongoing ideological assault on the basic norms for family and community.[24]

The "natural rights" of liberalism rely on negative obligations, which is to say the obligation to *not* interfere in the lives of others. Superficially this seems like a fine idea, particularly with respect to others' privacy, but freedoms all too often manifest themselves as freedoms *from* obligation, an emphasis on individuality for its own sake, rather than on individuals who may exercise their free will but are nevertheless bound to their people and their families (in short, their obligations). Such a state of affairs produces selfish and self-interested persons who

---

24 Reno, R.R., "Deadly Progressivism," November 4, 2015. *First Things*. Available at: www.firstthings.com/web-exclusives/2015/11/deadly-progressivism.

are no more than the sum of their base instincts and their shopping history. They are not individuals at all, but rather cogs in the machine. It is little wonder, then, that such people look for meaning in their lives and can scarcely find it.

Part Two: Economics

Chapter 6 - The Religion of Markets

"We're all clients."- The Red Chord, "Clients"

Just as Rome, before it succumbed to the barbarian incursions, attempted to advance its interests with the various tribes along its borders, often playing one off another, and incorporating them into their intricate military-economic web (to the extent in its waning days of settling tribes wholesale within the drawn boundaries of the empire, which, as we are seeing repeated today in the West, back-fired spectacularly – or is, from the globalist perspective, succeeding), many of today's governments with similar aspirations attempt to engage in the same kind of military-industrial dominance but on a fully global scale. This is the discourse of empire, an accepted model with prescribed roles within the seemingly all-encompassing military-industrial complex – rulers as CEOs, and subjects as clients.

With the fall of the Soviet Union, the most significant counterbalance to global capital was removed, and the carrion of the USSR was picked over by internationalists and domestic but ethnically alien oligarchs, perhaps most pronounced in Russia. Only with the rise of Vladimir Putin did the "Wild West" period of unbridled capitalism at the price of Russia's soul come to a close. While not perfect, the Putin regime is at present one of the few bastions against neo-liberalism in the world today. To understand the conflict in the Ukraine, it is vital to understand not just the ethnic component, but this fault-line between neo-liberalism and ethnic self-determination. "Communist" China is not much of an impediment to the spread of neo-liberalism, for though it is insular in many respects and aggressively seeks to advance Han ethnic interests, it remains very much "open for business" while enacting its neo-colonial agenda. In many crucial ways, the Chinese are actually vital to the neo-liberal system. Beyond the often superficial tensions between communism and capitalism, the centrality of globalization is the real story of the twentieth and twenty-first centuries, from Woodrow Wilson's Fourteen Points to modern American "nation-building." The struggle for ethnic self-determination and liberation from Mammon and the intervention of Market Forces is what really defines World War II. Contrary to the narrative, Germany was peacefully extricating itself from the global economy, a state of affairs that simply could not stand. This is why Iran finds itself squarely in John Bolton's crosshairs and why the "classical liberals" screech about women's liberation from mandatory head coverings and modesty laws, totally ignorant of the context of which they speak.

We are so deeply-conditioned to believe in this corrupted liberalism as a default that even many who are fairly far along in the process of greater awareness will often find the basis of their critique to be that particular ideologies have not embraced "Western pluralism." Case-in-point is that of Islam. In but one example of the inherent contradictions of liberalism, the hijab in Iran is construed as a sign of oppression, whereas amongst immigrants to the West, it is a symbol of empowerment. So, which is it? It depends on the agenda of course! Yet another war: hijab bad. Yet more immigrants resulting in the further splintering of the host culture: hijab good. Yes, some of Iran's laws and punishments are draconian, but we must remember that the Iranian theocracy is a direct response to: a) American meddling in their domestic affairs vis-à-vis the Shah, and b) "Westernization."

"Westernization" no longer refers to specific ideals and means of organization that one might correctly identify as "civilization," but rather the export of consumer culture and a loosening of morals, un-tethered from a nation's unique peoples and traditions. As with "diversity," "Westernization" makes everywhere the same, and in this deeply ironic way, the communistic impulse to characterless uniformity is expressed through consumer culture as a vehicle of totalitarian materialism at odds with the better natures of *all* peoples. Much like the Long March through the Institutions, previously forthright or reputable concepts have been hollowed-out and appropriated for something radically different than the original construction or intent. Whether it is a company like Disney or an idea like democracy, what it was and what it is are two different things entirely, and this is by design. It is the Trojan Horse of a particular globalist paradigm past our natural defenses. "Classical liberalism" is a Western invention, and it is imperialistic to expect the ready adoption of those values by other people. Democracy is the same. Now, both concepts have been perverted from their original iterations, such that neo-liberalism is neither democratic nor liberal if it ever was. What is clear is that in the countries where neo-liberalism is most prevalent, things are the worst.

The neo-conservative line about capitalism lifting more people globally out of abject poverty is exactly in line with Paul Treanor's observation that "the market" has become "an ethic in itself, capable of acting as a guide to all human action, and substituting for all previously-held ethical beliefs." By conflating the moral good of alleviating human suffering with material well-being – which, like all the most effective propaganda, does contain a grain of truth – "conservatives" may justify the dismantling of the middle- and working-classes in moral terms for "the greater good," while their counterparts on the Left use their own moral framework involving "privilege" and post-colonial theory and other Cultural Marxist constructions. These run social interference as often-incoherent noise, the only real uniting premise being that whites are bad, while the neo-liberal economic system is able to destroy ecosystems and entire nations and ethnic groups relatively unimpeded.

The entire global apparatus is in favor of obliterating all distinctions between different peoples – and between men and women – and restricting any real sense of identity beyond the superficial from group affiliation down to individual distinctions to a very rigidly-policed and -defined in-group. Sure multi-culturalism might encourage non-white groups in white nations to assert their unique cultural and ethnic identities *now*, but that is merely temporary as a tool for atomization. Eventually, in a grim irony, assimilation *will* occur, but this is a very different kind of assimilation than the civic nationalist ideal. This kind of assimilation looks like the Borg out of *Star Trek* – all unique cultures, all traces of individualism swallowed-up with a singular focus on consumption; consumption of that which stands apart, consumption as a *consumer*, it will all be centrally-controlled. In another irony, capitalism and communism eventually horse-shoe, with both defined by the predominance of a kleptocratic cabal of cosmopolitan interests. In this glorious future they have planned, the shuffling masses, "augmented" with their devices and smartphones, with no defining characteristics from race to culture to sex, will remain attached to and controlled by the Hive Mind, or plugged in to the Matrix if you like; in this Brave New World *not* having a sex change is a transgressive act and "rebellion" is synonymous with un-thinking conformity.

Most "popular culture" both within and exported by the United States is not organically "popular," with a few rare exceptions; it is, by and large, an alien imposition that glamorizes an alien inversion of morality: the anti-civilization. Not only are the means of production and dissemination such as the movie studios, radio stations, record companies, PR firms, and the like under control by a certain select group, but the financing of these ventures is as well. Through artificial manipulation, platforms such as YouTube promote or suppress whatever videos they like (and this of course extends to information), and the entire media apparatus colludes to provide the general public with pre-packaged "celebrities," "controversies," and "news."

In the absence of religion, celebrities and media figures now fill the deity function in the pantheon of "pop culture." That most of these people are disgusting degenerates, and artificial in nearly every respect, including their increasingly-grotesque physical features/augmentations, is not incidental. The nearly-universal exhortation of the media-entertainment-industrial complex is consume, consume, consume. Only in an environment of hyper-materialism and nihilism would we find such sentiments as the following sample lyric from Tove Lo, from "Talking Body": "Bodies! Our baby-making bodies we just use for fun. Bodies! Let's use them up 'til every little piece is gone."

Popular music, as one example, serves as a useful conduit to propaganda; think of "variety" radio stations: modern cross-platform music is shuffled into playlists with music of an intensely nostalgic variety. Essentially, there is modern "uni-genre" or "anything" music (a sort of antiseptic pseudo-rap/pop/electronic hybrid which is completely characterless, transitory, and thus highly consumable), nostalgia, and pop-oriented country-western. Those are your options, and the latter two are designed specifically to facilitate the listener's acceptance of the messaging and consumption of the former. Mainstream music is a powerful tool of control and has made for exceptional propaganda. By influencing impressionable youngsters with messages of materialism, carnality, and impropriety, the media moguls have crafted a "passively" auditory and easy-to-digest product, uniform in its outlook. Feminism, empowerment, consumerism, and sexual permissiveness are all conflated on the female side as evidenced by a recent hit song by Ariana Grande, "7 Rings":

Yeah, breakfast at Tiffany's and bottles of bubbles
Girls with tattoos who like getting in trouble
Lashes and diamonds, ATM machines

Buy myself all of my favorite things

You like my hair? Gee, thanks, just bought it
I see it, I like it, I want it, I got it

Wearing a ring, but ain't gon' be no "Mrs."
Bought matching diamonds for six of my bitches
I'd rather spoil all my friends with my riches
Think retail therapy my new addiction

Whoever said money can't solve your problems
Must not have had enough money to solve 'em
They say, "Which one?" I say, "Nah, I want all of 'em"
Happiness is the same price as red-bottoms

Feminism's (post-) modern iteration looks something like an insistence on black male-white female pairings nearly ubiquitous in advertisements and other propaganda (consider Grande's dating life, or that of other prominent celebrities such as the Kardashians, one of whom is now the world's youngest billionaire), pansexuality, gender confusion, and the like – all enfolded into one putrid package of "empowerment," so-called progressive politics, and consumerism. The target demographic here is obviously tween through early-thirties females, who will trade in their child-bearing years in order to become a cog in the corporate machine. Their sexual encounters will be "no strings attached," precisely the kind of transaction favored by the Establishment, and their adherence to Woke Capital ensures that this statement of empowerment and independence is at once political *and* consumerist. This marriage of the political and the corporate defines the modern era. When everything comes under the auspices of The Market, then everything is a transaction. In this way, neo-liberalism endeavors to make us all prostitutes, forever selling our bodies. The utter vapidity of popular culture and consumer culture – which are synonymous – leaves people with real internal value naturally feeling empty and depressed, which in turn causes them to surrender to the nihilistic excesses of consumer culture, and to seek remedy in narcotics and psycho-pharmaceuticals, or else to throw themselves into equally empty causes of "social justice." These badly-damaged vessels, particularly the so-called "feminists," are of little use to anyone except as shambolic consumers, misandrous shock-troops, and paper-shuffling wage-depressors.

Male "artists" fall into one of two camps: that of aggressive, typically black "alpha" with a preoccupation on genitalia and outward expressions of wealth or that of emasculated simperer of the Sam Smith variety. Occasionally "artists" such as Nicki Minaj or Cardi B will "cross over" and play the sexually aggressive female preoccupied with her genitalia, but such a role also seems generally reserved for darker-skinned performers. Going even further, Rihanna's "S&M" and its attendant music video feature explicit depictions of just that, and Minaj has performed while parading around with a rubber phallus on numerous occasions. The expression of same-sex desire is, however, usually reserved for white artists (the Britney Spears-Madonna MTV Video Music Awards kiss, Katy Perry's "I Kissed a Girl"[1] etc), as are

---

1   Perry's "rise" is an all-too-familiar tale of the apple-cheeked, wholesome white girl selling her soul for fame and fortune: "After singing in church during her childhood, she pursued a career in gospel music as a teenager. Perry signed with Red Hill Records and released her debut studio album *Katy Hudson* under her birth name in 2001, which was commercially unsuccessful. She moved to Los Angeles the following year to venture into secular music after Red Hill ceased operations and she subsequently began working with producers Glen Ballard, Dr. Luke, and Max Martin. After adopting the stage name Katy Perry...she

treatments of self-destruction and/or portrayals of being mentally ill (Bebe Rexha's "I'm A Mess" music video takes place in a psychiatric ward, as does Laday Gaga's "Marry the Night").

This intersects with the importation and veneration of Third World peoples in some crucial ways: they generally have high time preference and tend toward instant versus delayed gratification, and thus help power the hyper-consumerist engine of modernity. Additionally, as their "values" become increasingly represented in pop culture, pop culture feels less overtly alien as the *raison d'etre* of a Nicki Minaj is precisely represented in their music and performance – there is no "put on," as opposed to the corruptible naïve blonde-in-the-big-city from Wisconsin who "sells her soul" to Hollywood or the music industry. Then, as the traditional culture unconsciously absorbs aspects of pop culture, we have the normalizing effect of alien mores and behaviors as imposed from above.

These "values" don't quite extend to the neo-aristocracy pushing them on the general public, though. Sure, they luxuriate in nihilistic degeneracy themselves – virtually bathe in it, really – but they are ensconced in the failsafe of financial capital and numerous investments and in-group networking and nepotism, and are safe from the ramifications of the "diversity" they advocate for with their secure and homogeneous living arrangements. In short, they can have their cake and eat it, too, which is not too difficult when you're the architects of the economic conditions that have allowed the top 1% of Americans' wealth to triple over the past five decades while openly waging war on the middle- and working-class people of this country. The so-called "elites" marry and stay married, and can actually afford to have children while preserving a solvent familial unit, while they encourage carnality and recklessness for the "vulgar masses" and artificially suppress white birth-rates through onerous taxation and financial burdens.

---

signed a recording contract with Capitol Records in April 2007. Perry rose to fame in 2008 with her second album, *One of the Boys*, a pop rock record containing...'I Kissed a Girl.'" https://en.wikipedia.org/wiki/Katy_Perry.

Ours is truly a pitiful society where popular culture is nothing more than an open sewer, its music a funeral dirge, and its virtues nihilism, decadence, and ignorance, all painted over with a bright rainbow of tolerance-at-gunpoint. There is nary a scintilla of truth to what they're selling us, and all of the evidence we have contradicts the claims – slogans, really – emanating from the rainbow-colored globalist tyranny. No "white supremacist" society would feed and house tens of millions of non-contributing aliens at great cost, including that of even reproducing themselves.

The neo-liberal mind infection that convinces the third-most populous country in the world that they "need" more people and more labor – especially as automation makes millions of jobs redundant and outsourcing vanishes millions more – and that the height of compassion is to literally allow yourself to be raped, plundered, killed, and ultimately ethnically cleansed has become so pervasive *defending* your nation is now treasonous. *The people themselves are the nation*, not its GDP or some other abstraction. The land is ours, the culture is ours, the spirit is ours, but not in the eyes of the craven "elites," multi-national corporations, and the global financial establishment. As Mark Dyal illuminates:

> Homogeneity is the key that unlocks the ontological functions of multiculturalism. While globalists, corporate spokesmen, political leaders, and academics speak in glowing terms of a relativist multicultural humanism based on political and economic freedom, they are actively engaged in a two-pronged attack on human particularity and the defense thereof. First, multiculturalism is a moral regime that links progressive liberal ideas of tolerance, ecumenicalism, and cosmopolitanism in order to aggressively condemn racism or pride in one's particularity…Second, the State, having finally shed the pretense of existing as the will of a people, uses this moral regime at the bidding of the capitalist oligarchs… to spread a monolithic culture of liberal politics, feminism, anti-racism, and identity-based hyper-consumption. It calls for "one world, one race,"–the flip side of multiculturalism–and actively undermines any attempts to preserve the standards, values, and

traditions of local peoples, wherever they exist. Just as the State uses the World Trade Organization and World Monetary Fund to control the underdevelopment of the Third World, it uses global capitalism as a talisman to unlock any societies, peoples, States, or regions that remain overly local, xenophobic, or archaic, essentially capturing space for the purpose of its homogeneic valuation. But when the talisman does not properly entice, war is an ever-present possibility.[2]

The US military has been bandied about the globe over the last century-plus to scratch various ideological itches, itches that the American public does not, and unless the "elites" get their way and elect a new people, will not support. We have always been expansionist – Oswald Spengler's Faustian spirit is here reflected in the notion of Manifest Destiny and Thomas Jefferson's view that our race should people the entirety of the hemisphere – but this expansionism was for the most part confined to the hemisphere (the Pacific and the Philippines ventures notwithstanding), and it has also always existed in tension with a strong sense of isolationism. The United States is an exceptional nation, and is an historical aberration in many ways. Its seeming destiny as an empire has always contrasted sharply with its ideology of self-governance and the Founding Fathers' intent to have the United States remain a mostly agrarian, de-centralized society. The intent was certainly never to make money for Genie Energy, facilitate the mass migration of equatorial peoples into Europe by assassinating world leaders on its frontier, spend decades bombing innocent people into oblivion, or allow Israel to abuse its neighbors, murder US sailors aboard the USS Liberty despite being ostensibly allies, withhold crucial intelligence about the embassy bombing in Beirut or the 9/11 terrorist attacks, or provide safe haven to pedophiles, but here we are.

Whilst Baby Boomers were sold a bill of goods regarding "the content of our character," Generation X was treated to the cognitive dissonance of race-blindness and post-racialism coupled with affirmative action and the opening salvos of "political correctness." In spite of all of this,

---

2   Dyal, Mark, Foreword to Kerry Bolton's, *Babel, Inc.: Multiculturalism, Globalisation, and the New World Order*. Black House Publishing, Ltd: London. 2013.

in an interesting twist culturally, for a brief period of time from the mid-1990s until the early 2000s, we actually almost got the formula right, but continued job outsourcing, financial speculation, demographic transformation, and the ascendance and metastasizing of anti-Western and anti-white ideologies rushed head-long toward the corrupt and race-baiting Barack Obama presidency, which was meant to be an exclamation mark on the black-white racial healing process in the United States but in effect was simply George W. Bush 2.0 without the evangelical paint-job.

During the eight years of the Barack Obama banana republic, with power pretty much uniformly consolidated on the Far Left, the systemic, state-sanctioned persecution of ideological opponents was able to command the full force of the government apparatus: the IRS targeted conservative 501(c)(3)s; the Justice Department engaged in large-scale spying operations, including of a FOX News reporter, the Associated Press, and members of the Donald Trump campaign; the NSA had instituted numerous surveillance programs on average Americans that were undoubtedly unconstitutional; OSHA, the FBI, and the ATF were turned loose on Tea Party groups like True the Vote; and the list goes on.

Obama's race-baiting contributed to civil unrest and condoned a culture of enmity toward law enforcement. His clear view of the individual men and women of the armed forces to be used as nothing but cannon fodder for an imperialist agenda led to a number of veteran deaths due to VA negligence and fake waiting lists, and documents were forged to cover up the whole affair. The Justice Department moved to shield Obama's allies from scrutiny and was perceived as being so corrupt, that former FBI Director James Comey went public with his announcements on the Hillary Clinton investigation because he felt Loretta Lynch had been "compromised," especially after she met secretly with Bill Clinton and told Comey to refer to the investigation as a "matter." Comey himself is no peach, having allegedly been involved in some shady dealings with Turkey while with Lockheed Martin. What's more, three separate FBI field offices had requests to open public corruption cases against the Clinton Foundation denied by the Obama administration.

Even though voter ID laws are apparently racist according to the Left, the Justice Department saw fit to throw out lawsuits against the New Black Panther Party for intimidating white voters in the 2008 presidential election. Never one to shy away from identity politics, Attorney General Eric Holder claimed that criticism of the Fast and Furious debacle which resulted in a US law enforcement officer's death followed by a concerted cover-up of the details, even to the officer's family, was motivated by the fact that he and Barack Obama have a particular kind of relationship (Holder: "I'm there with my boy") and the fact that they are "African-Americans."

The sad fact is these incidents are just a small sampling of how disastrous the Obama administration was for the integrity of the United States. There's a depressing litany of other instances of cronyism, corruption, and cover-ups like Benghazi, Hillary Clinton's secret server, Lisa Jackson's fake identity, the bail-outs, Solyndra, and the GSA scandal, not to mention the complete albatross of Obamacare. Meanwhile Obama was busy hectoring the "hicks" of Middle America decimated by the former president's "green" policies that cost America over one trillion dollars and 125,000 jobs: "They get bitter, they cling to guns or religion or antipathy to people who aren't like them or anti-immigrant sentiment or anti-trade sentiment as a way to explain their frustrations." That or unlike the supposedly "intellectual" coastal elites, these people can clearly see what a commitment to globalism and progressivism is doing to our country.

While Bush rightfully was tarred by the opposition as a blood-thirsty warhawk and war profiteer (there used to be something called an opposition back then, although it was waning), Barack Obama spent every day of his presidency at war; the only clear division between the two beyond the obvious is in the former's final exhaustion of Ronald Reagan's "moral majority" and the latter's at-times antagonistic relationship toward Israel. Let's be clear about something, though: they essentially served the same master as two sides of the same coin. It is telling that, despite ostensibly representing Labour, Tony Blair and Bush were joined at the hip. Blair – the "third way" neo-liberal – and Bush – the neo-conservative – again represent complementary, not antagonistic, forces. When asked what Americans could do to help in Bush's "war on terror," he responded that Americans should get down to Disney World, or just go shopping.

To quote Michal Baranowski, director of Warsaw's German Marshall Fund office: "It's 'yes' to Europe, but what Europe?" Will it be a fierce defense of their national and ethnic identities or the limp-wristed childlessness of the EU? This open question applies to the whole of the West. Says Slawomir Debski of the Polish Institute of International Affairs, "The history is part of our identity, which people in other parts of the world don't understand. What is it to be a Pole?" Is it to be an imported Ethiopian who helps drive down wages and fracture national harmony and cohesion, or is it something deeper?

There's an inherent contradiction in the Leftist notions of diversity and communistic inter-changeability. If all people are basically the same – equal if you like – then why do we need diversity? And why do Leftists pine for the day when whites become a minority in their own countries, magically erasing all "racism" and inequality between groups? If diversity is a strength then why is one of the justifications for forcing it almost exclusively on white countries from non-white countries "revenge for colonialism," even if the country targeted for this revenge never participated in colonialism or the country exporting people never experienced it? Either way, though, surely depriving whites of the abundant benefits of diversity would be a greater punishment?

For the Left, the broad idea of dimension invariably evokes notions of direction and linearity. Even the notion of circularity (as in historical circularity and repetition) is purposefully undermined in several ways by bringing relativistic theories into provocative opposition; it is therefore helpful to consider direction and space in their wider implications. A discussion of direction necessarily includes verticality. Phrases such as "the height of the Roman Empire" occur frequently in historical discourse, and work to imply that empires – as a genus – move in one direction along a curve, either to a summit or a base.

There is no stasis; if an empire is at its height, it will continue to move forward, the trajectory eventually flattening out and falling. Retroactivity is not part of the "progressive" narrative. The Left seeks to further complicate fundamental conceptions of time, progress, and movement, and since upward movement implies adherence to the traditional slope archetype of progress, represented by the Conrad-Demarest Model of Empires, the Left seeks to dispense with the discourse of empire (another inherent contradiction, as the Left portrays itself as "progressive" – as in, progressing toward the socially harmonious utopia) while being itself instrumental in the expansion of the neo-liberal empire. We would do well to keep in mind that history like nature is, however, cyclical.

To hear the media mouthpieces tell it, to compassionate, to empathize, we must strengthen ourselves through diversity, through a fanatical fever dream of "equality" by enveloping the huddled and shivering masses in our warm embrace of consumerism. We must save them from themselves, and in so doing, we will become richer and more spiritually pristine! This is life in the fast lane of the Information Superhighway! And of course the exhortations to consume and copulate are reflected back at them by the high time preference, low impulse control brand-spanking-new population commissioned to plug-and-play their role in the media-entertainment-retail complex. The utopia of hyper-consumerism draws ever-nearer. As Noam Chomsky and Edward S. Herman write in their 2002 update of *Manufacturing Consent*:

The steady advance, and cultural power, of marketing and advertising has caused "the displacement of a political public sphere by a depoliticized consumer culture." And it has had the effect of creating a world of virtual communities built by advertisers and based on demographics and taste differences of consumers. These consumption- and style-based clusters are at odds with physical communities that share a social life and common concerns and which participate in a democratic order. These virtual communities are organized to buy and sell goods, not to create or service a public sphere. Advertisers don't like the public sphere, where audiences are relatively small, upsetting controversy takes place, and the settings are not ideal for selling goods. Their preference for entertainment underlies the gradual erosion of the public sphere under systems of commercial media, well exemplified in the history of broadcasting in the United States over the past seventy-five years. But entertainment has the merit not only of being better suited to helping sell goods; it is an effective vehicle for hidden ideological messages. Furthermore, in a system of high and growing inequality, entertainment is the contemporary equivalent of the Roman "games of the circus" that diverts the public from politics and generates a political apathy that is helpful to preservation of the status quo.[3]

Politics themselves have become a spectacle, a kind of kabuki theater in The Convergence. Nevertheless, the point still stands; the digital "community" has become preeminent, and it is essential for the continued expansion of the neo-liberal model. These "clusters" are creations of an extreme hyper-individualism that finds its expression – indeed, the very essence of identity – in consumer goods, tastes, styles, and other aspects of a commercialized "discourse."

The darker effect of the weaponizing of the racial oppression dialectic, however, is that ever-larger numbers of non-whites are internalizing this propaganda and are acting it out in increasingly violent ways. As the people of Europe are colonized by African and Middle Eastern migrants – roughly 75% of whom are fighting-age males – and their governments implement laws to crush any criticism of the native Europeans' dispossession, and as the rest of the West also fervently tries to dissolve itself through an abandonment of principles and an embrace of mass Third World immigration, when this all comes to a head, it has the potential to get very, very ugly.

The rapper Common venerates cop-killer Assata Shakur in his lyrics and has a lucrative commercial deal with Microsoft. Far be it from anti-white rhetoric being an impediment to career advancement, it seems these days to be a prerequisite (Sarah Jeong, etc.). This isn't

---

3   Chomsky, Noam and Edward S. Herman, *Manufacturing Consent*. Pantheon Books: New York. (2nd Edition). 2002. Intro p. xviii.

a culture war – it's a culture massacre, one that's on the precipice of turning literal. Though Francis Fukuyama and his ilk decided that the fall of the USSR meant "the end of history," it was only white Western liberals who bought into such a premise fully. Unfortunately, though, conservatives, so fixated on defeating the Reds, had missed the deep rot setting in their own culture while they vicariously fought Ivan Drago. They're now fighting ghosts. As Mark Point writes:

Millennials were taught from childhood that the highest moral good was serving the self-esteem of non-whites… According to the implicit demands of the experiment, whites and by extension what could be perceived as "white culture" was selected for strategic downsizing…It's unsurprising that when whites were encouraged to jettison the exigencies of tradition in favor of debasing themselves, that we ended-up with an entire class of people now lost in the wilderness without past or future. Over the past thirty years conservatives were busy building an entire culture around anti-socialism while the Left was busy pushing its cultural trojan horse to unleash a whole different kind of plague. Indeed, it's nice that wrangler-wearing boomers have had their war paint ready to conserve their nest egg from the perennial specter of Soviet style economics. Railing against socialized medicine and magazine limits is not without its merit, but for the sake of their grandchildren maybe they'd like to also counter the forces that seek to degrade whites and for the first time in 2,000 years, permanently disconnect culture associated with them. Is it not obvious that every group on the planet both within and outside the West is encouraged to embrace the legacy of their ancestors except for whites?...Don't expect the Japanese or Chinese to do anything but look in amazement and take notes as Ford F150 ten-gallon hat types indignantly yell "out of my cold dead hands!" meanwhile their grand daughter is likely to spend the same twilight years in a very dangerous world because her grandfather was too worried about his bumpstock or the return of Fidel Castro to take a stand against the toppling of his ancestors and the deracination of his heirs.[4]

---

4   Point, Mark, "Racism on the Rise," November 6, 2018. *American Thinker.*

Remind me again what we're trying to "conserve"? When you don't stand on solid ground, how can you stand for anything? For this brand of Useful Idiots and their trickle-down economics, the only thing trickling is the urine on our heads they call rain. The conservatives have stood athwart history and stopped nothing. Instead, they've been vaporized into a bloody mist by the bullet train of neo-liberalism. From mainstream conservatives the solution, as ever, is The Market. Just ask Ben Shapiro. As Noam Chomsky and Edward S. Herman write in their 2002 update of *Manufacturing Consent*:

> The triumph of capitalism and the increasing power of those with an interest in privatization and market rule have strengthened the grip of market ideology, at least among the elite, so that regardless of evidence, markets are assumed to be benevolent and even democratic…and nonmarket mechanisms are suspect, although exceptions are allowed when private firms need subsidies, bailouts, and government help in doing business abroad. When the Soviet economy stagnated in the 1980s, it was attributed to the absence of markets; when capitalist Russia disintegrated in the 1990s, this was blamed not on the now ruling market but on politicians' and workers' failure to let markets work their magic.[5]

The Market and its inscrutable mechanisms are only to be understood by the oracles on Wall Street or in the libertarian think tanks. For the rest of us peasants we rely on their divinations in order to understand the awesome cosmic power of the Free Market. We become totally subservient to the godlike omnipresence of transactions, debt accrual, compound interest, and other invisible "market forces" while everything around us becomes commodified and cheapened. When an economic system becomes sacrosanct, questioning its dogma becomes heresy. The True Believers on the Left have been totally taken in by the moralizing rhetoric running cover for both the economics and what is, at its core, a perverse and immoral system. It is, in fact, the

Available at: www.americanthinker.com/articles/2018/11/racism_on_the_rise.html#ixzz5X9kXgrJU.

5   Chomsky, Noam and Edward S. Herman, *Manufacturing Consent*. Pantheon Books: New York. (2nd Edition). 2002. Intro p. xvii-xviii.

anti-system, that which is most at odds with human nature and human dignity. As Anton Fedyashin and Anita Kondoyanidi write:

> With the loss of willpower, the Western democracies could offer the world nothing but "concessions, attempts to gain time, and betrayal." At the root of this malady lay "rationalistic humanism or humanistic autonomy" that produced a suicidal form of "anthropocentricity"...[ignoring] the intrinsic evil in man while simultaneously making him the universal point of reference. Even the American Founding Fathers' moral assumptions disappeared under the pressure of state secularism, producing materialist legalism, Solzhenitsyn argued. The twentieth century's technological achievements did not redeem its "moral poverty." Uncontrolled freedom encouraged licentiousness manifesting itself in the prevalence of "pornography, crime, and horror" in popular culture. "Life organized legalistically has thus shown its inability to defend itself against the corrosion of evil," Solzhenitsyn suggested.[6]

The modern anti-morality shows human beings may believe that they have dispensed with the need for religion, but in reality, the religious impulse of the Western liberal has merely been transferred into "social justice." For others, the displacement of particularized exalting, the singular, the cult of the self, has mutated into something horrific – nightmare-like and unreal – the modern superego inextricably intertwined in both the light of day and the dark recesses of night. In James Hillman's words:

> Today, cut off from this [sacrificial practices either for the gods or heroes] psychic background, the heroic becomes the psychopathic: an exaltation of activity for its own sake. The locus of its cult is not the burial mound on which the city and its deeds are founded, but in the human body itself, in the humanistic ego.[7]

---

6   Fedyashin, Anton and Anita Kondoyanidi, "The Conservative Dissident: The Evolution of Alexander Solzhenitsyn's Political Views," October 2009. *RIIM.* Available at: www.eseade.edu.ar/wp-content/uploads/2016/08/51_2_ fedyashin_kondoyanidi.pdf.

7   Hillman, James, *The Dream and the Underworld.* Harper & Row: New York. 1979. p111.

The cult of the self may be argued to have hit critical mass in a literary context with Bret Easton Ellis's *American Psycho*; the novel's central character Patrick Bateman espouses the virtues of self-exalting and consumerism. The inwardly-focused Bateman states: "It's impossible in this world we live in to empathize with others, we can always empathize with ourselves. It's an important message, crucial really." Bateman is the humanistic ego personified; his monstrousness is centered on the banal minutiae of his routine which, by extension, defines his existence. "Activity for its own sake," the performing of social rights-as-commitments, ultimately yields to Bateman's psychopathic impulses (real or imagined). For Leigh Claire La Barge:

American Psycho pushes the lifeless world of the brat-pack commodity-aesthetic to its limit with rambling descriptions of branded commodities newly rendered in deadening prose and broken by the representation of lethal violence. The novel is structured through short, interchangeable chapters that detail the habits and banalities of upper-middle class, urban consumerism, the contents of which are reflected in the titles, such as "Shopping," "Lunch," and "At Another New Restaurant." American Psycho is chronologically the last of the brat-pack releases; it contains a chapter entitled "End of the 1980s" and, indeed, the novel seeks to exhaust the period and one of its most contested literary aesthetics.[8]

Ellis was considered by critics to be a part of the "Brat Pack" of fiction in terms of the sheer number of pop-culture references and specific brand-naming; by attempting to saturate the text and combine "the labyrinthine, encyclopedic postmodern fictions of William Gaddis and Thomas Pynchon or, more recently, David Foster Wallace," the Brat-Packers were actually affecting a style, to quote La Barge, that "underwhelms rather than overwhelms, reading more like advertising copy." La Barge continues:

---

8   La Barge, Leigh Clare, "The Men Who Make the Killings: *American Psycho*, Financial Masculinity, and 1980s Financial Print Culture," 2010. *Studies in American Fiction* 37 (2). Available at: https://muse.jhu.edu/article/433373.

First reporting in 1982 on a new category of businessmen, the corporate raiders, the *New York Times* noted that "they have even developed their own language laced with images of aggression and sexual conquest." Soon after, periodicals quit analyzing this language and began employing it. Time's description of venture capitalist Arthur Rock, the man who arranged the initial financing for Apple, as one of "the men who make the killings," is one of many examples... Ellis's text uses financial, journalistic language to synthesize...different texts, all unified by the representation of the masculine financier and his violence.[9]

This interpretation is almost exactly correct, although the conflation of masculinity and violence through this lens does a disservice to masculinity; it is a *displaced* masculinity, not a true masculinity, which finds gain as the measure of a man. Such an internal conflation could only occur by a certain kind of man, in a certain set of social, political, and economic conditions. Call it war by other means, with the financier, the MP, or the CEO self-styled as a "warrior." Even, as was colloquially common to refer to Left-wing ideologues in the mid-2010s, the "social justice warrior." These are not warriors in any true sense – most are the exact inversion, in fact. But we live in times of inversion: the anti-civilization, as it were. The Doppelganger World. Everything must fall under the aegis of The Market's overlords, and in this Doppelganger World, it is the anarchists and communists who carry water for global capital.

On the Right, we take it as axiomatic that communism is unworkable and flies in the face of human nature; its horrors are well-documented (though obscured in mainstream discourse by politicians, historians, academics, and the media for a century-plus), but the false dilemma is one of a choice between oppressive totalitarianism, full systemic control, and genocidal slaughter on the one hand and...the same thing on the other via capitalism. The roads and methods may differ, but the destination is the same, and besides, the atrocities committed by the USSR, for example, would never have been made possible without Western state assistance and, more crucially, Western capital. There

---

9   Ibid.

is a third way, however, and it has been so effective as to become the basic default for almost the entirety of the West and huge chunks of the rest of the planet, and that is neo-liberalism.

The two ideological "poles" of communism and capitalism produce a lot of meaningless chatter, but in reality, unless one lives in Brooklyn or attends Bard College, communism as an ideology is totally discredited, though the vast majority of these people simply carry water for the neo-liberal establishment. Generally their sentiments revolve around regurgitated Cultural Marxist dogma and harming middle- and working-class white people because of "privilege." Possessing intelligence around one standard deviation below the average American, their thought process is pretty much whatever their handlers tell them it is. Occasionally their intersectional identities create problems for the Establishment, such as Ilhan Omar's criticisms of Israel and AIPAC, but they are generally minimized and mitigated. Omar quickly returned to the safe zone of anti-white boilerplate once the entire Establishment made it clear where her bread was being buttered. You do *not* bite the hand that feeds if you want to maintain your privileged position.

Chapter 7 - The Debt Regime

"Economists for the last 50 years have used the term 'host economy' for a country that lets in foreign investment. This term appears in most mainstream textbooks. A host implies a parasite. The term parasitism has been applied to finance by Martin Luther and others, but usually in the sense that you just talked about: simply taking something from the host. But that's not how biological parasites work in nature. Biological parasitism is more complex, and precisely for that reason it's a better and more sophisticated metaphor for economics. The key is how a parasite takes over a host. It has enzymes that numb the host's nervous system and brain. So if it stings or gets its claws into it, there's a soporific anesthetic to block the host from realizing that it's being taken over. Then the parasite sends enzymes into the brain. A parasite cannot take anything from the host unless it takes over the brain. The brain in modern economies is the government, the educational system, and the way that governments and societies make their economic policy models of how to behave. In nature, the parasite makes the host think that the free rider, the parasite, is its baby, part of its body, to convince the host actually to protect the parasite over itself."- Michael Hudson

According to a recently-published paper by Andrew Baker et al., a comparative assessment of the costs of "too much finance" in the form of lost growth potential driven largely by the City of London represented an astronomical £4.5 *trillion* over the time frame 1995-2015. The authors state that:

> The data suggests that the UK economy, may have performed much better in overall growth terms if: (a) its financial sector was smaller; (b) if finance was more focused on supporting other areas of the economy, rather than trying to act as a source of

wealth generation (extraction) in its own right. This evidence also provides support for the idea that the UK suffers from a form of 'finance curse': a development trajectory of financial overdependence involving a crowding out of other sectors and a skewing of social relations, geography and politics... If we add an additional category of excess rent to these calculations as a wider distributional cost with potential negative social implications, the costs rise to £5,180 billion.[1]

If the City of London and the financial sector does not represent the British people and is nothing but a grotesque over-grown leech or, perhaps more accurately as Michael Hudson characterizes it, a parasite, then for whose benefit does it exist? Though technically not an independent nation, the City of London acts like one. The City is a corporation with its own police force, its own representative to Parliament known as the "Remembrancer," and its own Lord Mayor, distinct from the Mayor of London. The City of London Corporation exists to protect the multi-nationals and the financial institutions and banks it houses, such as the Bank of England, which despite being nationalized in 1946 is itself still controlled by cosmopolitan interests such as the Rothschild family through more indirect means.

The Bank for International Settlements estimates that 46% of daily global revenue in the interest-rate derivative market is generated here, and within the confines of the City of London, you will find the London Stock Exchange, the London Bullion Market under the supervision of the Bank of England, HSBC's headquarters, Lloyds of London's headquarters, the Bank of England's headquarters, as well as the headquarters or offices of a slew of other major banks, financial institutions, insurance brokers, and multi-national corporations. The effective independence of the City is affirmed during a strange ritual where it is rumored that the monarch arrives at the entrance to the City and goes under a red cord raised by the City police, where allegedly

---

1   Baker, Andrew, Gerald Epstein, and Juan Montecino, "The UK's Financial Curse? Costs and Processes," September 2018. Sheffield Political Economy Research Institute. Available at: http://speri.dept.shef.ac.uk/wp-content/uploads/2019/01/SPERI-The-UKs-Finance-Curse-Costs-and-Processes.pdf.

the monarch then bows to the Lord Mayor inside the City (whereas the Lord Mayor bows to the monarch outside the City); the Remembrancer and other City officials are present, as is the State Sword carried by the Sword Bearer and the mace carried by the Sergeant-at-Arms – the sword and mace together symbolize the authority of the City of London Corporation and the Lord Mayor.

For as long as globalist and usury-based banking families like the Rothchilds have been positioned to do so, private interests have been maneuvering to acquire control over the major financial entities that now control the majority of the world's money supply and approximately 80% of the world's wealth. Much of it radiates outward from the City of London as well as several hubs in the United States, but regardless of location, the global financial system is deeply inter-connected and reflects the interests of the few, either through the banks themselves or through various institutions such as the IMF. Through control of the money supply and the banks in the US, the UK, and elsewhere, these interests can be reflected in IMF policy despite its ostensible "accountability" to the nation-states that comprise it. The US, for example, has 16.52% of the voting shares in the IMF, almost three times that of the next-closest nation, and is able to wield its significant influence as an extension of these interests, especially when colluding with the other hijacked nations of the neo-liberal axis.

In 1913, the Federal Reserve Act was passed by Congress, handing over control of America's money supply to these international cosmopolitan interests. The Federal Reserve has twelve regional banks, each with private shareholders. To be a member of the Federal Reserve system, commercial banks are legally required to own shares of stock in these regional Federal Reserve banks. The Federal Reserve Board of Governors is government-appointed, however the true power and the control of the money supply is largely out of the government's hands. And besides, beyond simply economic control – indeed, largely *because of* the economic control – cosmopolitan interests such as the Rothschild family have major influence over the politics of most major Western nations, hence the claim that the public-private dichotomy is increasingly meaningless. There are direct ties between the Rothschilds and prominent political figures such as Emmanuel Macron, Felix Rohatyn, Rene Mayer, Georges Pompidou, Gerhard Schröder, and Jacob Rees-Mogg. A deep history of the Rothschilds, let alone any of these prominent banking families, would fill volumes, and in any case, this work has been done elsewhere. For brevity's sake, I use the Rothschilds as emblematic as this exercise could be easily replicated for any of the major banking families or major financial institutions, such as Malcolm Turnbull, Gary Cohn, Henry Paulson, Steve Mnuchin, and Mark Carney, et cetera's ties to Goldman Sachs.

The entire system is inter-connected, and virtually every country on earth is enmeshed to some degree in this global network. It is abetted by organizations such as the International Monetary Fund (IMF), the World Bank, and the World Trade Organization (WTO). In 1944, the IMF and the International Bank for Reconstruction and Development (IBRD, now part of the World Bank) were formed at the Bretton Woods conference to "regulate international economies and payment settlements." In practice, what this looks like today is any nation that wanders off the neo-liberal plantation is subject to "international pressure" under various guises ranging from sanctions to "off the books" military intervention. The most common strategy is the intentional tanking of the local economy in order for said nation to be forced into accepting ludicrous interest rates from the IMF, their fiscal policy then dictated by the internationalist consortium of organizations such as the IMF and World Bank. No two situations are exactly the same nor do they always follow the same sequence of events, but we can see some common threads that often align with the tried-and-true World Bank-IMF *modus operandi*, also known as the Four Step Strategy outlined by former Senior Vice President and Chief Economist of the World Bank, Joe Stiglitz:

- Step 1: Privatization.

- Step 2: All laws taxing trans-border money are abolished. This is the repealing of any laws that taxes money going over its borders: Initially cash comes in from abroad to speculate in real estate and currency, then when the economy in that country starts to look promising, this outside wealth is pulled straight out again, causing the economy to collapse. The nation then requires IMF help and the IMF provides it under the pretext that they raise interest rates anywhere from 30% to over 80% austerity. This happened in Indonesia and Brazil, also in other Asian and Latin American nations. These higher interest rates consequently impoverish a country, demolishing property values, savaging industrial production and draining national treasuries.

- Step 3: Market Based Pricing. This is where the prices of food, water and domestic gas are raised which predictably leads to social unrest in the respective nation, now more commonly referred to as, "IMF Riots." These riots cause the flight of capital and government bankrupcies. This benefits the foreign corporations as the nation's remaining assets can be purchased at rock bottom prices.

- Step 4: Free Trade.[2]

The IMF is also granted a slew of immunities in the process: immunity from judicial processes and search, requisition, confiscation, or expropriation; immunity from taxation and customs duties; immunity of archives; and freedom of assets from restriction, regulation, or moratoria. In essence, the project is designed to turn us into perennial share-croppers, where *no one* may leave the globalist plantation.

One of the more ingenious accomplishments by the globalist hegemony is convincing a huge swathe of the population that by aligning themselves with these ruthlessly exploitative corporations that one is "#Resisting" the Establishment. Liberals used to be vehemently opposed to globalism (remember "Buy Local"?) and would bemoan the fact that the World Bank, the World Trade Organization, and the IMF have basically ravaged the entire Third World. No longer. It is now far more vital to purchase rainbow-colored consumer products than to

---

2 Stiglitz, Joseph. 2016. Available at: https://new.euro-med.dk/20160602-rothschilds-imf-how-the-elite-can-rob-us-untaxed-and-unpunished-and-accuse-others-of-corruption.php.

realize that independently-minded leaders who reject the machinations of global finance must be removed and replaced with ones much more amenable to the IMF, WTO, and World Bank dictating policy in order to effectively control their nation's economy. As Charles Eisenstein writes in *Sacred Economics:*

> Ex-economist John Perkins describes the basic strategy in *Confessions of an Economic Hit Man:* first bribes to rulers, then threats, then a coup, then, if all else fails, an invasion. The goal is to get the country to accept and make payments on loans-to go into debt and stay there. Whether for individuals or nations, the debt often starts out with a megaproject - an airport or road system or skyscraper, a home renovation or college education-that promises great future rewards but actually enriches outside powers and springs the debt trap. In the old days, military power and forced tribute were the instruments of empire; today it is debt. Debt forces nations and individuals to devote their productivity toward money. Individuals compromise their dreams and work at jobs to keep up with their debts. Nations convert subsistence agriculture and local self-sufficiency, which do not generate foreign exchange, into export commodity crops and sweatshop production, which do.[3]

The global "free market" subsists on child labor and wage slavery, another state of affairs liberals of yore were once committed to combating. Now Nike with its sweatshop-made products has made Colin Kaepernick the face of its new advertising campaign. "Standing for something," even if it means kneeling, might cost you everything – or it might just cost you next to nothing in labor expenses if you're Nike. When the Women's March claims to be pro-mass immigration and pro-labor, this gross contradiction, once again, is never "called out." It is literal Nazism to support ICE, despite the fact that they work diligently to combat the now-$32 billion-annually human trafficking business.

---

3   Eisenstein, Charles, *Sacred Economics*, Chapter Six. North Atlantic Books. 2011. Available at: https://sacred-economics.com/sacred-economics-chapter-6-the-economics-of-usury/.

The relationship between finance and nation is at present completely inverted; countries are being treated as assets to be stripped and scrapped for parts, or else run along the lines of a multi-national corporation. Those who fear socialism and venerate our present "free market" have it exactly wrong: the greatest danger is not the nationalization of banks, but the bankization of nations. What are constituents then? What redress of grievances do they have with a corporation or a bank, let alone a hedge fund manager, when they are not shareholders nor do they have a financial stake? How many nations have been victims of the Toys R Us model of asset stripping? How many more will be? As Anton Fedyashin and Anita Kondoyanidi write:

[Solzhenitsyn] considered shock therapy reforms criminal. "So this is how this reform, which made no sense economically, began," he told Remnick. "It showed no compassion toward people. The government never even asked what the people will do. Its own people live well, after all. Yeltsin said: 'I congratulate the people for not rebelling.' It's as if I were to meet you in the street, rob you, strip you, and congratulate you for not offering resistance" (Remnick, 2006:181). Solzhenitsyn articulated his criticism of Yeltsin's government and also proposed a pragmatic solution to Russia's problems, in Russia in Collapse, which reiterated his belief that spirituality and patriotism were organically connected. Solzhenitsyn criticized both domestic and foreign attempts "to erase Russians' national identity" by grafting Western values and institutions onto the country...privatizing the spoils of the Soviet economy under the guidance of the IMF.[4]

All that happened after the fall of the Soviet Union was the acceleration of neo-liberal global dominance, not the end of history. All told, according to the Institute of International Finance, global debt is estimated to have exceeded $257 trillion by the end of the first quarter of 2020. For perspective, the annual global gross domestic product

---

4   Fedyashin, Anton and Anita Kondoyanidi, "The Conservative Dissident: The Evolution of Alexander Solzhenitsyn's Political Views," October 2009. *RIIM*. Available at: www.eseade.edu.ar/wp-content/uploads/2016/08/51_2_ fedyashin_kondoyanidi.pdf.

(GDP) is estimated to be approximately $80 trillion, and the collective global wealth is about $300 trillion. For Michael Snyder:

> Much has been written about the men and women that control the world. Whether you wish to call them "the elite", "the establishment" or "the globalists", the truth is that most of us understand who they are. And how they control all of us is not some sort of giant conspiracy. Ultimately, it is actually very simple. Money is a form of social control, and by getting the rest of us into as much debt as possible they are able to get all of us to work for their economic benefit...over the past 10 years, student loan debt in the United States "has grown 250 percent" and is now sitting at an absolutely staggering grand total of $1.4 trillion... The total amount of auto loan debt in the United States has now surpassed $1 trillion...If you want to own a home, that is going to mean even more debt. In the old days, mortgages were commonly 10 years in length, but now 30 years is the standard. By the way, do you know where the term "mortgage" originally comes from? If you go all the way back to the Latin, it actually means "death pledge." And now that most mortgages are for 30 years, many will continue making payments until they literally drop dead. Sadly, most Americans don't even realize how much they are enriching those that are holding their mortgages. For example, if you have a 30-year mortgage on a $300,000 home at 3.92 percent, you will end up making total payments of $510,640. Credit card debt is even more insidious. Interest rates on credit card debt are often in the high double digits, and some consumers actually end up paying back several times as much as they originally borrowed...Total credit card debt in the United States has also now surpassed the trillion-dollar mark. Overall, U.S. consumers are now nearly $13 trillion in debt. As borrowers, we are servants of the lenders, and most of us don't even consciously understand what has been done to us.[5]

---

5   Snyder, Michael, "How the Elite Have Enslaved the Rest of the World," October 17, 2017. *Charisma News*. Available at: www.charismanews.com/marketplace/67780-how-the-elite-have-enslaved-the-rest-of-the-world.

As the apocryphal quote attributed to Albert Einstein goes, "Compound interest is the eighth wonder of the world. He who understands it, earns it...he who doesn't...pays it." Debt and compound interest go hand in hand. To quote Michael Hudson, "Mathematically, debts grow exponentially at compound interest. Banks recycle the interest into new loans, so debts grow exponentially, faster than the economy can afford to pay." The 1% invest in speculation within the finance sector, which in the United States has tripled since the 1980s. Meanwhile the real economy has shrunk and labor's share of income has declined. This is not coincidental, as the US continues to orient itself along a FIRE (finance, insurance, real estate) axis, which comprises the rent and interest paid by debtors and rent payers. If this seems like a Ponzi scheme, that's because it is, just on a global scale and calling itself something else.

Much like their Cultural Marxist peers do with concepts like "privilege" and "gender," modern bankers literally create money out of thin air. Their vampiric globalism "lives" on the blood of nations with compound interest and debt. Mortgages and college tuition are the two largest debt sources for modern Americans; the former traps people as prisoners in the homes they can't afford and the latter prevents the young from even getting on the property ladder. As Max Weber wrote: "Unreserved political idealism is found if not exclusively at least predominantly among those strata who by virtue of their propertylessness stand entirely outside of the strata who are interested in maintaining the economic order of a given society." Is it any wonder so many disaffected Millennials seem to believe Bernie Sanders-esque socialism is a viable option? They've been sold a bill of goods and they are furious. Unfortunately, they've been trapped into a false binary of Democratic Socialism, or "Social Democracy" as it was called before re-branding, versus the "free market." Quoting Gottfried Feder:

> Social-Democracy is doomed because it is based on Marxist ideology, which does not recognize the radical difference between industrial capital and loan-capital. Social-Democratic government, as a moderate application of Marxism that fails,

paves the way for Communism. The contemptible bourgeois and two objections from the bourgeois perspective...Is big loan-capital really not in some way productive? Only labor is productive.[6]

The rest is illusory and built on obscure proprietary formulas only the bankers and day traders could possibly understand. Most people have been so conditioned by this false dilemma of socialism/communism versus capitalism in the American political system that they are wholly unfamiliar with any ideas outside this binary. The debt machine that is the university system pushes activism and Democratic Socialism on its students while even its professed adherents in the political realm are owned by the very Establishment of which they are so publicly critical. Despite the tough talk, it appears Sanders doesn't walk the walk – he received huge campaign contributions in the 2020 Presidential Election cycle from the likes of PACs representing and/or individuals with Alphabet Inc., Apple, Microsoft, AT&T, Amazon, Wal-Mart, Kaiser Permanente, UC Berkeley, Boeing, IBM, UPS, the City of New York, and the Army, Navy, Air Force, and the US Department of Defense. In fact, his donor list was pretty much interchangeable with the rest of his "competition."

Many Americans have the unfortunate tendency to view economic growth as synonymous with the health of the nation. This is clearly not the case, because though the FIRE economy is positively molten, the nation has never been in worse shape by any metric, from the mental to the physical.

Neo-liberalism causes, exacerbates, and profits from human misery; in its exponential growth model we see the effects of mass immigration on the (formerly in many cases) working class while the 1% benefits. As Michael Hudson illuminates:

If the economy is growing, people want to employ more workers.

---

6   Feder, Gottfried, *The Manifesto for the Abolition of Enslavement to Interest on Money*. Joseph C. Hubers Verlag: Munich. 1919. Translated into English by Hadding Scott, 2012. p. 6.

If you hire more labor, wages go up. So the 1% always wants to keep unemployment high – it used to be called the reserve army of the unemployed. If you can keep unemployment high, then you prevent wages from rising. That's what's happened since the 1970s here. Real wages have not risen, but the price of the things that the 1% owns has risen – stocks, bonds, trophy art and things like that.[7]

This is in no small part why, despite over one third of eligible Americans not participating in the labor force and increasing automation making certain jobs redundant, immigration continues to rise. Male labor force participation in particular in this country is plummeting, a trend that began in the late 1960s just a few years after the Hart-Celler Immigration Act of 1965 re-opened America to mas immigration, though this time from drastically different cultures and regions than before. Male labor force non-participation has accelerated alongside the war on masculinity and the exponential increase in immigrants more alien and at odds with American values than ever before, and the effects have been predictably devastating.

During the 1996–2016 period, the nonparticipation rate increased the most for younger men of prime working age, those age 25 to 34. In 2016, over seven million men in the key working age range of 25-54 were out of the workforce in the United States. As women mate hypergamously, the perception of viable mates has become badly skewed, with the knock-on effect of fewer families, more broken and dysfunctional relationships (or lack of relationships in the form of, variously, one-night stands and/or casual sexual encounters, or perhaps nothing at all), general dissatisfaction, and other ramifications most recently recounted excellently in Tucker Carlson's *Ship of Fools*. There are other factors at play here, too, but suffice it to say that our "elites'" decision to hollow out the middle of the country has gone about as poorly as can be expected for our social fabric, but wonderfully for their bottom lines. As Douglas Himes writes:

---

7   Hudson, Michael and Bonnie Faulkner, "The Slow Crash. The Shrinking of the Real Economy," April, 2016. Global Research. Available at: www. globalresearch.ca/the-slow-crash-the-shrinking-of-the-real-economy/5532131.

Over the last two decades, the increase in nonparticipation was less pronounced among men at the extremes of the educational attainment spectrum, those with less than a high school education and those with a bachelor's degree or more education (note: though this is not to say that these two groups were not also affected). One possible explanation for the larger increase in the nonparticipation rate among men in the middle educational categories is that "job polarization" has decreased the demand for middle-skill workers while increasing the demand for both lower skilled and higher skilled workers. What both the low-skilled jobs (such as food preparation, cleaning, and security and protective services) and the high-skilled jobs (such as managerial, professional, and technical work) have in common is that they are not easily amenable to automation and computerization. In addition, demand for many of the middle-skilled jobs (for example, jobs in manufacturing) has been decreased by technological changes that make workers more productive and by increased offshoring and globalization. [Didem] Tüzemen maintains that this reduction in the demand for middle-skill workers accounts for most of the decline in labor force participation among prime-age men. Sadly, the lack of employment may be the start of a vicious cycle of inactivity, depression, and other health problems that, in turn, become additional obstacles to gainful employment.[8]

Runaway automation also presents a huge problem. In a nation which has seen its industrial sector and increasingly service sector outsourced, coupled with workforce saturation for the few remaining jobs, a massive under-class is forming, and economic inequalities are growing exponentially. The middle class stands to see its economic standing continue to erode as well, and not just due to obscenely high tax bills to re-distribute their earnings. Off-shoring is an omnipresent threat for virtually every position outside the boardroom.

While Douglas Himes is correct in his assertions regarding the more

---

8   Himes, Douglas, "Men's declining labor force participation," May, 2018. *Monthly Labor Review*, US Bureau of Labor Statistics. Available at: www.bls. gov/opub/mlr/2018/beyond-bls/mens-declining-labor-force-participation.htm.

extreme decline in labor force participation in the "middle" due to the detonation of solidly middle- and working-class jobs as a consequence of automation and outsourcing, what we have witnessed so far is just the beginning. If the current system remains in place, labor force nonparticipation can only increase and polarization will become even more extreme. As Andrew Yang discusses in his book *The War on Normal People,* if and when "Intellectual Manual Labor" jobs such as pharmacist, dentist, and even surgeon, which are more or less slight variations on replicable tasks, become automated, many upper-middle-class and higher-educational-attainment jobs will vanish as well. Quoting from Yang:

> The Federal Reserve categorizes about 62 million jobs as routine – or approximately 44% of total jobs. The Fed calls the disappearance of these middle-skill jobs "Job Polarization," meaning we will be left with low-end service jobs and high-end cognitive jobs and very little in-between. This trend goes hand-in-hand with the disappearance of the American middle class and the startlingly high income inequality in the U.S. The vanishing jobs are due in part to the incredible development of both computing power and artificial intelligence.[9]

Despite the fact that tens of millions of jobs may soon be automated out of existence, the vast majority of our political figures are clamoring for "The Greatest Number of Immigrants Ever." For the low-educational-attainment workers, untold millions of illegal *and* "legal" aliens have flooded that particular labor market, driving wages down. Many of these jobs, such as fast food restaurant cashier, are not immune from the dangers of automation, either. For the more specialized worker, H-1B visas do a fine job of wage suppression and American worker dislocation as well – and don't think AI can't "learn to code." Speaking of which, regarding journalists, Yang continues:

A company called Narrative Science produces thousands of

---

9   Yang, Andrew, *The War on Normal People.* Hachette Books: New York City. 2018. Accessed via: www.yang2020.com/blog/the-jobs-that-will/.

earnings previews and stock updates for Forbes and recaps of sports stories for fantasy sports sites in real-time. The company's bots won't be winning any Pulitzers in investigative reporting, but in the coming years, the quality of AI-produced writing will go from acceptable to very good – and those journalists who write routine stories like this will find their jobs increasingly at risk.[10]

Between mass immigration, automation, and outsourcing, the economy twenty years from now at the current pace will be extremely polarized. Think Amazon on steroids. Already, eight men now have as much wealth as the poorest 3.6 billion people living on the planet combined. Sure, most people outside of Africa have been lifted out of abject poverty by capitalism, but they remain in relative poverty and most will remain there if things go unchanged. Arguably even worse, however, is the state of affairs in the "post-industrial" world, where many people now face an existential crisis of meaning in their lives.

Our leaders don't care about the ramifications of automation because they already treat us like widgets in the economy. They treat entire populations as units to be moved around the globe to wherever it suits them best. They don't care about the social costs because they don't have to bear them. These are called "externalities" and "externalities" like a ruined environment, entire countries falling apart, life expectancies declining, and the rotten blossom of human misery do not have any negative bearing on the bottom line. In fact, they help it.

The ruling class doesn't care about radical inequality because they are the beneficiaries. In 2018, 82% of the wealth generated went to the richest 1% of the global population. Yet "magically" labor is taxed at twice the rate of capital, and societies are transformed into playgrounds for the rich. Giant companies such as Netflix and Amazon pay nothing or next-to-nothing in corporate taxes. Furthermore, in the United States, we actually have a regressive tax system, where the middle class and upper-middle class are actually hit hardest. Soon we'll all be serfs on the lord's manor once again – very progressive! When money

---

10   Ibid.

is god-like, it becomes easy to play as gods on Olympus with the fates of the "mere mortals" below. For Ellen Willis:

> The locus of oppression resides in the production function: people have no control over which commodities are produced (or services performed), in what amounts, under what conditions, or how these commodities are distributed. Corporations make these decisions and base them solely on their profit potential. It is more profitable to produce luxuries for the affluent (or for that matter for the poor, on exploitative installment plans) than to produce and make available food, housing, medical care, education, and recreational and cultural facilities according to the needs and desires of the people.[11]

The total hours worked in the United States have risen by 43% since 1980 while the middle class share of the nation's aggregate income has declined precipitously, from 62% in 1970 to 43% in 2014. Median wealth – assets minus debt – fell 28% from 2001 to 2013. The middle class ceased being a numerical majority in 2015. In the UK, "The economic downturn has meant an increase in the supply of unemployed residents in a labor market where migrants have been playing an ever-increasing role."[12] 70.7% of US adults are either overweight or obese, and in 2014, 62% of adults in England were classified as overweight or obese. The total number of prescriptions filled for adults and children in the US increased by 85% from 1997 to 2016, while the US population only increased by 21% in the same period.

Between 1981 and 2008, average income in the United States grew by around $12,000, but 96% of that went to the top 10%. The ratio of pay between CEOs and their workers went from 35 to 1 in 1980 to 185 to

---

11   Willis, Ellen, "Women and the Myth of Consumerism," June, 1970. *Ramparts*, Vol. 8, No. 12. Accessed via: http://fair-use.org/ellen-willis/women-and-the-myth-of-consumerism.

12   Anderson, Bridget, "British Jobs for British Workers?: Understanding Demand for Migrant Workers in a Recession," 2010. *The Whitehead Journal of Diplomacy and International Relations*. Available at: http://blogs.shu.edu/diplomacy/files/2012/05/11-Anderson_Layout-1a.pdf.

1 today. Beyond the economic, or perhaps more appropriately *because of* the economic, meaningful necessities of life for most people like family formation are, to quote Michael Hendrix, "becoming a luxury" and as such, "isolation is more likely to be the province of the poor," but it is not limited to the poor, just most pronounced.[13] As Sir Michael Marmot, professor of epidemiology at University College London reports from his extensive study of British civil servants working in the government bureaucracy based in Whitehall Street in London:

> There are two striking findings. The first was that there was about a threefold difference between the top and bottom in mortality. That's absolutely enormous. The second was that it wasn't just a difference between the top and bottom; it was what I called a social gradient. There was a stepwise relationship between your socioeconomic position and your health. Your readers who are not at the bottom [may want to know] that the second from the top had worse health and higher mortality than the top and the third was worse than the second...In Whitehall, we're not dealing with poverty. We're dealing with people in stable white collar employment and [still we see] this graded relationship between where they are in the hierarchy and health...[Smoking and lack of exercise] accounted for about a third of the gradient, [but]...you have to look for the causes of the causes (the reasons that the lower classes might be driven to smoke, drink, take drugs or indulge in sweet, fatty foods).[14]

---

13 "We found clear social inequality in loneliness across Europe: loneliness was around 10% more common in the poorest group than in the richest group. Similarly, frequent participation in social activities was around 10% more common in the wealthiest groups, compared to the least wealthy... among the poorest groups, those who often took part in social activities had a similar risk of loneliness to the wealthiest groups, suggesting that participating in these activities may be protective against loneliness. We found the greatest risk of experiencing loneliness among the least wealthy men who did not participate in social activities very often." Claire Niedzwiedz, "Loneliness is an Issue of Inequality," July 28, 2016. Centre for Research on Environment, Society and Health. Available at: https://cresh.org.uk/2016/07/28/loneliness-is-an-issue-of-inequality/.

14 Szalavitz, Maia, "How Economic Inequality Is (Literally) Making Us Sick," October 19, 2011. *Time*. Available at: http://healthland.time.com/2011/10/19/how-economic-inequality-is-literally-making-us-sick/.

Echoing these findings, George Monbiot writes:

A series of fascinating papers suggest that social pain and physical pain are processed by the same neural circuits...Opioids relieve both physical agony and the distress of separation. Perhaps this explains the link between social isolation and drug addiction... It's unsurprising that social isolation is strongly associated with depression, suicide, anxiety, insomnia, fear and the perception of threat. It's more surprising to discover the range of physical illnesses it causes or exacerbates. Dementia, high blood pressure, heart disease, strokes, lowered resistance to viruses, even accidents are more common among chronically lonely people. Loneliness has a comparable impact on physical health to smoking 15 cigarettes a day: it appears to raise the risk of early death by 26% (note: another estimate found that loneliness increased a person's odds for early death by 45%, Holt-Lunstad, Smith, and Layton 2010). This is partly because it enhances production of the stress hormone cortisol, which suppresses the immune system. Studies in both animals and humans suggest a reason for comfort eating: isolation reduces impulse control, leading to obesity.[15]

Sedentary lifestyles, poor dietary choices, and environmental factors are causing a whole host of health problems, not least of which include tanking testosterone levels for men and neurological and cognitive decline. A number of studies have shown that high sugar diets result in impaired brain function. There are also studies that show worsening symptoms of mood disorders caused by unhealthy diets, such as worsening depression. Serotonin, which regulates cognition and mood, is primarily located in the digestive tract. Therefore, it is reasonable to understand why the food a person eats will affect their mood. A litany of studies show that eating junk food has been linked to increases in depression. Those who are on traditional diets are at 25% to 35% lower risk for depression. Further, the production of serotonin

---

15 Monbiot, George, "Neoliberalism is creating loneliness. That's what's wrenching society apart," October 12, 2016. *The Guardian*. Available at: www.theguardian.com/commentisfree/2016/oct/12/neoliberalism-creating-loneliness-wrenching-society-apart.

is influenced by "good bacteria" which also play an essential role in health. Studies have been conducted finding that people who take probiotics, which contain these "good bacteria," have lower levels of anxiety and stress compared to those who do not take probiotics.

The ingestion of food releases hormones in the body such as insulin and they circulate to the hippocampus in the brain. Once the hormones reach the hippocampus, they activate signal-transduction pathways that affect learning and memory. When a person becomes insulin resistant, among other things, it restricts the ability to think properly and make new memories. The hippocampus is known to influence our memory and our mood and it is particularly sensitive to the negative effects of a diet high in processed foods. The size of a hippocampus is directly correlated to the quality of diet that a person is on. "If substances from 'low-premium' fuel (such as what you get from processed or refined foods) get to the brain, it has little ability to get rid of them. Diets high in refined sugars, for example, are harmful to the brain. In addition to worsening your body's regulation of insulin, they also promote inflammation and oxidative stress."[16]

A poor diet causes a lack of production in proteins in the brain that help with the growth of new neurons. Not only that, but it also causes cognitive deficits in the brain which are visibly noticeable within one week of a high processed food diet. A cognitive deficit is the impairment of a person's mental processes that are associated with the learning of information and knowledge. While omegas are good fats for you brain, long term consumption of other fats, like trans and saturated fats, may compromise brain health. "Bad diets have been linked to dementia due to high blood pressure and cholesterol disrupting the blood supply to the brain. Research now confirms that junk foods can prevent brain cells from responding properly to insulin... Eating an excess of fatty foods and sweets can increase an individual's insulin level. This causes the muscles, fat and liver cells

---

16   Selhub, Eva, "Your brain on food," April 20, 2018. *Nutritional Psychiatry.*
      Available at: https://mcmsouth.com/2018/04/20/nutritional-psychiatry/.

to no longer respond to the hormone."[17] High quantities of sugar are known to be bad for both physical and mental health. Food addiction is in large part caused by the brain pathways developing a response to natural reward. Sugar is extremely addictive. "The global increase in obesity rates has been tied to the rise in junk-food availability and consumption. Increasingly, children are exposed to a junk-food diet during gestation and early development. Excessive consumption of junk-food during this period may negatively impact the development of brain motivation and reward pathways."[18] This natural reward is activated by sugar which releases dopamine and endogenous opioids. Dopamine causes a feeling of satisfaction while opioid involvement is seen through food deprivation causing withdrawal. This leads to a cycle causing excessive eating.

Eating junk food suppresses hormones that tell the brain to stop eating. The higher the fat or sugar in a person's diet, the more he or she will crave this type of food because the hormones in his/her brain are being affected. Between the hormone suppressions, and the presence of dopamine and opioids, this cycle has terrible effects on the brain. This type of eating is associated with many other physical effects as well. Research in a host of various disciplines clearly shows that it is our modern diet of refined foods, trans fats, and sugar, coupled with a sedentary lifestyle, that is the root of so many degenerative diseases including obesity, cancer, and diabetes. Individuals with a body mass index (BMI) that's considered "obese" spend 42% more on direct health care costs than adults who are a healthy weight.

The deleterious effects of simple sugars, from the tanking of testosterone to blunting insulin sensitivity, cannot be under-stated. Lastly, the ingestion of 75 grams of sugar per day can reduce testosterone by as much as 25%, and frankly, we need all the testosterone we can

---

17 "How junk food affects the brain," October 31, 2018. Australian Institute of Personal Trainers. Available at: www.aipt.edu.au/articles/2018/10/what-happens-your-brain-when-you-eat-junk-food.

18 Lesser, Ellen Nacha, et al., "The impact of junk-food diet during development on 'wanting' and 'liking,'" January 15, 2017. *Behavioural Brain Research*, Vol. 317. Available at: www.sciencedirect.com/science/article/pii/S0166432816306295.

produce. If Henry Ford is credited with the creation of the Model-T, then the modern ruling class must be credited with the creation of the Model Low-T:

> Men today – compared to the men who lived a century ago – have a decreased level of testosterone; heightened levels of estrogen; and – most worrisome on a practical level, perhaps – decreased sperm counts. Maybe you have heard stories or anecdotal laments, suggesting that today's men just aren't quite as... well, manly as the men who came before. We're here to tell you that this isn't just anecdotal. There's real science behind it. One prominent journal reports a "population-wide decline" in testosterone levels – a development that's worrying, to say the least. You might be shocked at the extent of this trend...[A] journal report, focusing on the Boston area population, found a 1.2% annual drop in testosterone levels from 1987 through 2004. That's about a 17% dip overall, both in individuals and in the population as a whole. The report adds this, too: "The decline is consistent with other long-term trends in male reproductive health, including decreases in sperm quality and increases in testicular cancer, hypospadias and cryptorchidism."[19]

Men with low testosterone and higher estrogen are also at much greater risk for prostate cancer, which also has significant long-term implications for the current transgender mania.

According to one 2012 study, it isn't actually much to do with the natural process of aging, despite the higher median ages of Western countries versus the Third World. "Declining testosterone levels are not an inevitable part of the aging process, as many people think," says Gary Wittert, MD, professor of medicine at the University of Adelaide in Adelaide, Australia. "Testosterone changes are largely explained by smoking behavior and changes in health status, particularly obesity

---

19   "Why Men Today Have Less Testosterone Than Ever – and What Can Be Done About It," January 8, 2016. Physicians Age Management Centers. Available at: www.pagemc.com/about-us/physicians-age-blog/95-why-men-today-have-less-testosterone-than-ever – and-what-can-be-done-about-it.html.

and depression." There is ample research linking depression and low testosterone. Testosterone is essential for many bodily functions, including maintaining a healthy body composition, fertility, and sex drive. "It is critical that doctors understand that declining testosterone levels are not a natural part of aging and that they are most likely due to health-related behaviors or health status itself," Wittert says, and adds that "regular sexual activity tends to increase testosterone."

Environmental factors are also a major consideration. Hormones cannot be filtered properly; despite the Safe Drinking Water Act of 1974, compliance with harmful chemical restrictions isn't monitored carefully, and most wastewater-treatment systems aren't designed to remove hormones, antidepressants, and other drugs. 77 million Americans are served by water systems that violate testing requirements or rules about contamination in drinking water, according to the Natural Resources Defense Council.

Plastics are also a major culprit – BPA exposure has been linked with lower test. Further, per the Physicians Age Management Centers, "A big factor [in the precipitous decline in Western men's testosterone] is the array of hormone disrupters – also known as xenoestrogens – that are so common in our modern world. These environmental toxins mimic estrogen and impact our body chemistry in subtle yet significant ways." There are many environmental sources of xenoestrogens such as the common, plastic water bottle. These synthetic, estrogen-like chemicals are commonly used in industrial products and in a variety of consumer goods. Xenoestrogens are clinically significant because they can mimic the effects of endogenous estrogen and have been implicated in precocious puberty and other disorders of the reproductive system. Xenoestrogens are a modern phenomenon, having only been introduced to the population over the last 70 years, and as such, it's not improbable by any means that they've contributed to the testosterone declines in the West that have occurred during the same time span. Some specific ways in which xenoestrogens negatively impact body chemistry are:

• Increasing estrogen and thus decreasing testosterone. One of the primary causes of low testosterone is a high estrogen level.

Estrogens can be endogenous (produced by your body) or exogenous (from the environment, also known as xenoestrogens). Estradiol and Estrone (two of the three kinds of estrogen produced by your body) feed back to the hypothalamus and pituitary and shut off testosterone production.

- Inflammation as a result of high estrogen levels. Not only do high estrogen levels decrease testosterone in men, they also increase inflammation. Inflammation, just like stress, is a biochemical process. Inflammation is the natural result of the immune system. Inflammation, in the right setting, is actually the body protecting itself. However, when the immune system becomes imbalanced or chronically activated, the immune system causes damage through inflammation. For example, chronically activated immune cells in the brain (glial cells) play a pivotal role in the development of Alzheimer's, Parkinson's, and Multiple Sclerosis. Inflammation is also a leading factor in diabetes, high blood pressure, obesity, and countless other medical conditions.[20]

Estrogen is replacing testosterone in many American men and anabolic steroids, which are all derivatives of the male sex hormone testosterone, were perfectly legal for use until Joe Biden spearheaded a campaign in 1990 to make them illegal. So your ability to counter-act the slew of environmental factors artificially lowering your testosterone with low-dosages of test in an above-board manner was suddenly off the table. This, to my mind, was totally intentional. How could it not be?

Higher testosterone is associated with particular cognitive functions in addition to its physiological effects, which include denser bones and increased muscle mass. Testosterone is also neuro-protective, meaning you stay sharper longer. A trio of studies published in 2005 and 2006 linked androgen deprivation therapy with *impaired* performance on various cognitive function tests. Additionally, as compiled by the Harvard Medical School:

---

20   Ibid.

- A 2005 study of 565 World War II veterans found that higher testosterone levels in midlife were linked to better preservation of brain tissue in some, but not all, regions of the brain in late life.

- A 2004 study of 400 men age 40 to 80 found that higher testosterone levels were associated with better cognitive performance in older men.

- A 2004 report from the Baltimore Longitudinal Study of Aging evaluated 574 men over a 19-year period. Low free testosterone levels predicted an increased risk of developing Alzheimer's disease, even after other dementia risk factors were taken into account.

- A 2002 study of 310 men with an average age of 73 found that higher levels of bioavailable testosterone were associated with better scores on three tests of cognitive function.

- A 2002 study of 407 men between the ages of 51 and 91 found that men with higher free testosterone levels achieved higher scores on four cognitive function tests, including visual and verbal memory.

- A 1999 study of 547 men between the ages of 59 and 89 found that high testosterone levels in older men were associated with better performance on several cognitive function tests.[21]

Neurologically, those with higher testosterone are more emotionally detached and exhibit stronger abilities to problem-solve and engage in linear reasoning. Lower testosterone results in more "emotional reasoning" and mood swings. *The Guardian* is verklempt over the fact that middle-aged men have started using testosterone replacement therapy to look and feel younger. This is obviously a bad thing for the ruling class because low T keeps men sick, weak, mentally foggy, and unwilling to resist their displacement and replacement. Furthermore, citing a 2018 study published in *Political Psychology*

---

21 Available at: www.health.harvard.edu/newsletter_article/Testosterone_aging_ and_the_mind.

entitled, "Upper-Body Strength and Political Egalitarianism: Twelve Conceptual Replications," we learn:

> Animal models of conflict behavior predict that an organism's behavior in a conflict situation is influenced by physical characteristics related to abilities to impose costs on adversaries. Stronger and larger organisms should be more motivated to seek larger shares of resources and higher places in hierarchies. Previous studies of human males have suggested that measures of upper-body strength are associated with measures of support for inequality including Social Dominance Orientation (SDO), a measure of individual differences in support for group-based hierarchies. However, other studies have failed to replicate this association. In this article, we re-examine the link between upper-body strength and support for inequality using 12 different samples from multiple countries in which relevant measures were available. These samples include student and locally representative samples with direct measures of physical strength and nationally representative samples with self-reported measures related to muscularity. While the predicted correlation does not replicate for every single available measure of support for inequality, the overall data pattern strongly suggests that for males, but not females, upper-body strength correlates positively with support for inequality.[22]

This must be why the *Daily Mail* ran an article with the headline "Too Much Exercise Can Kill You – Especially if You're a White Man." It appears, however, that, per usual, just the opposite is the case. By removing meat from your diet, you run a significantly elevated risk of vitamin deficiencies as well as "brain fog," decreased brain volume, and other cognitive deficiencies, not to mention difficulty in gaining or even maintaining lean muscle mass, as protein from plant sources has lower bio-availability, fewer essential amino acids, and is

---

22 Petersen, Michael Bang and Lasse Laustsen, "Upper-Body Strength and Political Egalitarianism: Twelve Conceptual Replications," September 16, 2018. *Political Psychology*, Vol. 40, Issue 2. Available at: https://onlinelibrary. wiley.com/doi/abs/10.1111/pops.12505.

generally of an inferior quality. Red meat is vital for our diets because it has iron and other fat-soluble vitamins we need. It also has creatine, which is good for heart health and for building lean muscle. More lean muscle means a higher metabolism and less body fat. Vitamins B6, B12, and folic acid are micronutrients that protect the brain from diseases and mental decline. Vitamin B12 is naturally found in animal products, including fish, meat, poultry, eggs, milk, and milk products. Vitamin B12 is generally not present in plant foods.

In addition to the resource consolidation and speculation element, it is also clear why the ruling class does not want men especially eating meat, and it has nothing to do with ethics. German politicians from the Social Democrats (SPD) and the Greens recently proposed raising the value added tax (VAT) on meat to the rate of 19%, supposedly in the interest of combating climate change. In reality, it's because they want men unable to defend their country from hostile foreigners imported en masse, they want them to be less rational and thus more receptive to emotional appeals, they want them too stupid or foggy to comprehend what's happening, they want them sick and dependent, and they want them just overall docile or – even better – ridden with the impotent soy-angst that lashes out at so-called fascists and holds signs proclaiming Refugees Welcome while ceding ground at every possible turn. In a similar vein, the United Nations recommends everyone eat less red meat and Goldsmiths, University of London has banned beef as part of a wider effort to reduce its carbon footprint. The alternative pushed on Western populations, soy, has significantly harmful effects on the environment and the body – soybean oil consumption lowers immunity, increases susceptibility to infectious disease, and promotes cancerous growth. Are you seeing how all these things are connected?

Chapter 8 - Feminism and Consumer Capitalism

"This is a Lifetime movie on a global scale."- The Acacia Strain,
"Baby Buster"

In 1929, Lucky Strike cigarettes employed Sigmund Freud's nephew
Edward Bernays to market their cigarettes to the largely-still-untapped
female market. In keeping with the cultural shift of "women's liberation,"
Bernays cleverly framed women's "choice" to publicly smoke cigarettes
as an act of defiance, and a "bold" assertion of a woman's independence.
Countering "gendered stereotypes" of smoking cigarettes as a masculine
activity, Bernays adeptly wove together three disparate elements of
advertising-cum-propaganda into one highly-successful pitch: celebrity
spokeswomen, the use of cigarettes as weight loss agents, and, as
mentioned, "torches of freedom" for the newly-"liberated" woman.
Somewhere in the ether, Emma Lazarus was applauding. This pattern
has been repeated basically *ad infinitum* to mass market women's choices
for them in the ninety years since. Cornerstone Capital's "Advancing the
Gender Lens Framework" report states that:

A 2014 Goldman Sachs report notes that closing the credit gap
for women...results in improvements in other areas, making
gender equality a self-reinforcing phenomenon. The report also
notes that as women become more educated, join the workforce
and earn more income, women gain bargaining power. Growing
gender equality and women's increasing household spending
coincides with rising incomes and rapid growth in the global
middle class. As more women enter the labor force and/or grow
their own businesses, they show a higher propensity to use their
increased earnings to buy goods and services...This can create
a cycle where female spending fuels economic growth...This

added spending generates more revenue for global companies and economies.[1]

Sounds good, right? Unfortunately, not so much, as we will see. According to the Women's Institute for a Secure Retirement and National Center for Women's Retirement Research, the average woman spends 15% of her working years outside of the workforce caring for children and elderly parents compared to the average man's 1.6%. Imagine the productivity and earnings if you didn't have those burdens! Well, that is precisely where we are headed and a major reason why our society is falling apart.

In 1960, over 70% of Americans were married, whereas today traditional nuclear families with two married heterosexual parents are now a minority. Much of this can be attributed to demographic change, as non-white, non-Northeast Asian population groups (the Igbo excepted) have extremely high out-of-wedlock birth rates and generally do not emphasize monogamy, but the disintegration of the family is accelerating in the white community as well. Women are also waiting longer than ever to have children or opting not to reproduce at all. Quoting Melanie Notkin:

> There has been a steep rise in childless women from 1976, when the U.S. Census first began recording fertility rates. Then, 35% of women of fertile age were childless. Today, that number is 49 percent. Still, it's often assumed that all adult women are mothers, as if we've inverted the "W" for woman to the "M" for mother. And while the majority of women do eventually give birth, it's later than ever. For the first time, more than half (54%) of American women aged 25-29 are childless, as are nearly a third (31%) of women aged 30 to 34. By the end of our fertile years, about one sixth of women (17%) are childless.[2]

---

1   Bush, Heidi, Craig Metrick, Jennifer Leonard, and Katherine Pease, "Advancing the Gender Lens Framework," 2019. Cornerstone Capital. Available at: https://missioninvestors.org/sites/default/files/resources/Advancing%20the%20Gender%20Lens%20Framework%20-%20%20Cornerstone%20Capital.pdf.

2   Notkin, Melanie, "Glamourising the 'Childfree Life' Ignores Reality for Most

60% of US women 18-29 are single and just 26% of US adults 18-32 are married. There was a 31% increase in the number of US single women 30-34 between 2007-2012. According to Pew Research, 46% of Millennial Moms believe the institution of marriage has become obsolete, and 51% of Millennial women giving birth are single mothers.

RoxAnna Sway, executive director of Retail Intel, predicts that one in four Millennials will remain single for life. As Hans-Peter Blossfeld highlights, "Gender role change has been generally asymmetric, with a greater movement of women into the traditional male sphere than vice versa."[3] Per the Bureau of Labor Statistics, by 2011 71.3% of mothers with children under 18 years of age were participating in the workforce, and that percentage has risen. The categories of single mother and childless woman continue to grow while the married woman with children category continues to shrink, and those women are waiting longer and having fewer children at that, economic conditions often necessitating such decisions. From "The New Roles of Men and Women and Implications for Families and Societies" (2014) by Livia Sz. Oláh, Rudolf Richter, and Irena E. Kotowska:

> Given declining birth rates and marriage rates, increasing instability of couple relationships and a nearly simultaneous growth of female labour force participation, women's increasing economic independence has been seen as a main cause of family changes in economic theorizing, which identified gender role specialization as one of its main paradigms (see Becker, 1991). In sociology, it has been argued that ideational changes, such as the spread of individualism and thereby greater emphasis on self-realization, together with changing aspirations for paid work,

---

Childless Women," May 13, 2018. *Quillette*. Available at: https://quillette.com/2018/05/13/glamourising-childfree-life-ignores-reality-childless-women/.

3   Blossfeld, Hans-Peter, "Linked Lives in Modern Societies. The Impact on Social Inequality of Increasing Educational Homogamy and the Shift Towards Dual-Earner Couples," in *From Origin to Destination. Trends and Mechanisms in Social Stratification Research,* Stefani Scherer, Reinhard Pollak, Gunnar Otte, and Markus Gangl (eds.) The University of Chicago Press: Chicago. 2007. p. 284.

are the main driving forces behind the postponement of family formation (both marriage and childbearing) and the increasing fragility of couple relationships in modern societies. See, particularly, the Second Demographic Transition theory (van de Kaa, 1996; Lesthaeghe, 2010). Less attention has been paid to other factors affecting men, even though the decline in male wages and men's labour force activity, together with growing labour market uncertainty, have been recognized (Oppenheimer et al., 1997; Booth et al., 1999; Mills et al. 2005).[4]

The resultant instability is readily apparent, and the ramifications wide-reaching. We will return to the consequences later, but first we must consider *why* familial break-down and "women's independence" are being incentivized. 96% of Millennial women believe that "being independent" is their single most important life goal and 87% define success as being able to shape their own future. Sounds benign, but what does that actually look like?

The social control aspect is obvious: people without genuine ties to family, friends, and community are easier to manipulate and they have no support system. Atomized people also make for better workers and consumers, and they can be moved around to fill labor needs more easily without any real roots to speak of. As opposed to investing in the future and building a familial foundation with their time and energy, single women with disposable income are inclined to treat consumer goods and travel as a substitute for family. One in four women have participated in a "girlfriends' getaway" and 39% plan to do so at least once in the next three years, per AAA. 73% of travel agents surveyed by The Gutsy Traveler noted that more female travelers embark on solo trips than their male counterparts, and according to 68% of those travel agents surveyed, most female clients taking trips in small groups are over the age of 45. The Travel Industry of America concurs: The average adventure traveler is not a 28-year old male, but a 47-year-old female who wears a size 12 dress.

---

4 Oláh, Livia Sz., Rudolf Richter, and Irena E. Kotowska, "The New Roles of Men and Women and Implications for Families and Societies," 2014. Families and Societies Working Paper Series 11. Available at: http://www.familiesandsocieties.eu/wp-content/uploads/2014/12/WP11OlahEtAl2014.pdf.

Many women waste their reproductive years working as mid-level functionaries and HR commissars, and by the time they feel they are "ready" to have children, it is already too late. Quoting Julie Falcon and Dominique Joyce from their paper "More Gender Equality, More Homogamy?" in the *Swiss Journal of Sociology* (2017), "Given that reconciling work and family is extremely difficult, women tend to choose between employment and family."[5] If a woman's loyalty is to her employer above or in lieu of her family, the incentive structure changes dramatically, and one of the great ruses of our time has been the ruling class's successful conflation of "women's empowerment" with "financial independence" and becoming a cog in the corporate machine. Counterintuitively, "independence" and the ability to shape one's own future often prove to be mutually exclusive. For Mary Lou Roberts:

> Singlehood tends to force the acquisition of non-traditional consumer skills...Both Elkstrom and Kahne point out that single women are disproportionately represented in the labor force... While the social implications of women's ability to control their fertility cannot easily be overstated, there are also important implications for consumer behavior...In examining the effects of women's employment, Kohen points out that, while leisure is important to the working woman, it is frequently less fulfilling to them than is their work...We should not overlook the fact that women's employment is creating for them another role--- customer for business goods and services.[6]

Nielsen NeuroFocus research has found that the female brain is hard-wired with "evolutionary strongholds to create a very specialized customer" whose purchasing power "has never been stronger."

---

5   Falcon, Julie and Dominique Joyce, "More Gender Equality, More Homogamy?" November 2017. *Swiss Journal of Sociology*, 43 (3). Available at: Available at: www.researchgate.net/publication/321955927_More_Gender_Equality_ More_Homogamy_A_Cohort_Comparison_in_Six_European_Countries.

6   Roberts, Mary Lou, "Women's Changing Roles–a Consumer Behavior Perspective," in *Advances in Consumer Research*, Vol. 8, Kent B. Monroe (ed.), Association for Consumer Research: Ann Arbor, MI, 1981.

Between 2007 and 2016, female-owned firms grew five times faster than the national average. As of 2018, women held about 40% of global wealth; the highest percentages of female billionaires were in North America and Europe, and that is expected to continue to increase. According to a 2009 study from Boston College's Center on Wealth and Philanthropy, women will inherit 70% of the money that gets passed down over the next two generations – excluding the increasing amounts they earn on their own. Earnings of full-time female workers have risen by 31% since 1979, compared to a 2% rise in male earnings.[7]

By 2015, just over half of American personal wealth was controlled by women, according to the Bank of Montreal's Wealth Institute. Two years later, American women controlled 60% of the country's personal wealth. By 2030, women are expected to control two-thirds of the nation's personal wealth. Some forecasts have women in control of as much as 75% of household discretionary dollars worldwide by 2028. Women are responsible for between 85-90% of consumer spending. Women spend more money per shopping trip than men and make far more trips.

Regarding the concept of the "Connected Spender," 92% of women pass along information about deals or online recommendations to others. 44% of women say they prefer ads during the Super Bowl to any other aspect of the game, according to a 2013 Lab42 Research Study. According to Influence Central, 69% of Millennial Moms use blogs to learn about new products, while 64% use other social platforms. Additionally, "Millennials multi-task while in-store: going online to seek out new information, and ensure they've identified the best product for the best price. Moreover, they don't limit themselves to one-stop shopping, and their path to purchase remains fluid, with external choices making a key impact. Ultimately, these outside factors hold far more sway than in-store advertising." 44.4% of women say social media is a good way to keep up with the latest content, and 56%

---

7   "Women in America," US Department of Commerce, Economics and Statistics Administration, 2011. Available at: www.census.gov/library/publications/2011/demo/womeninamerica.html.

of women in the US use social networking sites. 58% of Facebook users are women, 64% of Twitter users are women, and 82% of Pinterest users are women. 95% of Millennial Moms own a smartphone. 50% of women say staying current on a brand's latest offerings is a top reason to follow brands on social media sites (Burstmedia, 2012).

Women watch more video than men, though both groups are spending more time watching it. In the fourth quarter of 2012, women 18 and older watched an average of 191:34 hours of video per month, up from 184:12 hours in the same period of 2011. Comparatively, men watched 174:51 hours in the recent fourth quarter, up from 170:06 in the previous year. Women are also more active than men online. In December 2012, 116 million American women were active online, compared with 102 million males. Women make up the majority of visitors to career, shopping, and social media sites, and account for more of the unique visitors to Netflix and Hulu. "Lesbian, Gay, Bisexual, Transgender (LGBT)-inclusive programs" were 24% of broadcast primetime scripted and reality shows, garnered 28% of broadcast primetime TV viewing, and 22% of ad dollars, according to Nielsen data. Within the 25-49 age demographic, "LGBT-inclusive programs" (and its advertisers) were most likely to reach college-educated white females, small white collar households, and "budding families" (those with 3 or fewer members).

With the increased connectivity of everything, and the mutually-reinforcing nature of digitized consumer capitalism, the Establishment's social, political, and economic "values" can be more readily inculcated, and certain population groups are more receptive to the messaging/ propaganda/advertising. Our daily lives are saturated with media and advertisements, and, increasingly, no one aspect can be isolated. This is well-understood and, naturally, encouraged by the "elites." This "intersectional capitalism" is a logical and intentional extension of media- and academia-generated concepts of "intersectionality" as it regards identity. From Cornerstone Capital:

At Cornerstone Capital Group, while we recognize the importance of using a "traditional" gender lens analysis in the investment review process, we also recognize that gender inequality will not be eliminated without additional efforts to tackle problems at their root. We recognize that inequality is embedded in a variety of institutional and systemic practices that have been in place for centuries if not millennia. We also recognize that the systems of oppression which keep gender inequality in place are multi-faceted and that issues of race and ethnicity, socioeconomic status, physical ability, sexual orientation and geography (among others) intersect with gender and in some cases reinforce gender inequality...Climate change, poverty and health are gendered issues – they affect men, women, boys, girls, and transgender and gender nonbinary people differently. In fact, in many cases women, girls and trans/gender nonbinary people experience the most acute impacts of major societal and environmental challenges. They are also major influencers of change and play a critical role in such existential issues as climate change.[8]

None of these claims are substantiated, as we might expect, and yet they rhetorically form the basis of this "progressive investment" in women, transgendered, et cetera. It is not based on compassion, that much is clear. It is not based on any empirical data other than a few debunked "climate change" studies and the easily-explained "gender wage gap." Third World poverty? Also easily explained. The central assumption that equity/equality – they are interchangeable in this context – is in and of itself "good" relies on faulty and dubious premises that are taken as axiomatic. Due to decades if not a good century-plus of constant and evermore pervasive propaganda, "liberalism" and "progress" are the defaults, with the academy as a particularly noxious "finishing school," which women, in greater proportion than men, are run through. Due to higher levels of empathy and emotionality, women are more susceptible to "emotional reasoning," and their natural instincts may be more easily perverted and channeled into destructive nonsense and consumerism. All these things are by design and are mutually-reinforcing.

---

8   Bush, Heidi, Craig Metrick, Jennifer Leonard, and Katherine Pease, "Advancing the Gender Lens Framework," 2019. Cornerstone Capital. Available at: https://missioninvestors.org/sites/default/files/resources/Advancing%20the%20Gender%20Lens%20Framework%20-%20%20Cornerstone%20Capital.pdf.

In 2013, women surpassed men in terms of education. There were 21% more women than men obtaining an undergraduate degree, and 48% more women attaining a graduate degree than men. Women now hold the majority (52%) of management, professional, and related positions in the US. 44% of women ages 18 to 24 were enrolled in college or graduate programs as of October 2010, compared with just 38% of men in the same age group. In addition, 36% of women ages 25 to 29 had a bachelor's degree, compared with only 28% of men in the same age group – a record-high divergence, per Pew Research Center.

Women accounted for 58% of students in two-and- four-year colleges in the US by 2009. Overall, 140 women graduated in 2013 with a college degree at some level for every 100 men. Women earned 61.6% of all associate's degrees, 56.7% of all bachelor's degrees, 59.9% of all master's degrees, and 51.6% of all doctoral degrees in 2013. Since 1982, women have earned 4.35 million more bachelor's degrees than men. Returning to Livia Sz. Oláh, Rudolf Richter, and Irena E. Kotowska:

In the diffusionist perspective, highly educated women are often regarded as trendsetters with regard to family formation and partner relations (Salvini & Vignoli, 2011). Research has indicated that a stronger commitment to the labour market exposes women with higher education to a stronger conflict between work and family life than their less educated counterparts. For instance, the largest discrepancy between ideal and actual family size occurs among the highly educated (Testa, 2012). If well-educated women are considered as trendsetters, their childbearing behaviour is likely to influence fertility levels for the rest of the society... The micro-economic theory posits that as women receive more education and gain access to better positions in the labour market, the costs of childbearing may increase. This primarily relates to opportunity costs, in the form of foregone earnings, slower human capital accumulation and depreciation of professional skills, because raising children requires considerable parental and especially maternal time and may force women to take time away from employment. The scale of opportunity costs is revealed by studies on the motherhood wage penalty (Kühhirt & Ludwig,

2012; Gough & Noonan, 2013). Assuming that education reflects income potential, the theory predicts that women with higher education will have fewer children than less-educated women, as the former have more to lose in terms of foregone earnings and career opportunities.[9]

This higher educational attainment for women means more disposable income, which can be funneled into consumer and "activist" capitalism. As evidenced earlier, women also control the majority of the country's personal wealth and are responsible for between 85-90% of consumer spending. Considering the aforementioned factors, more women are opting – sometimes by necessity or perceived necessity – for "non-traditional" roles as single and childless, single mothers, or as one of the non-traditional economic roles within the nuclear family, such as primary or dual earner; the hollowing-out of blue collar work and declining earning and educational opportunities for men contrasted with women's hypergamous tendencies all intersect and at great social and civilizational cost.

Historically, marriages in which wives were more educated than their husbands faced a higher risk of divorce, compared to couples in which husbands were more highly-educated.[10] On top of that, continuing with Oláh, Richter, and Kotowksa:

> The decline of fertility rates below or far below the replacement level, have been paralleled by a substantial increase in female labour force participation over time (Bernhardt, 1993; Jokinen & Kuronen, 2011; OECD, 2011)... Van Bavel (2012) suggested that the concept of marriage market and the related notion of marriage squeeze should be extended in order to investigate the implications

9 Oláh, Livia Sz., Rudolf Richter, and Irena E. Kotowska, "The New Roles of Men and Women and Implications for Families and Societies," 2014. Families and Societies Working Paper Series 11. Available at: http://www.familiesandsocieties.eu/wp-content/uploads/2014/12/WP11OlahEtAl2014.pdf.

10 Schwartz, Christine R. and Hongyun Han, "The Reversal of the Gender Gap in Education and Trends in Marital Dissolution, 2014. *American Sociological Review*, Vol. 79 (4). Available at: https://pdfs.semanticscholar.org/b1c9/979fd73 7060aff4e008f1da033ef63c2b101.pdf.

of the reversal of the gender imbalance in education for union formation…In a traditional marriage market, a good education has been considered particularly important for men because their income and occupational prestige largely determined the socio-economic status of the family. Therefore, women have tended to prefer men with a high(er) level of educational attainment. …In times with poor and uncertain economic prospects, men who are unable to fulfil the role of the breadwinner will not be attractive marriage partners and/or fathers…[Oppenheimer] argued that employment uncertainty for men impedes assortative mating and may therefore delay marriage. In such times, cohabitation becomes a less binding living arrangement, more suitable to the uncertain times…Concerning family formation, most research confirms that men with higher socio-economic status exhibit higher marriage rates than men with lower status, in line with theoretical expectations. …Existing research on men indicate that disadvantaged men have little chance to become fathers and to have multiple children in stable unions or as single fathers (Guzzo & Hayford, 2010).[11]

Women want to marry above their station, and when there are four college-educated women for every three college-educated men in the dating pool, this becomes virtually impossible, especially when manufacturing and other blue-collar jobs that supplied men with a steady income have virtually disappeared: from 2000 to 2016, rural America's aggregate share of GDP declined from 46% to 36%. As Alex Berezow reports, this decline is hitting blue-collar men in particular extraordinarily hard: "The deadliest occupational group for men was 'construction and extraction,' with a suicide rate of 53.2 per 100,000 in 2015. For women, the deadliest group was 'arts, design, entertainment, sports, and media,' with a suicide rate of 15.6 per 100,000."[12]

---

11   Ibid.
12   Berezow, Alex, "Suicide Rates by Sex and Occupation," November 16, 2018. American Council on Science and Health. Available at: www.acsh.org/news/2018/11/16/suicide-rates-sex-and-occupation-13604.

Men and women were never meant to be pitted in competition, but rather to function as complementary units to raise families. When we push against nature's will, the results are predictably disastrous. Our society has been so atomized, even the most basic building blocks are part of the rubble. The ramifications of such a sea change in wealth re-distribution simply cannot be understated. Despite the obligatory celebration of such a gross inequality as a landmark achievement of "equality," given the biologically-encoded mating habits of men and women, the resultant societal disintegration is to be expected. It was, after all, engineered by the ruling class. Traditional, intact nuclear families are antithetical to social engineering and are a major impediment to profits:

> Findings in family and life course research indicate major changes in women's and men's lives as they enter parenthood (Moller et al., 2008; Doss et. al., 2009; Ahlborg et. al, 2009). Both parents have less time for leisure and personal interests (Nomaguchi and Bianchi, 2004; Claxton and Perry-Jenkins, 2008) and they have more contact with close kin and less with friends (Gameiro, et al., 2010; Kalmijn, 2012). With regard to the division of labour, the transition to parenthood is a period where parents are likely to experience a reinforcement of their gender...Most often, however, even couples who practiced a non-traditional division of labour before pregnancy show a more traditional gendered division after the birth, usually attributed to traditional gender norms prevailing more or less under the surface (Kuehirt, 2012).[13]

We can understand why "challenging traditional gender roles" is so important for the Establishment. There is also a class component; the white working class in this country has been absolutely decimated. This is significant for a host of reasons, but continuing in the same vein as earlier:

---

13   Oláh, Livia Sz., Rudolf Richter, and Irena E. Kotowska, "The New Roles of Men and Women and Implications for Families and Societies," 2014. Families and Societies Working Paper Series 11. Available at: http://www.familiesandsocieties.eu/wp-content/uploads/2014/12/WP11OlahEtAl2014.pdf.

- Working-class women have been slower than middle-class women in breaking with traditional roles, and have tended to react negatively toward changes which appear to threaten established values.

- For ethnic working-class women [e.g. Italian, Greek, etc.], especially, religious institutions tend to reinforce traditional values.

- The working-class woman tends to be part of a tightly-knit social group composed primarily of female kin.

- Working class husbands and wives tend to adhere to traditional household roles and to engage in sex-segregated leisure activities, even if wives work.

- Wives' employment is often viewed as threatening by the working class husband whose ability to provide for the family is often the major source of his sense of self-worth (Samuels, 1975).

- Working-class women are more likely than their middle-class counterparts to feel that their adult life is better than their childhood.[14]

Regarding marriage itself, according to one survey conducted by SheSpeaks, married women were significantly more apt than single women to describe themselves as "thrifty" (73% to 58%) and less likely to say they "love to spend" (27% versus 42%). "This predisposition is reflected in their expenditures for clothing: 43% of the singles, vs. 28% of the marrieds, reported spending more than $1,000 per year on clothes. Conversely, 40% of the marrieds, vs. 26% of the singles, said they spend less than $500 per year in that category."

From an evolutionary biology perspective, this can be understood as single women channeling their instincts for attracting a mate into consumer behavior. Continuing with this perspective, as women are generally more compassionate and empathetic, brands are able to cynically market to them by using sentimentalized appeals that tap

---

14   Roberts, Mary Lou, "Women's Changing Roles – a Consumer Behavior Perspective," in *Advances in Consumer Research*, Vol. 8, Kent B. Monroe (ed.), Association for Consumer Research: Ann Arbor, MI, 1981.

into the "social justice" instinct – and besides, the entire culture has been transformed along these lines.

As outlined on Cornerstone Capital's website, "For companies, greater inclusion (sic) is associated with improved brand reputation. The most progressive companies seek to integrate their values into their operations, using their financial clout to push back on harmful practices (sic) even if they risk additional costs in the near term." The number of wealthy women in the US is growing twice as fast as the number of wealthy men. Women represent over 40% of all Americans with gross investable assets above $600,000. 45% of American millionaires are women and 48% of estates worth more than $5 million are controlled by women. Women control 39% of the country's total investable assets, according to Morgan Stanley, and they "prefer to invest in companies they perceive to be making a positive difference in the world."

Per the Spectrum Group, the number of wealthy women investors in the US is growing at a faster rate than that of men. In a two-year period, the number of wealthy women in the US grew 68%, while the number of men grew only 36%. RBC Wealth Management found that two-thirds of women believe they have more opportunity to tackle societal issues through impact investing, compared with 56% of men. Millennial women agree they have greater opportunity to tackle social issues that personally interest them: 83% compared with 65% of older women and 66% of men. 73% of UK female business owners say it's important that their business make a positive charitable impact on the communities in which it operates, compared with only 48% of men. As Avery Tucker Fontaine writes:

> Though traditional philanthropy has shown continued growth in total dollars, it typically hovers around 2% of the U.S. Gross Domestic Product and rarely goes higher than that. Newer models, however, are showing that Americans' capacity for giving is not maxed out. According to the Global Impact Investing Network, measurable investments in impact vehicles reached $502 billion in 2018, which is 1.2 times larger than the philanthropic market

of $427 billion. These vehicles, which fall under the umbrella of "social finance," do more than just pursue a positive societal or environmental impact; they also seek to offer a satisfactory financial return, blurring the line between traditional charitable giving and investing. While traditionalists and baby boomers might find this hybrid approach to be unorthodox, younger givers see no conflict. To them, environmental, social and governance issues are intertwined with financial health and long-term, corporate sustainability.[15]

This hybrid model has been extremely useful in amplifying profits for the neo-liberal establishment and catalyzing a sea-change demographic and structural transformation.

In order to address the ruling class's manufactured concerns "and all the major issues of our time," impact investing advisory firm Cornerstone Capital has "turned to the UN's 17 Sustainable Development Goals (SDGs)." Using their "proprietary methodology," Cornerstone CEO Erika Karp has explicitly stated that they will "invest with Jewish values" and facilitate global serfdom, I mean *equality*:

Just as gender lens investing yields economic benefits beyond those accruing to women and girls, we believe it yields broader social benefits that come from greater inclusion of historically marginalized communities. Access to the internet enables women to obtain education, employment, government services, and financial services that are otherwise hard to reach, and to increase personal income. Women's online participation also sparks systems-level change, as it enables them to organize and mobilize around important policy and decision-making processes. A McKinsey report opines that the market potential of offering gender equality in the telecommunications sector alone could add an incremental $20 billion in annual revenue globally

---

15 Fontaine, Avery Tucker, "From Philanthropy to Social Investment: A New Way of Giving," 2018. BNY Mellon Wealth Management. Available at: www. bnymellonwealth.com/articles/vision/from-philanthropy-to-social-investment-a-new-way-of-giving.jsp.

by 2025. This estimate does not consider the economic multiplier effect on additional income arising from women's access to telecommunication services globally. The intersectional nature of gender lens investing offers a rich variety of ways one can deploy investment capital to drive gains in gender equity. A conscious focus on improving access to products and services that benefit women and girls creates economic benefits extending to families and entire communities and can fuel economic growth more broadly.[16]

Maybe so, but as Adam Barrett puts it, "On a finite planet, endless economic growth is impossible. There is also plenty of evidence that in the developed world, a continued increase of GDP does not increase happiness." A study from *The Quarterly Journal of Economics* found that when women out-earned their husbands, the chances that the couple felt they were in a "happy marriage" fell 6 percentage points.[17] A wife out-earning a husband also resulted in lower testosterone for the husband, higher testosterone for the wife (!), and greater incidence rates of divorce.[18] They also had less sex. It should here be noted that 44% of women are now the primary breadwinners in their households, an almost four-fold increase since 1960.

---

16 Bush, Heidi, Craig Metrick, Jennifer Leonard, and Katherine Pease, "Advancing the Gender Lens Framework," 2019. Cornerstone Capital. Available at: https://missioninvestors.org/sites/default/files/resources/Advancing%20the%20Gender%20Lens%20Framework%20-%20%20Cornerstone%20Capital.pdf.

17 Bertrand, Marianne, Emir Kamenica, and Jessica Pan, "Gender Identity and Relative Income Within Households," 2015. *The Quarterly Journal of Economics*. Available at: https://faculty.chicagobooth.edu/emir.kamenica/documents/identity.pdf.

18 Oláh, Richter, and Kotowksa: "For marital stability, the role of women's social and economic independence has been of interest for social scientists in response to growing female labour force participation and increasing divorce levels. Economic models of marriage assume that women's employment destabilises marital unions because it endangers role specialisation within a couple (Becker, Landes, & Michael, 1977)." See also: Christine R. Schwartz and Hongyun Han, "The Reversal of the Gender Gap in Education and Trends in Marital Dissolution, 2014. *American Sociological Review*, Vol. 79 (4). Available at: https://pdfs.semanticscholar.org/b1c9/979fd737060aff4e008f1da033ef63c2b101.pdf.

And yet, according to a recent Irish study, more than two-thirds of women who stay at home and have a third-level education do not want to return to a paid job.[19] Every marker of happiness for women has been on the decline since they've entered into the workforce in appreciable numbers, and it has only accelerated downward since the fruits of the so-called "Sexual Revolution" have begun to rot.

The likelihood that most women will marry "below their station," known as "hypogamy," is slim,[20] and this is doubly-damning, for both men and women. The top 78% of women on the popular dating app Tinder are vying for the top 20% of men, and yet Tinder is 75% male and 25% female. The Gini coefficient for the "Tinder economy" is 0.58, which means that it has a higher inequality than 95% of the world's national economies. Far from glamorous, for most the single life leads to increased isolation, alienation, depression, and despair.

A recent survey in England found that a quarter of young women between the ages of 16 and 24 have harmed themselves, and one in eight have post-traumatic stress disorder (PTSD). Psychological disorders such as anxiety, depression, various phobias, or obsessive-compulsive disorder (OCD) affect 26% of these young women. Feminism, the so-called Sexual Revolution, and hormonal contraceptives such as the birth control pill have similarly wreaked havoc on women. Women who take "the pill" are nearly 10% worse at recognizing subtle expressions of complex emotions like pride or contempt, "blurring social judgement" according to new research.[21] Hormonal

19   Available at: www.independent.ie/irish-news/news/more-than-two-thirds-of-women-on-home-duties-with-higher-education-do-not-want-to-return-to-workforce-says-new-survey-38069447.html.

20   Though it is happening with a relatively higher frequency, according to Julie Falcon and Dominique Joyce, from their paper "More Gender Equality, More Homogamy?" in the *Swiss Journal of Sociology* (2017), "This rise in female hypogamy is nevertheless essentially driven by structural changes." As in, it is artificial and is generally characterized as what we might call "settling." This has its own negative ramifications.

21   Science News, "Oral contraceptives could impair women's recognition of complex emotions," February 11, 2019. *Frontiers in Neuroscience.* Accessed

contraceptive users, in contrast with non-users, were found to have higher rates of depression, anxiety, fatigue, neurotic symptoms, sexual disturbances, compulsion, anger, and negative menstrual effects, in addition to the physical effects, such as an increase in the risk of breast and cervical cancer, blood clots, and high blood pressure. Current contraceptive use was associated with an increased rate in depression, divorce, tranquilizer use, sexual dysfunction, suicide and other violent and accidental deaths. The definitive link between birth control usage and depression and other harmful side effects cannot be emphasized enough. These, in turn, contribute to and/or are exacerbated by other toxic by-products of modernity.

Interestingly enough, however, the depression may not be attributable to the hormones themselves, but rather, "The evidence suggests that most of the side effects of hormonal contraception are a result of a psychological response to the practice of contraception. It is reasonable to hypothesize, given the present data, that contraceptive activity itself is inherently damaging to women."[22] In other words, women become depressed due to a subconscious acknowledgement that they are artificially suppressing the natural instinct toward motherhood. Even more harmful, women then transfer their nurturing impulse toward destructive nonsense like "welcoming all refugees" or becoming a "dog mommy" – the latter of which is obviously not mutually exclusive with having children – and/or seek to alleviate or mask their depression through harmful behaviors and other kinds of transference. Add to the mix the dehumanizing and depression-inducing state of modern "living" – being a corporate cog, living in cramped quarters, poor nutrition, light pollution, etc. – and it is clear to see why women are so miserable. There is a knock-on effect with men, too, and capitalizing on women's (and men's) alienation are the very same parties who've created these conditions in the first place.

---

via Science Daily at: www.sciencedaily.com/releases/2019/02/190211083216. htm.

22 Robinson, SA, M Dowell, D Pedulla, and L McCauley, "Do the emotional side-effects of hormonal contraceptives come from pharmacologic or psychological mechanisms?" 2004. *Medical Hypotheses*, 63 (2). Available at: www.ncbi.nlm. nih.gov/pubmed/15236788.

Although it is obviously not universally true, women tend to prefer to stay in the home and nurture their children, as the "patriarchy" has ubiquitously "forced" women to do in virtually every civilization regardless of era, geography, or race.

Where women can't be cleaved off from the family or never start one in the first place, there are still ample profits to be had. In a 2011 GFK MRI Survey of the American Consumer, 74.9% of women identified themselves as the primary shoppers for their households. Women purchase over 50% of traditional male products, including automobiles, home improvement products, and consumer electronics, make 70% of all travel decisions, 90% of household healthcare decisions, 93% of over-the-counter pharmaceutical purchases, and 93% of women say they have significant influence on what financial services their family purchases per the *Harvard Business Review*. Most women don't have a preference for male or female financial advisers, sans two groups – divorcées and widows, according to a 2014 study from financial services firm Pershing (oh and by the way you *should* hire a female investor because according to a recent study by Caltech, the Wharton School, Western University, and ZRT Laboratory, testosterone apparently interferes with males' abilities to make smart financial decisions, which is blamed on "impulsivity" – and which also runs contra to all understanding of the *mature* male brain). Despite in essence controlling the wealth of the country, the average woman will nevertheless have a negative fiscal impact of $150,000 by the end of her life. As Nicolas Kilsdonk-Gervais informs:

Men and women spend approximately the same amount on both education and health...With the exception of the age group between 45-59 years old, women cost more to the state than the tax they provide. In contrast, men generate more tax revenue than they cost between 23 and 65 (a 43 year span). In the brief period in which women generate more or as much tax money than they consume, men outscore them by at least 3 times...While feminists are demonizing men for benefiting from all liberties and rights they have constructed, they have oddly remained silent over the fact that anonymous male tax payers are paying women to exist...The fact that feminists want a stronger government is not a coincidence. While historically, women had to choose a wealthy husband for resources, they can now stay single, be lesbians, marry a poor man, or use the sperm bank, and the state will still transfer male taxes to them. Interestingly, within 10 years of women's suffrage, the government doubled their tax revenue and expenditure in the USA.[23]

As a nice knock-on effect for keeping women voting more Leftward, *irrespective of race,* women *always* vote more conservatively after marriage on a population level.

Another nice benefit from the ruling class's perspective is the cycle of dependence state-subsidized single-motherhood produces. As Josh Park notes, "The biggest indicator of poverty is neither the quality of one's job nor one's educational attainment; the biggest indicator is single motherhood (or, to a lesser extent, single fatherhood)." Only 8% of Americans who finish high school, marry before having a child, and postpone marriage past the age of twenty end up in poverty; conversely, for those who do not make such decisions, 79% are impoverished. Clearly, then, for a whole host of reasons it makes sense to use women against men and against themselves, and, intersecting with the "diversity" agenda, the very notions of commitment in monogamy and family, and by extension community and nation.

---

23 Kilsdonk-Gervais, Nicolas, "Research finds that as a group, only men pay tax," 2016. Available at: http://archive.is/xwarB.

Chapter 9 - Identity Politics Works

"Diversity sells." - Ana-Christina Ramón

The neo-liberal establishment is almost completely uniform in its support for "diversity." For starters, there is an entire industry catering to "unconscious bias training," "diversity and inclusion" initiatives and seminars, and a host of other services. Beyond that, Big Capital recognizes the financial windfall produced by increased diversity. To illustrate this point, consider CEO Action for Diversity and Inclusion, "the largest CEO-driven business commitment to advance diversity and inclusion within the workplace...More than 800 CEOs of the world's leading companies and business organizations are leveraging their individual and collective voices to advance diversity and inclusion in the workplace...[and] to promote diversity within our communities." Well, not in their communities, but in yours, anyway. Past the newspeak that increasing diversity will "alleviate racial, ethnic and other tensions," we get to the crux of it: "Diversity is good for the economy; it improves corporate performance [and] drives growth."

Co-signing the pledge to advance "equity and inclusion" is a veritable who's who of corporate, financial, media/entertainment, and academic players, as well as a number of other organizations, including, but not limited to: AT&T, Bain Capital, 21st Century Fox, American Express, HSBC, Hyatt, the Hispanic Association of Colleges and Universities, American Airlines, Papa John's, PayPal, Impossible Foods, JP Morgan Chase, Jack in the Box, JC Penny, Accenture, the Ad Council, Katten Muchin Rosenman LLP, KeyBank, PepsiCo, L'Oreal, Marriott, Major League Baseball (MLB), Minor League Baseball, the PGA Tour, McKinsey, Morgan Stanley, the National Basketball Association (NBA), Netflix, Standard Beverage Corp., The New York Times Company, Yum! Brands Inc., Citigroup, the Federal Home Loan Banks of Chicago, Des Moines, Indianapolis, and San Francisco, and more.

The evidence for browns and blacks, especially, as ideal hyper-consumers is ample. Blacks are more aggressive consumers of media and they shop more frequently, averaging ten more shopping trips annually than the national average. American blacks spend $1.3 trillion annually, though that number is expected to grow to $1.5 trillion by 2021; the "all cash" lifestyle of check cashing services, prepaid debit cards, and cash apps on cell phones results in greater spending and less saving. Blacks and Hispanics are less likely to be homeowners or have retirement accounts.

In a 2013 survey, Prudential Research found that 40% of blacks considered themselves to be spenders and just 9% had made any kind of investment. A dollar circulates a mere six hours in the black community as opposed to seventeen days in the white community, twenty days in the Jewish community, and thirty days in the Asian community. Compared to all groups, blacks spend 30% more of their total income – despite making $20,000 less than the average household. Per Pew Research, "About a quarter of all Hispanic (24 percent) and Black (24 percent) households in 2009 had no assets other than a vehicle, compared with just 6% of white households. These percentages are little changed from 2005." High time preference populations are also more susceptible to cash app and checking-cashing scams, taking loans at astronomical interest rates or relying on various forms of credit or cash advances with high interest rates, and using assets as collateral with a high likelihood of losing said assets (only to be re-acquired at a later date and often in a cyclical nature).

We can attribute this to high time preference and low impulse control, in addition to a highly externalized view of status through a commercial lens. "Blacks on the average are six times more likely than Whites to buy a Mercedes, and the average income of a Black who buys a Jaguar is about one-third less than that of a White purchaser of the luxury vehicle," writes Earl Graves of *Black Enterprise Magazine*. Per Nielsen:

> In terms of sheer dollars, African Americans spent considerably more money in the general beauty marketplace last year. Black

shoppers spent $473 million in total hair care (a $4.2 billion industry) and made other significant investments in personal appearance products, such as grooming aids ($127 million out of $889 million) and skin care preparations ($465 million out of $3 billion)... African Americans make up 14% of the U.S. population but have outsized influence over spending on essential items such as personal soap and bath needs ($573 million), feminine hygiene products ($54 million) and men's toiletries ($61 million). Nielsen research also shows Black consumers spent $810 million on bottled water (15% of overall spending) and $587 million on refrigerated drinks (17% of overall spending). Luxury, non-essential products such as women's fragrances ($151 million of a $679 million industry total), watches and timepieces ($60 million of $385 million in overall spending) and even children's cologne ($4 million out of $27 million) also play well to an audience that's keen on image and self care.[1]

Each year, blacks spend more than $47 billion on Lincoln automobiles, $3.7 billion on alcohol, $2.5 billion on Toyotas, $2 billion on athletic shoes, and $600 million on McDonald's and other fast foods, according to Target Market News Inc. Black women are 12% more likely than white women to purchase jewelry. By 2053, the median net worth of blacks in America is projected to be zero dollars, meaning everything that comes in goes out – in short, the perfect consumer. Blacks and Hispanics are the primary drivers of retail spending. Nikolai Roussanov, Kerwin Kofi Charles, and Erik Hurst found that:

Blacks and Hispanics spend up to 30% more than whites of comparable income on visible goods like clothing, cars and jewelry...This meant that, compared to white households of similar income, the typical black and Hispanic household spent $2,300 more per year on visible items...blacks and Hispanics do not spend more than whites on items, such as home furnishings, that

---

1   Nielsen Research Group, "Black Impact: Consumer Categories Where African Americans Move Markets," February 15, 2018. Nielsen. Available at: www.nielsen.com/us/en/insights/article/2018/black-impact-consumer-categories-where-african-americans-move-markets/.

could serve as status symbols but aren't seen by as many people... blacks and Hispanics spend 16% and 30% less, respectively, on education than whites of similar income. They spend 50% less on health care. Spending on health and education is not as visible to as many people as spending on cars and clothes, so it does not contribute as much to one's status.[2]

Because the visibility factor is so crucial to one's status in the black and brown communities especially, we would naturally expect social media to play a key role in the cultivation of these markets, especially when we consider the amount of time these two groups spend on social media and consuming media in general. According to Nielsen, black women aged 18 and older are 29% more likely to spend three to four hours on social media per day and are 86% more likely to spend five or more hours on social media per day than white women. Blacks are 44% more likely than whites to interact with brands on social media or to use social networks to support companies and brands. They are also 44% more likely than the average to create a social media account. Black women are 25% more likely to use social media to show support for their favorite companies or brands and 12% more likely to use social media find out about products or services than white women. We also learn from Nielsen:

African-Americans are exuberant and reflective – optimistic about present-day advances in income, education, entrepreneurship and health care, and determined to forge a better future as influential leaders and catalysts of social awareness against discrimination and social injustice...African-American Millennials are forging ahead in their use of technology and social media to raise awareness and evoke a national discussion on civic and political issues. African-American Millennials are expanding the use of mobile devices (particularly smartphones with a 91% penetration rate for all African-Americans).[3]

2   Roussanov, Nikolai, Kerwin Kofi Charles, and Erik Hurst, "Conspicuous Consumption and Race: Who Spends More on What" May 14, 2008. The Wharton School of Business. Available at: https://knowledge.wharton.upenn. edu/article/conspicuous-consumption-and-race-who-spends-more-on-what/.

3   Nielsen Research Group, "Young, Connected and Black," October 17, 2016.

Blacks watch 37% more television than any other group, averaging a whopping seven hours and seventeen minutes daily.

Crucially for the cultivation of the "elites'" Connected Consumers of the future, as Nielsen reports, "African American consumers no longer see their virtual actions as distinct from 'in real life behavior.'" 38% of blacks between 18 and 34 and 41% of those 35 and older say they "expect the brands they buy to support social causes," 4% and 15% more than their total population counterparts, respectively. 45% of Hispanics say that the brands they support must also support "social causes." They are also 29% more likely to agree that, "A celebrity endorsement may influence me to consider or buy a product." This is important to note in this context because of the increasing prevalence of "celebrity activism" and hence an overt infusion of "celebrity culture" with the political – and vice versa. Furthermore, "Our research shows that Black consumer choices have a 'cool factor' that has created a halo effect, influencing not just consumers of color but the mainstream as well," says Cheryl Grace, Senior Vice President of US Strategic Community Alliances and Consumer Engagement for Nielsen. "These figures show that investment by multinational conglomerates in R&D to develop products and marketing that appeal to diverse consumers is, indeed, paying off handsomely."

Every aspect of this system is inter-connected to some degree and each "arm" serves to reinforce the others. 52% of Hispanics 18 and older spend at least one hour per day on social networking sites (compared with 38% of whites) and 24% spend three or more hours per day (compared with 13% of whites). Hispanics over-index the general population in smartphone ownership. Hispanics spend the most time on social media and they are five times more likely to share the content they consume in comparison to whites. Per Nielsen, "This is especially true for U.S. Hispanics aged 18-49, who are more active when using YouTube, Instagram, Google+ and Snapchat." Further:

Available at: www.nielsen.com/us/en/insights/report/2016/young-connected-and-black/.

88% of Latinas own a smartphone, and they are 15% more likely than non-Hispanic white women to own such a device. On average, Latinas spend 22 hours each week watching videos and using apps or the Internet on their smartphones. They are also early adopters of newer tech gadgets, as they are more likely than non-Hispanic white women to own smart watches…Latinas of all ages spend most of their time watching TV…19% of Latinas say they use social media to show support for their favorite company or brand, compared with 16% of non-Hispanic white women. And 19% of Latinas say they use social media as an important source for reviewing or rating a product or service, compared with 17% of non-Hispanic white women. As for actual platforms, Latinas used certain apps more than their non-Hispanic white women counterparts. During a 30 day period, Latinas use Snapchat at a rate 96% higher than non-Hispanic white women, Instagram at a rate 64% higher, Spotify at a rate 59% higher and both Google+ and Pandora at rates 58% higher.[4]

70% of Hispanics say they follow performers on social media sites, a percentage well above that of whites. Asians also have specific market niches beneficial to the current economic order, most noticeably reflected in the fact that they are 50% more likely to use the internet and apps for consumer reviews than the general population and Asian women subscribe to online music services 30% more than the general population. Neither the Hispanic or Asian markets in the US are small potatoes, either: Asians have $1 trillion in annual buying power and by 2023, Hispanic spending power in the US is projected to top $1.9 trillion – well over the GDP of Mexico and a number greater than that of Canada by over $200 billion.

If almost all of the GDP growth from immigration accrues to the immigrants themselves, then of course it makes sense to keep the borders pried wide open, otherwise retail growth in particular is going

---

4   Nielsen Research Group, "Latinas are Avid Tech Users, Voracious Video Consumers and Social Trendsetters," September 12, 2017. Nielsen. Available at: www.nielsen.com/us/en/insights/article/2017/latinas-are-avid-tech-users-voracious-video-consumers-and-social-trendsetters/.

to slow way down, and as only retail and the FIRE economy are producing any economic growth in the post-industrial West, this is absolutely essential. At a certain point, though, once each individual consumer is maxed-out in their consumption habits even after the extension of more credit for the debt regime to help keep things afloat at least temporarily for those already here, you must continue to import huge numbers of those populations primed for hyper-consumption to keep growing the retail market. That maxing-out of the domestic population is already starting to happen, particularly among blacks and to a lesser extent Hispanics, and as Kasey M. Lobaugh, Bobby Stephens, and Jeff Simpson inform:

The retail market has been growing and continues to expand. In fact, in 2017, retail grew a healthy 2.3 percent. However, per capita retail spending remained flat for the most part of the period, meaning that population growth, rather than greater spending per person, was the primary driver of the increase in spending.[5]

With the exponential growth model in mind, immigration must continue to rise along with both personal and public debt, as wealth transfers from the middle class also power both FIRE and retail, top and bottom. The governments themselves are cashing in on immigration in all the ways we would expect, but some unusual ones, too: *The Times* found that the Home Office made £500 million in 2018, up from £260 million in 2014 just from collecting fees from immigration applications alone.[6]

One of the major difficulties the Establishment is going to face is that childless people are better consumers than those with children, and they are working very hard to suppress birth rates amongst whites, especially as whites are by far the worst race from a consumer

---

5   Lobaugh, Kasey M., Bobby Stephens, and Jeff Simpson, "The consumer is changing, but perhaps not how you think," May 29, 2019. Deloitte. Available at: www2.deloitte.com/us/en/insights/industry/retail-distribution/the-consumer-is-changing.html.

6   Available at: www.gulbenkian.co.uk/home-office-made-500m-from-immigration-fees-in-2018/.

standpoint. Destroying the family has helped produce more social dysfunction (good from a social engineering standpoint) and atomized consumers, but the coupon-clipping single mother who pinches pennies is just one major stumbling block. The equatorial world is being used as a nursery for childless and/or pathological whites (and homosexuals) to adopt from and add consumers into the market. Good on the one hand, bad on the other. We can already see several tension points here that will eventually cause the system to start breaking apart. The Establishment will push the expansion as far as it will go, though, because it's the only thing keeping it going. There are no brakes: there is no stasis for neo-liberalism and that will ultimately prove its undoing. For now, though, the paradoxically inherently-isolating platforms of social media are a major locus of control for the Establishment, and the inter-connected nature of propaganda, commerce, entertainment, and "activism," all merge, work synergistically, and spread with increasing rapidity across the globe. Commercial brands understand this, and have amplified profits by becoming "political," but it is nothing more than the next evolution, or mutation, of a convergence that finds distinctions between public and private, political and corporate, increasingly meaningless.

Is it a coincidence brands have made "social justice," "sustainability," and the like such major selling points of late? Most of what passes for "change" and activism by celebrities, politicians, and the like is what Mark Steyn refers to as "striking attitudes": in the same way designer fashions are modeled and displayed on the catwalk, public figures slip into and out of whatever position or viewpoint is most fashionable or politically and socially expedient with the ease of changing an outfit. Like models, these threads are chosen for them by designers behind the scenes: the Mugatu Left.

In essence, many consumers have come to view entertainment, activism, status, and consumption as often inter-connected, the significance of which simply cannot be understated. Among the digitized youth, which is rapidly approaching majority non-white (92% of the total growth in US population from 2000 to 2014 came from "multicultural" groups), per Nielsen:

Our purchasing behavior and habits are often shaped by the media content we consume across our devices. Generation Z adult consumers clock over six hours daily with their digital devices – almost 20 minutes more than their non-sustainability conscious Generation Z peers. And about one-third of their overall time with digital devices is spent social networking...Viacom's Generation Change platform celebrates those who inspire media creation as well as those who are inspired to act because of the media they engage with.[7]

It is a kind of vicarious play-acting where passive consumption is framed as activism. In fact, politics becomes itself both a pre-scripted drama and a spectacle to consume, political participation "in" the drama analogous to watching a film or television show on the couch – one is "invested" and a "participant" insofar as their vicarious fantasy carries them. Their investment has no bearing on the outcome, and they remain physically separated on the other side of the fourth wall. They feel as though they are a part of the process, though, and that is what makes all the difference. "Diversity," in all of its present dimensions, is a boon to both capital and the political in terms of social control. Jeffrey Klaehn explicates:

> Media, according to this framework, do not have to be controlled nor does their behaviour have to be patterned, as it is assumed that they are integral actors...fully integrated into the institutional framework of society, and act in unison with other ideological sectors, i.e. the academy, to establish, enforce, reinforce and 'police' corporate hegemony. It is not a surprise, then, given the interrelations of the state and corporate capitalism and the 'ideological network', that the propaganda model has been dismissed as a 'conspiracy theory.'[8]

---

7   Nielsen Research Group, "Gen Z Sustainable Consumers Go Digital – And Use Activism to Shape a Smarter Market," November 4, 2019. Nielsen. Available at: www.nielsen.com/us/en/insights/article/2019/gen-z-sustainable-consumers-go-digital-and-use-activism-to-shape-a-smarter-market/.

8   Klaehn, Jeffrey, "A Critical Review and Assessment of Herman and Chomsky's 'Propaganda Model,'" June 1, 2002. *European Journal of Communication.*

What we have here, then, is a system that operates not only in terms of political control, but in terms of corporate and financial control. What's more, these aspects are becoming, and to a large extent already have become, so enmeshed as to be indistinguishable. Given its interconnected nature, neo-liberalism must be understood synergistically, yet each component must also be understood on its own terms. Each element feeds, reinforces, covers for, and/or amplifies the others. Diversity is essential in order for the ruling class to create its dream society of atomized hyper-consumers, and until the various populations of the world can be blended into a nondescript serf class, the more violence-prone groups will be weaponized against those who are less so, terrorizing them into compliance and their turtle-shell existences of long commutes, streaming services, and online purchasing habits. As we know from Robert Putnam's findings, diversity causes atomization of society, the fraying of communal bonds, and a general feeling of negativity and despair. Putnam wrote in his "Diversity and Community" paper that those in more diverse communities:

> Distrust their neighbors, regardless of the color of their skin, [and tend] to withdraw even from close friends, to expect the worst from their community and its leaders, to volunteer less, give less to charity and work on community projects less often, to register to vote less, to agitate for social reform more but have less faith that they can actually make a difference, and to huddle unhappily in front of the television…People living in ethnically diverse settings appear to 'hunker down' – that is, to pull in like a turtle.[9]

This in turn creates better consumers and more easily-controlled, atomized people who are also more depressed and de-moralized. As Yuri Bezmenov wrote under his pseudonym Tomas Schuman in *Love Letter to America*, de-moralization is step one to the subverting group consolidating power, and people are very clearly demoralized.

Available at: https://journals.sagepub.com/doi/abs/10.1177/0267323102017002691.

9   Putnam, Robert, "*E Pluribus Unum*: Diversity and Community in the Twenty-first Century," 2007. *Nordic Political Science Association*. Available at: http://citeseerx. ist.psu.edu/viewdoc/download?doi=10.1.1.515.6374&rep=rep1&type=pdf.

Diversity is decidedly not a strength. Beyond the sheer multitude of studies showing that by every marker quality of life goes down the more diverse an area is, most intuit this as well, but have been conditioned to dismiss this as "racism." Perish the thought. What the ruling class is trying to do on a global scale is to create one indistinguishable mass of hyper-consumers, willing to work for less and in worse conditions, more easily propagandized, and with fewer objections to decrepit living conditions and infrastructure. That this "new population" would, paradoxically, be more violent is easily understood as a mechanism to terrorize the law-abiding, fracture their communities, and drive them indoors.

Provided the violence remains quarantined in favelas, ghettoes, or the wreckage of once-working-class towns and cities, it is of little consequence to the ruling class. The social unraveling would be reason enough for "white flight," but the violence and criminality puts the blood-red cherry on top of the sundae. Clearly, then, the "diversity" project is not based on sound, logical premises in order to benefit the host population, but rather it is based on ideological principles and done only in the name of greed and malice, despite the supposed GDP-boosting and cuisine-option-expanding window-dressing, and that is terrifying. There can be only one conclusion: this is being done *to* us, not *for* us.

The most vociferous supporters of mass immigration into the United States are almost to a person among the nation's most privileged. The advocates who proclaim their support for "social justice" are no different, but far from their motives being pure, they desire the importation of a new serf class of hyper-consumers. The social justice ideology imbues the economic decisions with a moral imperative (and also excuses naked attacks on whites done out of spite). The Establishment machinery is entirely geared toward the entrenchment, perpetuation, and expansion of neo-liberalism, which necessitates breaking down any obstacles to the free movement of people, goods, and capital. Along with the exponential growth model, this is the defining characteristic of neo-liberal economics.

Whites are subjected to ruthless, USSR-esque conditions while the immigrants run roughshod over them. The productive finance the un-working and imported scab labor, automation, and the outsourcing of jobs squeeze the life out of the middle- and working-classes. While anarcho-tyranny rules the day, Westerners are being crushed by a steady diet of Cultural Marxism while "free trade" continues to erode their sovereignty. It is the worst of both worlds, an unholy alliance of over-weaning bureaucracy, soulless corporatism, consumerism-masquerading-as-individualism, and ultimately genocidal demographic replacement, all with a bright plastic smile.

We cannot ignore the many clear consequences of imposed demographic change. Whites are the only demographic which consistently polls in the majority for support of absolute free speech, which is an extremely harrowing thought. A recent Gallup poll showed that a majority of California Democrats (and disconcertingly almost half of Republicans) felt that the free speech of white nationalists should not be protected. So much for the freedom for the thoughts that we hate. Another Gallup poll showed that a majority of college students polled believed that diversity and inclusion were more important than free speech. This is the consequence of both the shifting racial demographics of the United States and the prevalence of Cult-Marx propaganda. The foundational precepts and the philosophical inheritance of American republicanism and the Constitution simply cannot survive in an environment where groups who are hostile to them are growing in numbers at an accelerating rate. We'd like for it to not be true, but the adage demography is destiny is once again bearing itself out.

According to the Cato Institute's 2017 *Free Speech and Tolerance* survey, 56% of blacks and 58% of Hispanics polled believed that the government should legally prohibit "hate speech." 61% of all Democrats polled believed that racial epithets toward blacks should be made illegal, and 53% believed anti-Semitic statements should be banned. South Carolina was eager to comply with its 2018 Anti-Semitism Awareness Act. 65% of Hispanics believed it should be illegal to say anything offensive about them, and 62% of blacks felt the same about their own racial group. For point of comparison, 26%

of whites felt that offensive speech about whites should be banned. 51% of self-identified liberals stated that it was morally defensible to "punch Nazis," and 59% of this group believed that the United States should have, "a law that would require people to refer to transgender persons by their preferred gender pronouns, not their biological sex." 75% of blacks and 72% of Hispanics polled agreed with the statement that, "Hate speech is an act of violence." 66% of Democrats agreed. 62% of Hispanics and 59% of blacks believed that "disrespectful people" don't deserve free speech.

90% of blacks, 80% of Jews, 77% of Asians, and 69% of Hispanics voted Democrat in the 2018 mid-term elections; these overwhelming percentages voted for the present radical, anti-white iteration of the Democrat Party. Using CNN's exit polling data, 79% of the respondents who answered that electing more racial and ethnic minorities was "very important" were Democrats. 87% of respondents who felt that whites were favored in society today were Democrats as opposed to 69% of the Republicans who felt that no group is favored. This is depressing on two fronts: one, a whole lot of Republicans, mostly whites, either have their heads in the sand or are so deeply marinated in post-"Civil Rights" propaganda that they refuse to see the reality playing itself out before them, and two, that most Democrats are just as delusional in feeling that whites, with all of the venom and anti-white policies directed at them, are somehow a privileged group.

Another aspect of the atomization of society that occurs with increased diversity is the zero-sum nature of politics. On a practical level, multi-culturalism has made identity politics an inevitability. As Jared Taylor writes, "When minority communities grow they exert a powerful attraction on their members that fosters parochial loyalties. At the same time, when other minorities turn their backs on assimilation and carve out alternative identities for themselves – and gain clear advantages for doing so – the temptation to do likewise is strong." Racial identity (for all but whites), and its tribal hostilities, are on the rise in American politics, unsurprising when you consider Finnish researcher Tatu Vanhanen's findings of a correlation of .726 between ethnic conflict and ethnic heterogeneity (diversity) scores.

Consider that on the first day of Democrat control of the House of Representatives in 2018, we were treated to the following by their party members: a comparison of President Trump to Adolf Hitler by Representative Hank Johnson; a pledge by Representative Rashida Tlaib that, "We're gonna impeach the motherfucker"; an introduction of the articles of impeachment against Trump by Representative Brad Sherman; an introduction of a bill to grant Washington, DC (which went 90.8% for Hillary Clinton in the 2016 presidential election, 5.1% for various independent candidates, and 4.1% for Donald Trump) statehood by Representative Eleanor Holmes Norton; and the introduction of a bill to abolish the electoral college by Representative Steve Cohen. For those keeping score at home, Johnson is black, Tlaib is a Palestinian-Muslim, Sherman is Jewish, Norton is black, and Cohen is Jewish. Not long after, a bill to abolish ICE was introduced by House Democrats Adriano Espaillat (Dominican), Pramila Jayapal (Indian), and Mark Pocan (gay and Jewish).

This is the reality of American politics now, and increasingly that of many other Western nations: a censorious racial spoils system closely managed by a hostile foreign "elite" and the remnants of the Old Guard willing to collaborate for material gain and to stake a claim in the new globalist paradigm. Buffeted from every direction in a sea of alienism, native Americans find themselves ear-marked by the "elites" as casualties of globalism. Globalism is the antithesis of the nation, its cosmopolitan nature belying an origin totally at odds with the European philosophical inheritance. It is alien, it is oppressive, and it is, most crucially, destructive. That is obviously the intent: to have so thoroughly detonated the foundations of normal life, to have people so atomized and alienated, so awash in chaos and misery, that they become like putty in the hands of the ruling class. People are often moved to violence in the throes of emotional fervor, and the danger of crowds is the dispersal of responsibility that occurs when a crowd turns into a mob. The only kind of democracy or democratization (if you can call it that) our ruling class truly finds acceptable is that of the targeted lynch mob – online or in person. Organizations like Antifa are only on the more extreme end of what is tacitly approved in an anarcho-tyrannical society. Diversity fractures communities and causes people to turn inward, and feminism weaponizes one half of the population against the other. It turns natural complements into antagonists. It is the age-old strategy of divide-and-conquer, and every "-ism," every grievance or aggrieved group another potential fissure to exploit.

Chapter 10 - LGBT Consumers and Commissars

"If I had to pinpoint a time where it all coalesced, I'd have to say it was in 2015 when I was made aware that Goldman Sachs was flying a Pride Flag on their flagpole next to the American Flag."- Woke Capital

Like feminism and "diversity," so-called "LGBTQ rights" superficially seem reasonable enough. If each is about love and healing and empathy and equality, you'd have to be a monster to oppose them. That instinct, predominant among whites, is what has been manipulated and used against us. Would it just be about equal rights, protecting legitimate refugees until it's safe for them to return to their respective countries, and otherwise preventing undue harm to people, but that is a far cry from what these Trojan horse causes are all about. Each successive "wave" – blacks, women, immigrants, homosexuals, now transgenders – has been weaponized against the American Nation for ideological purposes. This has been the rough pattern for the other subverted nations of the West as well, although though the earlier importation of millions of African slaves has added another layer of difficulty, to put it mildly, in the American context. Reconciliation may well have been possible – and I will include aborigine peoples here for the former colonies such as the US, New Zealand, Australia, and Canada as well – had the subverters not organized and weaponized these peoples for ideological and commercial purposes, but that ship seems to have sailed.

In any case, homosexual and transgender "concerns" now carry far more weight with "our" leaders than do the very real concerns of the average American or Canadian or Australian. Homosexuals and transgenders are natural enforcers of the globalist order and they make for great HR commissars and busy-bodies, loyal to their masters above all others, jealously guarding their new position in the hierarchy. Homosexuals and transgenders are the perfect extension of the Establishment – they are ideal consumers and their hyper-narcissism and insecurity in their status makes them viciously effective as cultural commissars. As such, they have a vested interest in not just the System's survival, but its expansion. With no genetic progeny to care for and an ethos predicated first and foremost on gratifying their carnal desires, homosexuals also make for ideal hyper-consumers. As regards their jealously-guarded role as cultural commissars, to quote Leon Trotsky, "There is no justice in bureaucracy for the individual, for bureaucracy caters only to itself." When coupled with the extreme narcissism of the Prideful, this self-perpetuating bureaucracy becomes almost solipsistic, and the concerns of the people outside of the "in crowd" not only cease to be relevant, they effectively do not exist outside of something to be ridiculed. There is also the matter of LGBTQ "social justice" as an investment, which intersects with ideological concerns as R.R. Reno explicates:

It is patently obvious that giving homosexuals and trans individuals access to the extremely powerful and coercive tools of civil rights law is bad social policy. It will further empower the powerful, allowing them to destroy anyone who resists their agenda. The gay rights establishment is flush with money. It has tremendous cultural power. Outside conservative evangelical churches, no significant American institution opposes this establishment... By the time we reached the Obama administration, the nexus of government agencies, lawsuits, and activist organizations had become so tightly woven that tens of millions of dollars in financial penalties for discrimination in home loans (a lawsuit based entirely on disparate impact doctrine) were funneled into activist organizations such as the Southern Poverty Law Center. These organizations are dedicated to the further expansion of the civil rights legal regime... The extension of the powerful weapons of post-1960s civil rights to homosexuals and transgender individuals is almost certain to be even more elite-oriented. Data show that gay men earn more than straight men. It has long been a truism in marketing that the gay community is a prime target.

Without the costs of childrearing, they not only make more but have still more to spend.[1]

The LGBTQ "community"[2] is more inclined to spend money than save it, recalling our discussions of ideal hyper-consumers. They have huge amounts of discretionary income to spend and though some do adopt, they are generally not encumbered by children. Marianne Puechl states that, "The incredible 'Dual Income, No Kids (DINK)' buying power of the gay and lesbian population is stirring things up in business these days."[3] From a corporate perspective, the windfall from the growth of dual income, no kids households, and hence more disposable income, has been a net positive regardless of sexuality.

Embattled Virginia Governor Ralph Northam explicitly stated in an interview regarding late-term abortions/infanticide where the fetus is "non-viable" that, "Reproductive freedom leads to economic freedom for women...It brings prosperity." It literally brings prosperity to Planned Parenthood when they sell dismembered baby parts, and it frees up childless women to work more and to consume more. Plus, all those children Western women won't have then necessitates more of the fecund, easily-controlled hyper-consumers to be funneled into the country in order to keep the exponential growth model humming. Abortions are essential to keep the country in the black.

The nuclear family represents in every way an obstacle to the Uni-Party's consolidation of power, from its inherent conservatism to its multi-generational investment both from a financial perspective and in the inculcation of specific values, such as temperance, responsibility, respect for elders and tradition, future planning, obligations to the

1 Reno, R.R., "How Gay Rights Empower the Rich," October 9, 2019. *First Things*. Available at: www.firstthings.com/web-exclusives/2019/10/how-gay-rights-empower-the-rich.

2 I'll use "community" for shorthand, though the reader should understand that such notions of a coherent "community" are largely artificial constructs designed for marketing and political purposes, the same as the "black community," etc.

3 Puechl, Marianne, "Boost Profits by Marketing to the Gay Community," November 22, 2013. Available at: www.businessknowhow.com/marketing/market-gay.htm.

familial unit, and more, which are antithetical to modern "culture." Furthermore, the childless especially can give everything to their jobs without, from the corporate perspective, a "dual loyalty" to their family. The modern emphasis is on instant gratification and the ready embrace of hedonistic abandon. From video streaming services to popular music, the message is uniformly the same: consume, consume, consume. To quote Will Durant, "A nation is born stoic, and dies epicurean."

Homosexuals, transgenders, high time preference peoples, Cool Wine Aunts, single moms, and Allies are all atomized figures, and atomized people make for fantastic consumers. Both from a political and financial point of view the assault on the traditional nuclear family by the Woke Establishment makes all the sense in the world. Regarding the homosexual vanguard in particular, E. Michael Jones writes:

> The homosexual is the consumer culture's version of the ideal citizen because he takes all of the strains of narcissism to their logical anti-essentialist conclusion. The homosexual qua homosexual can form no family and, as a result, no real community; in a culture which promotes sexual liberation as a form of control by breaking down family and community, homosexuality is the most exaggerated form of sexual individualism...By promoting homosexuality as a viable alternative lifestyle, the consumer culture is saying that fantasy can triumph over reality, which is the essence of the narcissistic personality disorder. Homosexuality is a function of father deprivation. The less father, the less reality. The less father, the less family. The less family, the less reality. The less community, the less reality. The reverse of all of those equations is also true. By fostering narcissism and promoting narcissistic personalities—homosexuals, rock stars, etc.—to positions of celebrity and prominence, the consumer culture weakens family and community and strengthens its hold over the weakened individuals who must struggle through life without support from community or family. The only thing they can hold onto without fear of reprisal is their narcissistic fantasies of themselves as grandiose and "special."[4]

4   Jones, E. Michael, "The Ideal Citizen is Homosexual," October 2014. *Culture*

This also applies to, perhaps even more so, the "transgender" phenomenon. Despite the never-ending rainbow onslaught, Paul Hiebert states that, "In America...66% of LGBT individuals report that they don't see their lifestyle represented enough in advertising, compared to 51% of the general public. The same pattern occurs in the UK and Germany, where the differences are 57% to 44% and 40% to 33%, respectively."[5] Interestingly, Frank Browning's research of contemporary gay culture found that the homosexual group often used consumption venues and activities to express their hostility and anger toward straight society. This has significant ramifications regarding homosexuals as a revolutionary vanguard and as ruthlessly effective enforcers of Establishment orthodoxy; after all, they are clear beneficiaries of the current system and would not want their privileged position jeopardized.

Many LGBTQ people are being unconsciously manipulated as well. The reader must understand the various rainbow identities as a market share, because businesses certainly do. They cultivate it, market to it, and commodify it. The media's incessant wailing about "Donald Trump's America" and the "erasing of trans identities" is actually extremely useful from a business perspective for, as Junghyun Kim writes, "Compensatory consumption refers to a goal-directed behavior that may resolve psychological threats (e.g., social exclusion, identity threats, etc.) by consuming products/brands reinforcing a desired self-view (Lisjak et al. 2015; Kim and Rucker 2012; Lee and Shrum 2012)."[6]

Consumers not functionally oriented are significantly affected by the symbols encountered in the identification of goods in the marketplace

---

Wars Magazine. Accessed via: www.thinkinghousewife.com/2018/07/the-ideal-citizen-is-homosexual/.

5   Hiebert, Paul, "The benefits of advertising to LGBT consumers," June 8, 2017. YouGov. Available at: https://today.yougov.com/topics/media/articles-reports/2017/06/08/benefits-of-advertising-to-LGBT-consumers.

6   Kim, Junghyun, "Lonely Consumers: When, How, and Why Does Loneliness Influence Consumer Behavior?" March 23, 2017. Virginia Polytechnic Institute and State University. Available at: https://pdfs.semanticscholar.org/c351/aae8545f1c42c1902d73064e95e7161cd954.pdf.

(Levy, 1959). Grubb and Grathwohl (1967) specified that self-concept is valuable to the individual, and behavior will be directed toward the protection and enhancement of self-concept (Sirgy, 1982), ie-the individual "seeing themselves" represented in or by some facet of the product.[7] Goffman (1951) suggested that products possess symbolic properties, which are somehow congruent with an individual's self-concept (Kates, 1998).[8]

"Diversity and inclusion are good for business, period," states Jonathan Lovitz, senior vice president of the National LGBT Chamber of Commerce (NGLCC). This is well-understood by wireless provider Verizon and its $130 billion in revenue. Verizon has partnered with PFLAG, the nation's oldest organization "uniting LGBTQ people and their families," to help it build programs, call centers and education resources in "underserved communities." Swedish furniture retailer IKEA partnered with the Human Rights Campaign (HRC) to release a Pride version of its shopping bag. Target launched a special 90-item Pride collection and donated $100,000 to GLSEN, an organization dedicated to "making schools safe and inclusive for everyone."[9]

John Hegarty of global advertising agency Bartle Bogle Hegarty says, "Gay men and blacks tend to be fashion leaders and sensitive to style-led advertising, so we keep half an eye on what they're doing." Echoing Cheryl Grace, Senior Vice President of US Strategic Community Alliances and Consumer Engagement for Nielsen's earlier statement about blacks' "cool factor"/halo effect, Pride also has that halo effect, and consumers get the double-dopamine-hit of feeling like they are advancing "equality."

---

7   Chen, Joseph, May Aung, Jianping Liang, and Ou Sha, "The Dream Market: an Exploratory Study of Gay Professional Consumers' Homosexual Identities and Their Fashion Involvement and Buying Behavior," 2004. *Gender and Consumer Behavior*, Vol. 7. Association for Consumer Research. Available at: http://acrwebsite.org/volumes/12074/gender/v07/GCB-07/.

8   Ibid.

9   Cerullo, Megan, "'Rainbow retail' a biz opportunity in Pride Month and beyond," June 27, 2019. CBS News. Available at: www.cbsnews.com/news/gay-pride-2019-rainbow-retail-a-big-business-opportunity-in-pride-month-and-beyond/.

Consider that Reykjavik's annual Pride event is attended by 100,000 people – out of Iceland's total population of around 350,000. It's not about "social justice," it's a marketing technique, and, to be blunt, it is pathetic that people would attach their identities to – or worse, derive their identities from – consumer goods. When people have been de-racinated and stripped of any meaningful aspect of what should form their identities, though, in many cases this is all they have left. These kinds of people are a financial goldmine and are very easily manipulated.

In this context, and considering that per a report by Community Marketing & Insights 78% of LGBTQ community members said they are inclined to support companies that market to and support LGBTQ people, the very public 2018 co-signing of a letter by the usual suspects – Apple, Amazon, Facebook, Google, etc. – supporting "equality under the law for transgender people" following a report that the Trump administration was considering limiting the definition of gender to birth anatomy makes all the sense in the world. This is not done out of compassion; it is done for profit.

A 2010 survey from Community Marketing Inc. found that of the 22,000 surveyed 88% of gay men and 91% of lesbians said that a brand's support of LGBT events favorably influences their buying decisions.[10] Combining this aspect with the LGBTQ halo effect "social justice" dopamine rush of liberals, not to mention the entire social orientation toward everything rainbow and "diversity," Pride events have become a grotesque orgy of all that's wrong with modern society:

This year, 16 Global Fortune 500 corporations, including Walmart, Delta, AXA, Netflix, Bud Light, Unilever, BNP Paribas, Nissan and Disney, sponsored the New York [Pride] event, a number that has almost doubled since 2012. T-Mobile was this year's presenting sponsor, the top level of corporate partnership, which

10 Heasley, Jessica, "Reaching Out to Gay and Lesbian Consumers," January 28, 2010. Event Marketer. Available at: www.eventmarketer.com/article/reaching-out-gay-and-lesbian-consumers-0/.

Frederick says usually costs about \$175,000. London's Pride, though half the size of New York's, has experienced similar growth in the past decade: its sponsorship revenue, which this year stood at £400,000, has grown 250 per cent since 2013... This year, NYC Pride included not only the march for which the movement is famous – during which two million spectators line the streets of Manhattan to cheer the passing floats of big brands and non-profit organisations – but also the party on the pier (a woman's event called Teaze), a VIP rooftop party and, at the start of the week, a Pride Luminaries Brunch, a \$50-a-ticket event serving canapés including cubes of French toast and pieces of bacon, held in clothes pegs suspended along a string...The event's budget has almost trebled in [ten years]. This year's total is an estimated \$2.4m; about half comes from sponsorship, which has increased by a factor of 10...the rest comes from ticket sales, fundraising events and float registration fees. Over the same period, the number of people attending the march has grown by a third...What was once a political protest has, over half a century, become a boozy, bacchanalian celebration.[11]

According to a Google Consumer survey, 47.4% of young Millennials stated that they were more likely to support a brand after seeing an "equality-themed" ad. 45% of consumers under 34 years old said they're more likely to do repeat business with an LGBT-friendly company, and of those, more than 54% said they'd choose an "equality-focused brand" over a competitor. "Pride advertising" is having a widespread impact online, according to YouTube and Google data.[12]

This leads to completely ridiculous spectacles like Burger King's staged unveil of its rainbow-wrapped Whopper:

In July 2014, Burger King and the advertising agency David

---

11   Ross, India, "The business of gay pride," August 10, 2016. *Financial Times.* Available at: www.ft.com/content/228207c6-5f46-11e6-ae3f-77baadeb1c93.

12   Snyder, Brendan, "LGBT Advertising: How Brands Are Taking a Stance on Issues," March 2015. Think With Google. Available at: www.thinkwithgoogle. com/consumer-insights/lgbt-advertising-brands-taking-stance-on-issues/.

launched a product called the "Proud Whopper" during San Francisco Pride. The only difference from its regular burgers was its rainbow wrapping, which opened to reveal the slogan: "We're all the same inside." (After eating the Whopper, a girl interviewed for the agency's promotional video says: "A burger has never made me cry before.")[13]

At NYC Pride, referencing North Carolina's "bathroom bill," there was a MasterCard-sponsored toilet that could be used by anyone applying their hands to a heart-shaped pulse sensor, so anyone with a heartbeat could use it. "This restroom accepts all humans," read the tagline. Pride Month is a retail bonanza for brands:

> Like Halloween, Christmas, and Valentine's Day that come before it, LGBTQ Pride Month...has become a major selling season in the American retail calendar. Brands ranging from Johnson & Johnson-owned Listerine mouthwash and Harry's, a men's care brand, to clothing makers Ralph Lauren and Michael Kors have rolled out rainbow-themed designs and products to celebrate the occasion. Restaurants have bit into the theme too, adding special-edition food items – in rainbow hues, of course – to their menus: Shake Shack is selling a Pride Shake (a cake batter shake topped with rainbow glitter sprinkles) and Fresh&Co has a special Pride Menu, including the Love Salad and Rainbow Sandwich, available for the month of June. Service providers like FlatRate Moving and New York City's subway and bus system are also celebrating the 50th anniversary of the Stonewall Inn uprising with rainbow decals and special edition metro cards.[14]

Oreo cookies, Honey Maid, Tiffany & Co., Cheerios, Microsoft, Wells Fargo, Hallmark, Apple, Budweiser, JCPenney, JetBlue, Volvo, Coors, Absolut, Burger King, T-Mobile, Levi's Jeans, Kohl's, Thomas

---

13   Ross, India, "The business of gay pride," August 10, 2016. *Financial Times.* Available at: www.ft.com/content/228207c6-5f46-11e6-ae3f-77baadeb1c93.

14   Cerullo, Megan, "'Rainbow retail' a biz opportunity in Pride Month and beyond," June 27, 2019. CBS News. Available at: www.cbsnews.com/news/gay-pride-2019-rainbow-retail-a-big-business-opportunity-in-pride-month-and-beyond/.

Cook, Home Depot, Target, Tylenol, Johnson & Johnson Baby, Nikon, Chobani, IKEA, Campbell's Soup, Benetton, Rizzoli, Philip Morris, Viking Books, Remy Martin, and Starwood Hotels are just a few examples of companies that have launched LGBTQ-specific marketing campaigns, and who can forget the infamous Lezbaru. McDonald's has rainbow-colored French fry containers. Companies like Burger King feel compelled to publish diversity statements on their websites and 91% of Fortune 500 companies have felt compelled to add additional "non-discrimination policies" based on sexual orientation.

ViacomCBS has an "LGBT wing" called Logo. CEOs posing as activists such as Tim Cook of Apple, Howard Schultz of Starbucks, and Mark Zuckerberg of Facebook have taken on the cause of "LGBTQ rights." Starbucks recently released a commercial featuring drag queens Bianca del Rio and Adore Delano. During Pride month, Adidas released a rainbow-flag Stan Smith sneaker. The NBA pulled its 2017 All-Star Game from Charlotte due to the "transgender bathroom bill." This is all because these corporations care so deeply about homosexuals and transgenders, just like they care about "diversity," right?

More likely they care about the fact that the "pink dollar" is approaching a $1 trillion market share in the US, and as both more people come to identify themselves with the omnipresent "movement" and hiring preferences for higher-paying jobs skew toward the LGBTQ set, that market share will only increase. According to GLINN (the Gay/Lesbian International News Network), from 1996-1998 the annual value of the gay and lesbian market was $514 billion, and LGBTQ buying power rose over $100 billion from 2013 (approximately $800 billion) to 2015 ($913 billion). 76% of gay and lesbian household incomes are above the national average. For gay men and women, the average household income is $81,500 per year. 7% of wealthy households in America "identify as   LGBTQ."[15] The combined global spending power of LGBTQ/+ persons is estimated at $3.7 trillion a year, according to a

---

15 "The 2018 US Trust Study of High Net-Worth Philanthropy," Bank of America and The Indiana University Lilly Family School of Philanthropy. Available at: www.privatebank.bankofamerica.com/articles/2018-us-trust-study-of-high-net-worth-philanthropy.html.

2015 report by LGBT Capital, a corporate advisory and investment management company focused on the LGBT consumer market.

Perceived traits such as style-consciousness, the early adoption of new products, and a higher-than-average disposable income make gay consumers a profitable target demographic, says Daphne Kasriel-Alexander, a consumer trends consultant at Euromonitor.[16] According to a recent survey conducted by Forbes and Experian, 49% of 25- to 34-year-old LGBTQ respondents reported having bad spending habits, admitting to overspending on dining out, travel, and personal hygiene.[17] According to one recent survey, LGBTQ respondents estimated they devote 16% of monthly income to discretionary spending, but just 11% to saving or investment.[18] Even still, homosexuals have 24% more equity in their homes.

Gay and lesbian households make 16% more shopping trips than the average American household. As Brad Fuller relates, "Male same-sex households are especially likely to spend more frequently, shopping nearly 30% more often than the average household. On average, that's $2,045 more per year spent on packaged goods in male same-sex households."[19] LGBT households spend 35% more on liquor than non-LGBT households. They also spend more on pet care (38% more) and men's toiletries (32%). Gay men spend an average of $33,822 on their weddings, and lesbians spend an average of $25,334. LGBTQ weddings have larger average guest lists and engagement ring spending continues to increase, with men spending $5,719 and women spending

---

16   Ross, India, "The business of gay pride," August 10, 2016. *Financial Times.* Available at: www.ft.com/content/228207c6-5f46-11e6-ae3f-77baadeb1c93.

17   Akim, Jim, "LGBTQ Money Survey: Attitudes, Challenges, and Opportunities," June 18, 2018. Experian. Available at: www.experian.com/blogs/ask-experian/lgbtq-money-survey-attitudes-challenges-and-opportunities/.

18   "Report examines LGBT spending habits," September 12, 2018. *Windy City Times.* Available at: http://www.windycitymediagroup.com/lgbt/Report-examines-LGBT-spending-habits/64037.html.

19   Fuller, Brad, "Here's How Some Brands Have Subtly Won Over the LGBT Community," June 23, 2013. *Business Insider.* Available at: www.businessinsider.com/lgbt-community-untapped-market-consumer-brands-2013-6.

$5,349 on average.[20] In a recent survey in Australia, 6.2% of straight men agreed with the statement, "I was born to shop," whereas 19.1% of gay men agreed with the statement. Gay men were also much more likely than straight men to agree that they "enjoy clothes shopping (41.9% versus 23.3%), and 37.6% of gay men said they would "buy a product because of the label" compared with 23.3% of straight men. Gay men in Australia account for 11% of the dollars spent by men on men's clothing.[21] Nielsen Research found that:

> The [LGBT] community spends 48% more on wine than non-LGBT households, and 43% more on technology...On-line shopping is also a thriving LGBT market. Each year gays and lesbians purchase 35% more online than their straight counterparts. Popular LGBT on-line items are snacks at 122% over non-LGBT, and household cleaners at 73%. Rounding out the list of keyboard driven purchases are coffee (69%) and medication (67%)...LGBT music fans over-index on spending on tickets to attend music festivals (index 123, or 23% more likely), subscribing to streaming services (126) and going to see a DJ they know perform (150). Non-white, professional Millennials without children also tended to watch LGBT-inclusive shows more frequently than primetime in general. 49% of all LGBT moviegoers said they had texted, tweeted or posted about the movie the same day they saw it (as compared with only 34% of heterosexual moviegoers) and they are more likely to purchase a physical copy or digital download of the movie at a later date than heterosexuals.[22]

40% of LGBTQ persons purchased a new smartphone within the

---

20   Jacobson, Ivy, "You've Got to Read These 15 Statistics from Our LGBTQ Weddings Study," 2017. The Knot. Available at: www.theknot.com/content/lgbtq-weddings-study-the-knot.

21   "Thinking pink: the purchasing power of gay Aussies," June 29, 2016. Roy Morgan. Available at: http://www.roymorgan.com/findings/6866-power-of-the-pink-dollar-201606271639.

22   Rawles, Timothy, "It's official: gay and lesbian dollars are fueling the US retail economy, Nielsen reports on where," August 5, 2015. *San Diego Gay and Lesbian News*. Available at: https://sdgln.com/news/2015/08/05/its-official-gay-and-lesbian-dollars-are-fueling-us-retail-economy-nielsen-reports-w.

past year; these figures all indicate fantastic Connected Consumers. In a recent survey, when asked if they use their phone to look for products and services seen advertised on posters and billboards, 43% of LGBT consumers in the US affirmed that they do, compared to 33% of Americans in general. Similar percentages were found in LGBT consumers in the UK and Germany as well. LGBT individuals are also more likely than the general population to research the products they see advertised on television.[23] Films and the retail industry were the top categories that drove advertising on LGBT-inclusive programming, devoting 28.3% and 27.6% of their ad dollars, respectively. Credit cards, telephone, and tech companies also spent a significant share of ad dollars on these so-called LGBT-friendly programs.[24]

Speaking of LGBT-friendly, the ruling class's new imported population isn't exactly so, and it leads to serious trouble in paradise. Britain's Labour Party – they of large-scale voter fraud, the shameless pandering to Britain's increasingly-irascible acid-flinging Muslim communities, and MP Naz Shah who re-tweeted the sentiment that the one million victims of "Asian" grooming gangs "just need to shut their mouths for the good of diversity" – has recently appointed "trans model" Munroe Bergdorf to be their LGBTQ adviser. You may recall Bergdorf for the comments that got her sacked by L'Oreal:

> Honestly I don't have energy to talk about the racial violence of white people any more. Yes ALL white people. Because most of ya'll don't even realise or refuse to acknowledge that your existence, privilege and success as a race is built on the backs, blood and death of people of colour. Your entire existence is drenched in racism. From micro-aggression to terrorism, you guys built the blueprint for this shit.

---

23 Hiebert, Paul, "The benefits of advertising to LGBT consumers," June 8, 2017. YouGov. Available at: https://today.yougov.com/topics/media/articles-reports/2017/06/08/benefits-of-advertising-to-LGBT-consumers.

24 "The New Mainstream 28% of TV Watching Spent on LGBT-Inclusive Shows," October 27, 2011. Nielsen. Available at: www.nielsen.com/us/en/insights/article/2011/the-new-mainstream-28-of-tv-watching-spent-on-lgbt-inclusive-shows/.

While Munroe Bergdorf has, shall we say the *privilege* of railing against micro-aggressions and condemning whites in relative safety, (all that jihad, anti-LGBT bigotry, and non-white criminality apparently following the white blueprint excepted) according to the Human Rights Risk Index, the following countries are classed as having "Extreme Risk" for the abuse of human rights: North Korea, Syria, Iraq, Iran, Saudi Arabia, Yemen, China, Vietnam, Afghanistan, Pakistan, Bangladesh, Myanmar, Turkmenistan, Uzbekistan, Russia, Zimbabwe, the Democratic Republic of the Congo, Equatorial Guinea, Nigeria, the Central African Republic, Sudan, South Sudan, Ethiopia, Somalia, Eritrea, Egypt, and Libya. The countries classed as having "High Risk" are basically the rest of Africa, Asia (minus Taiwan, Japan, and South Korea), and Central and South America (minus Argentina, Chile, and Uruguay). So before you decide to drown a perfectly good bowl of vanilla ice cream in hot fudge, you might want to spare a thought for those rainbow sprinkles.

30% of homosexuals have taken a major vacation within the last year. Community Marketing Inc. found that from 2001-2003 gay and lesbian travel accounted for $54.1 billion in annual spending in the United States alone. In 2009, that number was $63 billion. According to OUT NOW Consulting, in 2016 the LGBTQ traveling market was worth $211 billion globally. 59% of respondents to Community Marketing Inc.'s 2009 survey stated that their travel decisions were influenced by their "preferences and loyalties as an LGBT consumer."[25] Sensing a perfect opportunity, Orbitz became the first online travel company to launch a "microsite" dedicated to LGBT travel. Travelocity quickly followed suit. The International Gay and Lesbian Travel Association (IGLTA) joined the United Nations' World Tourism Organization (UNWTO) in November 2010:

> The two bodies jointly produced a 40-page "Global Report on LGBT Tourism" that was delivered this past January to the ministers of tourism of every WTO member nation. "This report

25 "Gay Travel Statistics," 2009. Home Around the World. Available at: www. homearoundtheworld.com/page/gay-travel-stats-2.

demonstrates the clear relationship between countries' progressive policies toward LGBT people and the economic benefits for their tourism sector," Javier Blanco, director of UNWTO Affiliate Members, said in a statement at the time of the report's release.[26]

As Antonio Zappulla writes, "In the words of the UN, the fight against homophobia is now, more than ever, a 'development imperative.' By forging an internal culture of inclusion that transcends national policies yet is aware of them, companies have a tremendous opportunity to leverage their global influence to shape socio-economic progress."[27] Something clearly must be done about those stubborn countries like Uganda and Nigeria and their so-called anti-homosexuality laws! Importing their people and cultural attitudes en masse into the West, however, is a harbinger of "progress." The wonders never cease. Maybe a good old-fashioned boycott like the infamous "transgender bathroom" one in North Carolina from a few years ago might do the trick, democracy be damned! Speaking of which, as Susanna Kim reported for ABC News in 2016: "Gender neutral bathroom signs are slowly growing in popularity, and signage designers and architects expect a boom in the business of making them." For Richard Corradi:

The medieval field of alchemy – the attempt to change base metals into gold and to find the philosopher's stone capable of bringing about human perfection, even immortality – is ludicrous to the modern mind, a relic of a prescientific time. Yet the ancient belief in transmutation is still with us. Current popular delusions are aspirations not to turn base metals into gold, but rather to transcend the laws of biology and transmute human nature. Among them is the popular belief that gender is fungible, so that whether we are born male or female is of no consequence.[28]

---

26 Kiesnoski, Kenneth, "With a big-spending reputation, gay travelers attract suppliers," May 22, 2012. *Travel Weekly*. Available at: www.travelweekly.com/ Travel-News/Travel-Agent-Issues/With-a-big-spending-reputation-LGBT-travelers-attract-suppliers.

27 Zappulla, Antonio, "The simple reason why so many businesses support LGBT rights," January 14, 2017. World Economic Forum. Available at: www.weforum. org/agenda/2017/01/why-so-many-businesses-support-lgbt-rights/.

28 Corradi, Richard, "Transgender Delusion," October 2015. *First Things*.

The neo-liberal establishment *is*, however, turning transgenderism – and all its other neighbors in the LGB et cetera acronym, not to mention women and most non-white groups – into gold.

Launched in 2015 at the Clinton Global Initiative Annual Summit, Open for Business is an organization that describes itself as "Business Action for LGBT+ Inclusive Societies," with the stated intention of "building a consensus amongst the business community that anti-LGBT+ policies run counter to the interests of business and economic development." This is in line with not only American foreign policy, but already appears to be the consensus among major corporations as well. I know, American foreign policy, corporate interests, I repeat myself. Open for Business's coalition features a number of major businesses, banks, and conglomerates, each with its own statement of "diversity and inclusion" on the organization's website, including: AT&T, Google, Thomson Reuters, Virgin, IBM, American Express, Barclays, Deutsche Bank, LinkedIn, MasterCard, McKinsey, Tesco, Burberry, and Accenture.

In just one example of how these various agendas intersect, Accenture has partnered with and provides consultations and digital services, as well as millions of dollars of financial support, to the United Nations High Commissioner for Refugees (UNHCR) and the 501(c)(3) "non-profit" Upwardly Global, which "helps immigrant, refugee and asylee professionals rebuild their careers in the United States." This is of course done purely for humanitarian reasons, not about training a cheap, semi-educated, and compliant workforce. Open for Business has disseminated materials to "activists" in Kenya, Taiwan, India, and Uganda, and their Local Influencer Program has "convened hundreds of business leaders from challenging markets to discuss LGBT+ inclusion, including Brazil, Bulgaria, the Caribbean, Hong Kong, Hungary, India, Kenya, Singapore and South Africa." Already, it has gotten the following institutions to adopt its "inclusiveness agenda":

Available at: www.firstthings.com/article/2015/10/transgender-delusion.

- The Vatican
- World Economic Forum (WEF)
- The Commonwealth Heads of Government Meeting
- European Parliament
- UN LGBTI Core Group
- UN Business and Human Rights Forum
- International Bar Association

Open for Business has also collaborated with George Soros's Open Society Foundations and receives funding from Tides, the Arcus Foundation, and the Oak Foundation (Barbara Rothschild sits on their Advisory Panel), among others.

Virgin founder Richard Branson has been adamant that Virgin will not do business in Uganda until it repeals its "anti-homosexuality" law and has stated that he will encourage other businesses and tourists to boycott Uganda until they capitulate to the globalist agenda. Love is love, after all, so we will crater your local economy until you realize it, and then we'll replace your people and scrap your nation for parts! Branson said it was not for any government "to ever make any judgements on people's sexuality," but apparently massive multi-nationals can. And besides, as we shall see, governments like Branson's most certainly do make positive judgements on, and advance the agenda of, subversive sexualities.

If global pressure in the form of boycotts, divestments, and economic sanctions don't work, there's always the globalist intelligence community and military establishment. NATO offers four "gender perspective" courses aimed at adopting a gender theory perspective in military affairs and "apply[ing] a Gender Perspective in scenarios of patrolling, checkpoints and engagement with the local population in a culturally sensitive manner." The preposterousness – and dangerousness – of this requires no comment, but it suggests the priorities of the Establishment.

In 2017, it emerged that the Australian military was penalizing recruiters who were failing to hit female acceptance quotas in order to "balance out" the "gender inequality" of the armed forces. The recruiters were exempt from punishment for failing to hit this acceptance rate if a larger proportion of the males were aborigines or Torres Strait Islanders. The Canadian military has set a goal of 25% of its armed forces consisting of women by mid-decade, as well as increasing the military's share of "visible minorities." Though Norway has been at the forefront of instituting "progressive" policies regarding women in the military, it has seen the female share of its military remain stuck at a "stubborn" 10%. Nevertheless, they've been experimenting with full "gender integration" with select 50-50 split male and female units that even share the same mixed sleeping quarters.

In late 2019, the United Nations placed strict gender quotas on a British Army "peacekeeping force" sent to Mali to "contain extremist activity" as part of its Uniformed Gender Parity Strategy 2018-2028, Department of Peace Operations – war is peace after all – that mandates quotas for female personnel in the name of equal opportunity. Forty-four French soldiers have died in the Sahel region as "peacekeepers" since 2013 and for what? Meanwhile their home country is being transformed beyond all recognition. Other salient points from the Uniformed Gender Parity Strategy "to ensure that the uniformed component of United Nations peacekeeping is diverse and inclusive of women, reflecting the communities the United Nations serve" include:

- OMA/Police Division to coordinate with the military/police component in each mission to include in their gender strategy and action plan relevant goals and actions to support the implementation of the Uniformed Gender Parity Strategy and ensure that all staff are appropriately trained.

- Training on overt and unconscious gender bias made available to staff involved in recruitment and selection boards, based on UN developed materials.

- Deliver annual Military Gender Advocate of the Year Award and the International Female Police Peacekeepers Award.

- Give priority during selection to officers from contributing countries that nominate at least 30% women candidates.

- Update calls for nomination to include an option to not accept nominations which contain only male candidates.[29]

Beyond the obvious insanity of putting women on the front lines of military action, policing, and fire and rescue for reasons physical, dispositional, emotional, and mental in the first place, beyond the fact that quotas will prevent the advancement of much more qualified candidates, beyond the lowered physical requirements for all recruits in order to get more women into front-line positions, beyond the presence of women interfering with the tight bonding process that occurs among teams or units of men in high-stress situations – and the not-at-all-inconsequential fact that mixed-sex units in military combat experience casualty rates multiples higher than male-only units, at least six times by one measure – using a concept invented out of whole cloth with no empirical backing or real-world applicability in the deadliest of situations shows just how delusional the Establishment's Useful Idiots truly are, and how far the true power brokers, the Soros types who regard themselves as "god-like," are willing to go in order to advance this deadly lunacy – and it will be enforced at gun-point. Any country that stubbornly resists the agenda will be bombed into submission and/or invaded. After toppling the regimes in Afghanistan and Iraq, the United States mandated gender quotas for members of parliament in the two countries' new constitutions.

Though here in the West the CIA and other intelligence agencies have been very helpful in facilitating our subversion, the military doesn't really need to be deployed if, as Aldous Huxley wrote, "The all-powerful executive of political bosses and their army of managers control a population of slaves who do not have to be coerced, because they love their servitude." (Anti-) cultural inertia and corporate uniformity – with government complicity and plenty of NGO help, of course – are doing the job pretty well here in the Occident, where the rainbow flag flies high signifying that you are a conquered population.

---

29 "Uniformed Gender Parity Strategy 2018-2028," Department of Peace Operations, United Nations: New York. Available at: https://peacekeeping. un.org/sites/default/files/uniformed-gender-parity-2018-2028.pdf.

Stonewall, "the largest LGBT rights organization in Europe," is a UK-based "charity" that, among other things, tracks and ranks the UK's "most LGBT-inclusive employers." Its corporate partners include the Premier League, Adidas, Asos, Absolut, eBay, Sky Sports, Aviva, Barclays, and Prudential. Some of the most "inclusive" employers will be unsurprising – Lloyds, JP Morgan Chase, Credit Suisse, Vodafone, a number of universities – others perhaps more so. MI5 – the United Kingdom's domestic counter-intelligence and security agency – was the fourth-most "LGBT-inclusive" employer in the entire country in 2019. So instead of preventing people from being run over, stabbed to death, or maimed with nail bombs in the name of the jihad, MI5 is concerned with whether or not it has enough homosexuals and transgenders in its ranks.

The gross failure and incompetence at all levels of the security apparatus, including the police, will soon become clear; also featured on the list were: the National Assembly for Wales and the Newcastle City Council, tied at number five (it emerged recently that a massive grooming gang had been operating with impunity in Newcastle); the Welsh Government (#8); the Ministry of Justice (#12); the Royal Navy and Royal Marines (#15); the Cheshire Constabulary (#18); Lancashire Constabulary (#36); the British Army (#51); Sheffield City Council (#61); the Royal Air Force (#68); Leeds City Council and the Scottish Government (#72, tie); Sunderland City Council (#76); Sussex Police (#81); MI6 – the foreign intelligence service of the government of the United Kingdom (#86); Northumbria Police (#88); Nottingham City Council (#95); and the National Crime Agency (#100). Cheshire Fire and Rescue clocked in at #4 on the 2018 list along with the House of Commons (#23), the Home Office (#38), Tyne and Wear Fire and Rescue Service (#59), and Police Scotland (#90).

Tower Hamlets Homes was apparently too busy basking in its inclusion on the inclusion list in 2017 (#12) to keep up with the basic maintenance and fire safety protocols of its Grenfell Tower, which went up in a massive conflagration on June 14th, 2017 and burned for sixty hours, resulting in the deaths of seventy-two people and injuries to several hundred others. It was the worst residential fire in the United

Kingdom since World War II. The fire spread so rapidly because the building's exterior did not comply with building regulations. An alternative cladding with better fire resistance was refused due to cost-cutting. The building was designed under the assumption that a full evacuation would never be necessary. There was no centrally-activated fire alarm and only a single central staircase. There was only one entrance and exit, and the building's fire doors would not close or seal properly. Most of its corridors were filled with garbage and many exits had been blocked by mattresses and other discarded items. For at least twelve years prior to the fire residents had complained about a lack of proper maintenance and fire safety equipment. In 2012, an official recorded that the firefighting equipment had not been checked in four years, and most of the fire extinguishers were expired. When one of the residents posted about this online, they were threatened with legal action. In June 2016, an independent assessor identified forty serious fire safety issues in the Tower that required immediate attention but were never addressed.

"Inclusion" and "diversity" once again revealed for the sham they are, Tower Hamlets was evidently more concerned with parading around its gay and transgender employees than it was ensuring the basic upkeep of its building. Of course, many of the residents bear some responsibility for clogging exits and hallways with mattresses and other detritus, and generally treating their living space as a garbage dump; in a dark harbinger of the Shape of Britain to Come, Grenfell Tower's residents were primarily poor, non-white recent immigrants to the country.

Conclusion (The Returner)

"Such is his conflict; in maintaining Family and State, he has been forced to sacrifice Family and State. Then when he has accomplished the deed of sacrifice, he must restore himself to what he has immolated. A hard task, a deeply contradictory process, whose end is, however, harmony; many will not be able to reach the latter stage, but will perish by the way. The Return is this great process of restoration after the estrangement." -Denton J. Snider

Whites especially are inherently dynamic in vision and thinking: without goals whites sink into a spiritual malaise, wither away, and die, both metaphorically and literally. Presently we have a civilization on the retreat from having subdued most of the globe, and we have a culture that is alien and utterly vapid; divorced from real meaning, people turn to escapism, often in very unhealthy ways. Literally millions of people die globally from alcohol abuse every year. In the United States, as in so many other Western nations, rampant opioid and anti-depressant abuse has given rise to a shocking number of deaths by despair, otherwise leaving individuals even more hollowed-out than before they began, numb and non-threatening. SSRI abuse may be one reason we seem incapable of resisting our demographic destruction; regarding the opioid epidemic, Jim Goad has an interesting theory, which draws the parallel between an opium-addicted China in the 19th century and its carving-up by the "Great Powers" and the immense profits which accrued to the Jewish Sassoon family.

The *only* system that will work for and not against its people is one which is in accordance with the natural order. To be fair, this is not a one-size-fits-all approach; each *ethnos* orients itself differently. In order to understand that which will be most conducive to allowing the Occident to not just survive but thrive once again, we must first understand its essence and the nature of re-birth.

Building on the ideas of Plato and Aristotle, Polybius's concept of anacyclosis as introduced in his *Histories* is that for each of the three just forms of government as derived from Plato, there is a corresponding pathological or anti- version. The pathological and corrupted version of a kingship is a tyranny; of an aristocracy, an oligarchy; of a democracy, an ochlocracy, or mob rule. He views the corruption of each as inevitable, showing an acute understanding of both human nature and the nature of history. For each system, the inevitable break-down occurs, followed by a reformation and transition to another form of government. This is contrasted with Roman Republicanism, which is meant to be more durable since it contains elements of all three, though this does not mean that republics are indestructible nor incorruptible.

This idea of the life cycle of societies and civilizations is one that a number of historians and philosophers have explored, in the modern world no one more compellingly than Oswald Spengler in *The Decline of the West*.

Spengler, interestingly, separated our modern Western culture (Faustian) from those of classical antiquity (Apollonian). Certainly by the fifth century Apollonian civilization in the western half of the Mediterranean was dead; the Byzantine Empire, however, flourished for another thousand years, and as one silver lining to its fall in 1453, many scholars and archivists fled west to a re-awakening Apennine Peninsula with an infusion of ancient texts thought lost. This conjoining of energies manifested itself in the Renaissance, which had powered the Western world to its centuries of unprecedented greatness. In 1865, on his eighth try, Englishman Edward Whymper climbed the Matterhorn with nothing but a small flask of tea and a ham sandwich. That same year Trollope, Zola, and Dostoyevsky published new works of fiction and in the six years on either end, the internal combustion engine, plastic, the bicycle, the typewriter, air brakes, the subway, traffic lights, and dynamite were invented, all by Europeans of course. Western greatness and the Faustian spirit have been driving human progress for seven hundred uninterrupted years (and intermittently for millennia). An America unconcerned with "diversity" invented flight and sixty-six years later was on the moon. Competence is clearly no longer on the agenda in this new landscape of "equality": Blacks are nearly four times as likely as Asians and nearly three times as likely as whites to be accepted to medical school with identical MCAT scores and GPAs. Why would this be necessary if all people were "equal"? We have become consumed with fanatical delusions, deeply pathologized, and shot through with disease, to borrow from William Gayley Simpson. Those energies of greatness appear exhausted now, and the question is what comes next?

Spengler postulated that we (Western, or Faustian Civilization) are in the "winter stage." A cursory evaluation of the world at large confirms such an observation; however disconcerting this may appear, however, it signals an opportunity for new growth. We must re-configure our set of cultural assumptions regarding "equality," "democracy," and the nation. As we have established, the nation is not just a parcel of land but a reflection of and testament to its people. Only in such conditions can a true democracy form. As Polybius wrote in his *Histories*:

> It is not enough to constitute a democracy that the whole crowd of citizens should have the right to do whatever they wish or propose. But where reverence to the gods, succour of parents, respect to elders, obedience to laws, are traditional and habitual, in such communities, if the will of the majority prevail, we may speak of the form of government as a democracy.

Liberalism is exactly wrong: it is in the *collective* that the individual finds strength, purpose, and meaning. I speak of the collective not as a hive-mind, but as the *natio* (nation). One need not sacrifice their individuality to the group, but rather a true citizen would subordinate their self-interest to the greater good:

> It should be emphasized that the Greeks saw no contradiction between individual freedom and the needs of the state; the two concepts were not opposites; rather, they were seen in harmonious balance, a symbiosis. Preparing oneself fully, developing one's body and spirit, was to prepare

oneself to participate in the activities of the state. The philosopher Aristotle would later define the state as, "an association of similar persons for the attainment of the best life possible." The clearest expression of the relationship between the individual and the state comes from Pericles himself in his "Funeral Oration": "We do not say that a man who takes no interest in politics is a man who minds his own business; we say that he has no business here at all." Individualism was later to become a problem for Athens, a source of the breakdown of traditional values and unity in time of war.[1]

For Aristotle, "The end of democracy is freedom; of oligarchy, wealth; of aristocracy, the maintenance of education and national institutions; of tyranny, the protection of the tyrant." For Edward Goldsmith, the overriding goal of Green politics is to re-establish a "natural social order...organised on the same plan and governed by the same laws [as] the Cosmos and the natural world," very much in keeping with this Grecian concept from classical antiquity, a similar concept of which we see expressed in Roman republican governance and in many other incarnations throughout European history, including in England and in many of the city-states of Italy in the Renaissance. Quoting Denton J. Snider:

The law exists as the first fact in the world, and will work itself out with the Gods as executors. Is not this a glorious starting-point for a poem which proposes to reveal the ways of providence unto men? The idea of the Homeric world-order is now before us, which we may sum up as follows: the Gods are in the man, in his reason and conscience, as we moderns say; but they are also outside of man, in the world, of which they are rulers. The two sides, divine and human, must be made one; the grand dualism between heaven and earth must be overcome in the deed of the hero, as well as in the thought of the reader. When the God appears, it is to raise man out of himself into the universal

---

1   Murphy, James J. and Richard A. Katula with Forbes I. Hill and Donovan J. Ochs, *A Synoptic History of Classical Rhetoric*. Hermagoras Press. (3rd edition). 2003. p. 21.

realm where lies his true being. Again, let it be affirmed that the deities are not an external fate, not freedom-destroying power, but freedom-fulfilling, since they burst the narrow limits of the mere individual and elevate him into unity and harmony with the divine order. There he is truly free.[2]

That freedom is in discipline and duty, not freedom from them. It is from a strengthening, not severing, of bonds. It is also a deep understanding of what that duty must be – not "global uplift," but a singular one.

While Christianity appears to have been taken hostage by the "social gospel," we must always remember that this was the original version of Christianity. It was not the faith of world-conquerors, but of slaves. Only in the late Roman Empire, after Caracalla had extended citizenship to all freemen in the Empire's confines and after the founding families had all stopped breeding and died off did Christianity become the state religion. It was only after Christianity had been modified from its original form from its fusion with local customs and pagan rites (think of shrines to the Saints with burnt candles and other offerings, or of prayer to the Saints as intermediaries between Man and God, or else of the Celtic tradition of Samhain followed the next day by All Saints' Day – these are but three small examples) and more importantly was imbued by the essence of those peoples that it became acceptable to Europeans. In short, Christianity had been made to adapt to Europeans, not the other way around. If it is a hindrance, then it must be burned away; its monuments preserved as testament to who we were and what we can do, just like those magnificent testaments to the accomplishments of classical antiquity, but as a belief system, if it keeps us in the terrestrial mud when it should be impelling us to transcend as it once did, then we must find that essence elsewhere.

It may be that it only needs a reinvigoration of the primal spirit of the Occident, for only in the modern world has Christianity become

---

2   Snider, Denton Jaques. *The Collected Writings of Denton J. Snider.* W.H. Miner Co. 1922. p. 17.

a universalist religion again, and we must reject this form for it will surely mean our oblivion. That is to say that the uniqueness of Western civilization stems from the fact that it is at once more egalitarian in its orientation than any other in terms of what we might call "rights," especially as it pertains to women (while simultaneously granting women a special status as pristine beings in need of protection from all that is harmful and foul), and in its emphasis on merit; but it is also more aristocratic, for its people – when unencumbered by alien ideas that warp this egalitarian impulse into something communistic and/or pathologically altruistic – are the primary drivers of innovation, creativity, and beauty on this earth. Just as the Renaissance harnessed the positive elements of classical antiquity and infused them with something new, we must be willing to do the same as we look to the future without forgetting our past.

The ability of Europeans to create something from nothing is astounding, be it global superpowers hacked out of the wilderness or notions of self-governance and right-to-rule. The progeny of Europe have been very concerned with various iterations and degrees of self-governance and right-to-rule from the Germanic tribes of antiquity to Athens to Rome to Iceland to England to America. It is in the DNA it would seem – just as the overwhelming majority of inventions that define human progress come from the European people so, too, do their concepts and inventions, as definitively catalogued by Charles Murray in *Human Accomplishment, Pursuit of Excellence in the Arts and Sciences, 800 BC to 1950*.

As in the United States and Canada, and other products of European exploration, expansion, and settlement such as Australia, New Zealand, and what remains of South Africa, their very existence is a testament to European dynamism. Returning to the notion of Western Man's Faustian spirit, for Ricardo Duchesne:

Oswald Spengler used [Faustian] to designate the "soul" of the West. He believed that Western civilization was driven by an unusually dynamic and expansive psyche. The "prime-symbol" of this Faustian soul was "pure and limitless space." This soul had a "tendency towards the infinite," a tendency most acutely expressed in modern mathematics. The "infinite continuum," the exponential logarithm and "its dissociation from all connexion with magnitude" and transference to a "transcendent relational world" were some of the words Spengler used to describe Western mathematics. But he also wrote of the "bodiless music" of the Western composer, "in which harmony and polyphony bring him to images of utter 'beyondness' that transcend all possibilities of visual definition," and, before the modern era, of the Gothic "form-feeling" of "pure, imperceptible, unlimited space" *(Decline of the West, Vol.1, Form and Actuality [Alfred Knopf, 1923] 1988, pp. 53-90).*[3]

We are the ones who first planted a flag on Luna, and if humanity is to transcend its present constraints, it is we who will subdue the heavens. This cannot happen if we are weighted down with a religion that enervates the undifferentiated mass, the ignorant flock in need of shepherding, or of an ideology that treats men and women as interchangeable yet in perpetual opposition. This could not be further from the truth, for we are meant to be complementary, but a system that abuses our notions of chivalry with this equality-with-an-asterisk sows resentment and destroys empathy for women, especially as they are conditioned to incapacitate themselves with drugs and alcohol but are absolved of any consequences as a result of their actions. In the #MeToo era, the sheer volume of false rape accusations as well as the conflation of rape with unwanted advances or even simply regret is generating a population of men who are indifferent to the sufferings of women at the hands of legitimate predators, many of whom have been imported from alien cultures that regard women as absolute inferiors and often chattel.

Europeans' restless, conquering spirit remains tethered to, and in many ways is born from, notions of fairness and trust, and the

---

3   Duchesne, Ricardo, "Oswald Spengler and the Faustian Soul of the West: Part I," September 4, 2014. Council of European Canadians. Available at: www. eurocanadian.ca/2014/09/oswald-spengler-and-faustian-soul-of-west-part1. html.

willingness to organize beyond kinship ties, but the collaborative and extra-kinship/contractual network of relationships that undergird and make possible Western advancements and achievements as mentioned above can be a double-edged sword. It makes us uniquely primed to appreciate "out-group" members, but it also diminishes our sense of the "in-group." Coupled with an innate sense of "fair play," the rules of engagement, and integrity, we become overly-trusting, and, by assuming everyone is playing the same "game" as us, allows us to be uniquely susceptible to deception. We also have a strong tendency to universalism and empathy, and when you combine these factors and that of the tendency to irreligiosity, the transference of the religious impulse, and the corruption/reversion of Christianity, the present state of affairs begins to take on a far greater degree of clarity.

Now all of this is not to say that we should throw the baby Jesus out with the bathwater, for a society that believes in nothing quickly grows nihilistic and decadent before its demise. As Polybius wrote in his *Histories*:

For I conceive that what in other nations is looked upon as a reproach, I mean a scrupulous fear of the gods, is the very thing which keeps the Roman commonwealth together. To such an extraordinary height is this carried among them, both in private and public business, that nothing could exceed it. Many people might think this unaccountable; but in my opinion their object is to use it as a check upon the common people. If it were possible to form a state wholly of philosophers, such a custom would perhaps be unnecessary. But seeing that every multitude is fickle, and full of lawless desires, unreasoning anger, and violent passion, the only resource is to keep them in check by mysterious terrors and scenic effects of this sort. Wherefore, to my mind, the ancients were not acting without purpose or at random, when they brought in among the vulgar those opinions about the gods, and the belief in the punishments in Hades: much rather do I think that men nowadays are acting rashly and foolishly in rejecting them.

In this yawning spiritual void, to quote Douglas Murray, "some of the absolute bases of Western civilization were...offered up for negotiation...Europe lost faith in its beliefs, traditions, and legitimacy." In their stead came the false doctrines of democracy and equality – the same doctrines, though in secular form, that powered the pre-European-infused iteration of Christianity. "Global uplift" becomes the suicidal rallying cry; democracy on a global scale can only turn ochlocratic for the global minority that is the white race. The feverish modern delusions of "democracy" are nothing but the veneration of the masses; in this way it is no different from communism. In practical terms, there is no difference between the kleptocratic conditions of communism and ruthlessly exploitative capitalism. The methods of control are the same, too.

In any case, the notion of Nietzsche's *Übermensch* is at once a terrific conceptual response to the existential challenges of the aforementioned frictionless lifestyle, and yet, from the Prologue of *Thus Spoke Zarathustra*, the *Übermensch* "*shall be* the meaning of the earth! I beseech you, my brothers, *remain faithful to the earth*, and do not believe those who speak to you of otherworldly hopes!" Nietzsche believed that high culture could fill the God-sized hole of Western civilization, and the closest anyone came to "playing God," as it were, in this respect was Richard Wagner (this concept is alluded to in the brilliant *Alien: Covenant*, with its dual-edged sub-text of both Wagner's philosophy of an all-encompassing high-cultural aesthetics and a Nazi-esque preoccupation with aesthetics and eugenics personified by the android David – witness the recurrence of Wagner's *Entry of the Gods Into Valhalla* as the android David, "the creator," enters the embryo room; alternatively, the film could be read as David-as-God-imposter, ushering in a new era of freakish amalgams and dysgenic and violent "neomorphs"). The ramifications of Nietzschean philosophy cannot be understated, as Lesley Chamberlain outlines:

He might just as well simultaneously have declared "reason" dead. Indeed, he did just that. For reason, in the idealist context, was not just some capacity of mind to prove propositions about experience true; it was, for Hegel, a supernatural force out there, moving the world towards progress. Nietzsche's rebellion was a way of saying that no great metaphysical forces governed human life and created a framework for meaning, every individual faced the possibly absurdity of existence alone... So, "God is dead," which means "Reason" with a capital R, the force out there that made possible the philosophy of Plato, of the intertwining of Reason and divinity throughout mainstream Christianity and western philosophy, cannot be used to explain the nature of "man." But that means that man, too, is dead. In fact, the most serious outcome of Nietzsche's death of God is the death of man, or mankind, as one entity, defined by rational capacity and slotted into a vision of "rational" progress.[4]

I must beg to differ slightly with Chamberlain here as Nietzsche was not presaging the death of Reason and Man entirely, but a certain *kind* of death, one which, paradoxically, must have a resurrection – a Renaissance if you like – in order for Man to transcend its present limitations onto a higher plane of existence. This has, as of yet, not happened, as we are presently in the death throes of the old order.

Faith need not be a concession to bovine, unthinking submission. It can be, as seen in Ephesians 6:11-13, folded into a conception of both the *Übermensch* and Kierkegaard's Pursuer of Difficulties who straddles this realm and the next (and it need not be literal – consider ideas such as "legacy" and "posterity"):

> Put on the full armor of God, so that you can make your stand against the devil's schemes. For our struggle is not against flesh and blood, but against the rulers, against the authorities, against the powers of this world's darkness, and against the spiritual forces of evil in the heavenly realms. Therefore take up the full armor of God, so that when the day of evil comes, you will be able to stand your ground.

To quote Whittaker Chambers, "[The West is] a creative force...

---

4   Chamberlain, Lesley, "The political message of Nietzsche's 'God is dead,'" February 7, 2012. *The Guardian.* Available at: www.theguardian.com/commentisfree/belief/2012/feb/07/political-message-nietzsche-god-is-dead.

whose mandate…impels men to die for it, not because they wish to die, but because they feel its shaping power so completely that they would rather die than live without it." We can also see, via Chamberlain, that progress in the Progressive sense is foundationally based on irrationality, but it also does much to illuminate the inherent contradiction in the image of a harmonious utopia of man on this terrestrial plane. Their philosophy is untenable, so as they continue to try and force this corrupted ideal on the West, the privileged classes either dismiss or simply do not comprehend the fundamental illogic of the undertaking, made more grotesque and terrible by their rigid adherence to an emphasis on the collective identities of the Other despite a preponderance of evidence *at the group level* that said groups are not exactly model citizens, let alone the next batch of Shakespeare's and Copernicus's and Voltaire's. It is, finally, the centrality of *logos* in Western civilization that has ultimately been supplanted by effete and unthinking *pathos*. Being of European Man, the *logos* is not a substitute for race as some might have it; it encapsulates our people's essence and our drive to understand the world *as it is* though not at the expense of ideals to strive for. According to Douglas Frame:

> Hierophanies of the sun have achieved real importance in few cultures, being all but limited to Egypt, Asia, and primitive Europe. Where they have become important, however, they have consistently gone hand in hand with a development toward rationality; hence the phenomenon that sun worship habitually ends by rationalizing itself out of existence, at least from the standpoint of its originally "ambivalent" nature. The "rationalizing" tendency of sun worship has an obvious bearing on the word *nóos*, which in attested Greek designates the "rational" faculty. When we consider the importance that this word attained in the Greek philosophical tradition, the notion of a rational "elite" also becomes important…I suggest that the history of Greek *nóos* also followed a course from "hierophany" to something more strictly rational…It must be remembered that the Homeric poems are themselves well along in the development of Greek rationalism.[5]

---

5   Frame, Douglas, *The Myth of Return in Early Greek Epic*. Harvard University

Expanding on this notion, we learn from Mircea Eliade's *Patterns in Comparative Religion*:

Sunset is not recognized as a "death" of the sun (unlike the moon's three days in hiding) but as a descent into the lower regions, into the kingdom of the dead. Unlike the moon, the sun has the privilege of passing through hell without undergoing the condition of death. Nonetheless, its predestined journey through the lower regions still confers on it the prerogatives relating to death and burial. Thus even when it no longer holds a front place in the pantheon or in the religious experience of a given civilization, as the Supreme Being who has become a sun god or a fecundator, the sun still manifests a certain ambivalence which makes it capable of undergoing yet further developments. This ambivalence might be expressed rather like this: though immortal, the sun descends nightly to the kingdom of the dead; it can, therefore, take men with it and, by setting, put them to death; but it can also, on the other hand, guide souls through the lower regions and bring them back next day with its light. That is its twofold function – as psychopomp to "murder" and as hierophant to initiate…It is worth underlining the close connection between solar theology and the elite – whether of kings, initiates, heroes, or philosophers. Unlike other nature hierophanies, sun hierophanies tend to become the privilege of a closed circle, of a minority of the elect. The result is the hastening of the process of rationalization. In the Graeco-Roman world the sun, having become the "fire of intelligence," ended by becoming a "cosmic principle"; from a *hierophany* it turned into an *idea*. . . . The philosophers, last among the "elect," . . . at last completed the secularization of what was one of the mightiest of all the cosmic hierophanies.[6]

Center for Hellenic Studies. 1978. Accessed via: https://chs.harvard.edu/CHS/article/display/4041.2-the-root-nes-in-prehistoric-greek.

6   Eliade, Mircea, *Patterns in Comparative Religion*. Sheed & Ward: New York. 1958. Introduction, University of Nebraska Press: Lincoln, 1996. First Bison Books re-print, 1996. p. 136.

CONCLUSION (THE RETURNER)

In the *Odyssey*, Frame writes, "Helios causes the ultimate destruction of the 'amorphous mass' of companions. What is most apparent is thus the negative side of the sun's ambivalent powers." This foreshadows the Return. As Denton J. Snider wrote, using Homer's Odysseus/ Ulysses as the avatar of Occidental or Western Man:

> Finally is Ulysses, not yet returned, but whose time has nearly arrived. In comparison with the others he is the Returner through the Occident...In spite of the grand estrangement, [the Greeks] have the aspiration for return, and for healing the breach which had sunk so deep into their souls. Did they not undergo all of this severing of the dearest ties for the sake of Helen, for the integrity of the family, and of their civil life also? What he has done for Helen, every Greek must be ready to do for himself, when the war is over...The true Returner, accordingly, gets back to the institutions from which he once separated; he knows them now, previously he only felt them. His institutional world must become thus a conscious possession; he has gone through the alienation, and has been restored...The new man after the restoration is the image of the complete self-conscious being, who has taken the negative period into himself and digested it.[7]

We see, then, in Occidental or Western Man the inextricability of the sun's journey from a kind of death as it passes through the house of the dead, which may carry the living to experience this death while not truly dying, a sort of temporary living death if you like. He re-emerges in the light having completed his journey through the underworld and his Return. But this process is cyclical; eventually, recounted by Frame:

> In Book 9 Odysseus encounters the Lotus-eaters, whose food causes anyone who eats it to lose his desire to return home. This loss of desire is a kind of "forgetfulness," as is revealed by two closely related collocations, both in verse-final position:

---

7   Snider, Denton Jaques. *The Collected Writings of Denton J. Snider*. W.H. Miner Co. 1922. p. 54-55.

nóstou te lathésthai, "to forget their homecoming," in line 97 and *nóstoio láthētai*, "that he might forget his homecoming," in line 102. What is suggested by the forms of *lanthánomai*, "to forget," in these collocations is that the loss of a "return" is at the same time a loss of "mind."…The lotus blossom, an integral feature of the episode, is a drug, and this fact sufficiently explains the use of the verb *lanthánomai*. One could compare the phrase *lathoíato patrídos aíēs*, "that they might forget their fatherland," in x 236, which describes the effect Circe intends her drugs to have on the companions of Odysseus…Balancing *lathoíato patrídos aíēs* in x 236 is the phrase *mimnḗskeo patrídos aíēs*, "remember your fatherland," in x 472, and balancing *nóstou te lathésthai* and *nóstoio láthētai* is the phrase *nóstou te médēai*, "(if) you are mindful of your homecoming," in xi 110 and xii 137. The verbs *mimnḗskomai*, "remember," and *médomai*, "be mindful of," have as much significance for the connection of *nóos* with *néomai* as does the verb *lanthánomai*…The above evidence suggests that Greek epic diction contained a regular opposition between "remembering" and "forgetting" one's "return," and that the phrases *nóstou te láthesthai* and *nóstoio láthētai* are to be seen in terms of this opposition... The argument may now be carried a step farther. Just as the connection between *nóos* and *néomai* is only latent in the encounter with the Lotus-eaters, so is the idea that a *nóstos* was originally a "return from death." But this idea, however latent, is still suggested by the verb *lanthánomai*. The noun associated with this verb is *lḗthē*, "forgetfulness," and this noun, in post-Homeric Greek, designates a place of oblivion in the lower world. The land of the Lotus-eaters, since it is also a place of oblivion, likewise suggests a kind of death… Particular attention is drawn to line 705, in which *lḗthē* is associated with a loss of *nóos* in the context of "death"; attention is also drawn to the several words designating the "intelligence" which enabled Sisyphus to "return from death."…It is very significant that *nóos* is associated with a "return from death" in a myth concerning a figure other than Odysseus.[8]

---

8   Frame, Douglas, *The Myth of Return in Early Greek Epic*. Harvard University

To forget, to remember, to return, to be restored. The sun is the light, the fire of intelligence. The Proto-Indo-European root recalls the Vedic *pra math*, "to steal," *pramathyu-s*, "thief," cognate with "Prometheus." Helios has both sacred cattle and sacred sheep. The association with intelligence in myths of the Sun's cattle has significant overlap with Vedic mythology, where cattle are associated with the sunrise; and according to Douglas Frame, "in particular, the 'winning of cattle' and the 'winning of light' are closely related mythical deeds." When Odysseus's men eat these sacred cattle, Helios calls for their destruction:

> "They perished by their own folly;" they would not obey the counsel of their wise man; they rejected their Hero, who could not, therefore, rescue them. A greater wisdom and a deeper suffering than that of Ulysses will be required for their salvation, whereof the time has not yet come. He would bring them home, but "they ate of the oxen of the sun;" they destroyed the attribute of light in some way and perished.[9]

They violated the natural order and they defied their leader, and in so doing were themselves destroyed. The "undifferentiated mass" was descended into darkness where the Hero yet still holds the promise of redemption and Return. He will need to "die," however, in order to be re-born. From Hesiod:

> Here stands the dread house of dark Night covered with black clouds. Before the house stands the son of Iapetus, holding fast the wide heaven on his head and untiring arms, at the place where Night and Day address each other as they pass, crossing over the great bronze threshold: one of them goes down within while the other comes out, so that the house never contains both of them, but one is always outside the house traveling over the earth, while the other is inside the house waiting for the time

---

Center for Hellenic Studies. 1978. Accessed via: https://chs.harvard.edu/CHS/article/display/4042.3-the-return-of-odysseus.

9   Snider, Denton Jaques. *The Collected Writings of Denton J. Snider.* W.H. Miner Co. 1922. p. 9.

of her journey to come; one of them brings the far-seeing light to those on earth, while the other, baneful Night covered with murky clouds, carries Sleep, the brother of Death, in her hands.

Frame explicates:

In Hesiod, when "Night and Day address each other as they pass, crossing over the great bronze threshold," we cannot help but be reminded of Tēlépulos, "where shepherd, driving in his flocks, cries out to shepherd, and the other, driving his flocks out, hears the call." At this point let us consider where Parmenides and Hesiod imagine the "gates" (or the "threshold") of day and night to be. Since Parmenides is "returning to light," his gates are presumably on the eastern shore of the world. Hesiod, on the other hand, mentions Atlas (*Iapetoîo páis* in l. 746), whom he has previously (l. 518) placed "at the ends of the earth, in front of the Hesperides," in other words, on the *western* shore of the world. This discrepancy arises from the very concept of a single point at which day and night pass, for, in reality, there are two such borders between darkness and light – one in the east, the other in the west. In the Hesiodic passage, Day and Night call out to each other, whereas in Homer "shepherds" do this. If "shepherds" are traditional in this context, do they not recall the cattle and sheep of Helios investigated earlier? Of course Homer, in the lines concerning the possibility of a "double wage," takes a rational and realistic view toward these shepherds. But what if the same shepherds were once represented as passing each other on their way into and out of the "house of night"? This house can have been nothing other than the cave at the ends of the earth which enclosed the herds and flocks of the sun.[10]

Approximately 5,000 years ago, the Indo-European (Aryan) people branched out in several directions, some arriving in northern India, some in Persia, some in Europe, bringing with them their warrior-like

---

10   Frame, Douglas, *The Myth of Return in Early Greek Epic.* Harvard University Center for Hellenic Studies. 1978. Accessed via: https://chs.harvard.edu/CHS/article/display/4042.3-the-return-of-odysseus.

yet aristocratic culture which found fertile ground in Europe especially, and ultimately proved to be a potent admixture with the extant hunter-gatherer European population's tendencies to relative egalitarianism and cooperation and the agricultural southerly middle wave's more structured rigidity and sophistication. We see, then, a powerful fusion of egalitarianism and merit, individual and group.

It is the Trojan War that forms the deep scission between East and West, Occident and Orient – the Hellespont a chasm between the Hellenistic world and the Oriental one. Yes, many Greeks remained in their millions for millennia along the coast of Asia Minor, but they always faced West. Only Christianity connects the Occident to the East, the one connection bridging that chasm which, paradoxically, grows weaker the further East one travels.

The syncretizing Biblical elements are found in Luke – "Because my eyes have seen your salvation, which you have prepared before the face of all people, a light for the revelation of the Gentiles" – and Matthew – "*Think not that I am come to send peace on earth: I came not to send peace, but a sword.*" For Denton J. Snider, "The *Odyssey* has two phases of Negation, both of which the heroes (father and son) must overcome." This synthesis and call to action are incumbent upon the natural aristocracy of our people, who – if enough remain – must seize the mantle of power and supplant the alien culture that has been poisoning our people with Mammonism, degeneracy, and self-hatred and restore order through the re-birth – the Return. For Snider:

> The taking of Troy…[is] the great opening event of the Greek world, as here revealed. For this event was the mighty shake which roused the Hellenic people to a consciousness of their destiny; they show in it all the germs of their coming greatness. Often such a concussion is required to waken a nation to its full energy and send it on its future career.[11]

---

11   Snider, Denton Jaques. *The Collected Writings of Denton J. Snider.* W.H. Miner Co. 1922. p. 7.

The Occident was born of struggle and the reverberations shook Greece to its heights.

Frame states that, "The nóos of Odysseus should properly reappear only when he reawakens in his homeland," sleep (Hypnos) and non-violent death (Thanatos) being twin brothers, sons of night (Nyx). "Waiting to give Odysseus advice when he returns is the goddess Athena. The striking feature of the encounter that follows is the attention given to 'intelligence,' particularly through the words nóos and nóēma." Athena here is of such vital importance, and a vessel of both knowledge and power, that we see the respect for, indeed veneration of, the power of women in European culture; the Return cannot be completed for Odysseus without Athena's help. Man and woman–complementary, just as rationalism and humanism are complementary. As Snider puts forth, Odysseus/Ulysses's aim is:

To restore Helen, to vindicate Family and State, and even Property. Troy is destroyed because it was itself destructive; it assailed the Greek domestic and civil institutions in the rape of Helen. So the destroying city itself is destroyed, but this leaves Ulysses a destroyer in deed and in spirit; home and country he is not only separated from but is destructive of–he is a negative man...Return must in the first place be within himself, he must get rid of the destructive spirit begotten of war...When he is internally ready, he can go forth and destroy the Suitors, destroy them without becoming destructive himself, which was his outcome at Troy...This destruction thus becomes a great positive act, now he restores Family and State, and brings peace and harmony...The main fact, however, of the Trojan cycle is the great separation, deepest in history, between Orient and Occident, through the instrumentality of Greece. The civilization of Europe and the West is the offspring of that separation, which is still going on, is a living fact...The great separation of Greece from the Orient...is the fundamental fact of the Trojan War, and of which the Homeric poems are the mighty announcement to the future. Troy, an Orientalizing Hellenic city in Asia, seizes and keeps Greek Helen, who is of Europe; it tears her away from home and country, and through its deed destroys Family and State. Greek Europe restores her, must restore her, if its people be true to their institutional principles; hence their great word is restoration, first of their ideal Helen, and secondly of themselves...This rounding-off of the Trojan cycle is, on the other hand, a final separation from the Orient; the scission is now unfolded, explicit, quite conscious. When Ulysses comes back to Ithaca, and re-establishes Family and State, Greek life is independent, distinct, self-determined. The Hellenic world rises and fulfills its destiny in its own way; it creates the Fine Arts, Literature, Science; it is the beginning of the Occident.[12]

Therefore, to quote Richard M. Weaver, "We are looking for a place where a successful stand may be made for the *logos* against modern barbarism." This is it.

When we talk about tactics, we have four separate spheres to consider: personal, local, national, and international. Unless you have George Soros or Michael Bloomberg money and influence, there's not much you are going to be able to do past the local sphere outside of educating people, most likely in either the digital space or through the spread of knowledge contained in a book, and though you may be able to provide some material support, it is certainly not going to be at the level or organization of a Soros or a Bloomberg (and besides, Soros and Bloomberg are not revolutionaries but avatars of the system itself). The cumulative effect of local action coupled with information dissemination will prove decisive, however, for the sturdy foundations are those which will survive. But we must be prepared for a protracted struggle and steel ourselves for what may come. The system will die, but there's no telling how long that will take. Certainly we will do what we can to hasten its demise.

Of particular concern to us in this book is the constructing of a platform which will not only enjoy the broad-based support of our

---

12   Snider, Denton Jaques. *The Collected Writings of Denton J. Snider.* W.H. Miner Co. 1922. p. 525.

people, but one which acknowledges their basic human dignity and puts their interests first and foremost. Donald Trump, for all of his short-comings, was able to achieve the presidency by tapping into this vein. Beyond enacting many of the policies President Trump should have already and which readers are no doubt familiar with (such as building a gigantic wall, enforcing the border, and deporting illegal aliens), what would such a platform look like? For starters:

- Revocation of dual citizenship; if a current American "citizen" is eligible for right-of-return or citizenship in their home country, they must exercise that right and relinquish American citizenship.

- Re-evaluation of the criteria of earning citizenship.

- Retroactive stripping of birthright citizenship for all American and Canadian "citizens."

- Retroactive stripping of all amnestied aliens in the United States.

- Treat temporary protections and refugee and asylum status as actually temporary.

- Address the opioid crisis; serious jail time for those responsible for over-prescription, distribution, and even more draconian punishments for those figures, such as the Sackler family, primarily responsible for addiction profiteering.

- In the United States, retroactive stripping of post-1965 naturalized citizenship; only those who have at least one parent's ancestry in this country extend to before 1924 may be considered citizens.

- Floors in European countries where the ethnic group belonging to the nation-state shall never fall below 90%.

- Some similar strategy regarding the founding stocks of New Zealand, Australia, and Canada; Quebec should be granted independence and also establish its ethnic floor to preserve its unique culture.

- Establish an independent state for the Boer in South Africa; establish an independent state for Rhodesians and other Anglo-Africans.

- Institute protectionary tariffs.

- Heavily tax remittances to foreign countries.

- Deport all illegal aliens and heavily punish companies or individuals who employ and/or harbor illegal aliens.

- Significantly curtail if not eliminate all foreign worker visa programs.

- Immediate cessation of property taxes and the ability of law enforcement to engage in civil asset forfeiture.

- End unnecessary foreign "aid."

- Institute severe penalties for job outsourcing and for offshoring.

- Forgive all interest-based accruals to student loans and establish a fair payment plan.

- End government subsidies of private oligopolies.

- Term limits for House Representatives and Senators.

- Ending of affirmative action and all race-, sex-, and sexuality-based hiring and collegiate acceptance quotas.

- Establish severe penalties for pollution.

- Increase the number of parks, land trusts, and general conservation efforts.

- Outlaw the barbaric practices of kosher and halal slaughter.

- Close all international army bases and end all foreign wars and entanglements.

- Repeal and/or allow to expire the provisions of the Patriot Act/ the USA Freedom Act and eliminate most of the surveillance state beyond what is absolutely essential; abolish the CIA as it has been compromised for some time and is nothing but a nation de-stabilizing cancer.

- Only permit bi-lateral trade deals and only allow for barter-based international trade such as that of the economic miracle in the mid-1930s in central Europe.

- Banning of all seditious NGOs, advocacy groups, 501(3)(3)s, and racial caucuses.

- Outlaw all subversive "disciplines" in the academy and establish compulsory courses in public education relating to civics, home economics, rhetoric and philosophy, and national history; protect the arts and expand subsidies to the arts, including music.

- Provide for free trade school and certification courses such as commercial driving licenses.

- Ensure no foreign interference in elections; this includes private censorship such as that conducted by Facebook in the Irish abortion referendum or Google's manipulation of search results in the 2016 presidential election; outlaw all other foreign interest groups such as AIPAC.

- All contributions from outside the specific region of the election in question (town, county, state, etc.) may only originate from persons residing in that region; all corporate and special interest campaign contributions must be outlawed.

- Immigration moratorium or reform along the lines of current Japanese immigration policy or that of the United States in 1924 – in short, protecting the ethnic composition of the nation as it should be.

- Peaceful repatriation and stipends for establishing new lives in their old homelands for all aliens affected by citizenship status changes.

- Establishment of an ethno-state for American blacks whose ancestors were involuntarily brought to the United States.

- Interest-free loans and loan forgiveness programs for young people to become home owners; create incentive programs for American couples to have two or more children (at least until replacement-level stasis is achieved).

- Tax breaks for small businesses and family farms.

- End affiliation with NATO, the United Nations, and other globalist organizations.

- Total overhaul of the tax code.

We will rebuild the middle class; end financial speculation, addiction and war profiteering; put the dignity and prosperity of our people above corporate interests; and regain our sovereignty from internationalist and alien interests. All alien peoples will be re-patriated to their respective homelands and will be compensated for their property and/or given a financial stipend to start new lives where they belong.

These policies are both good for our people and would enjoy popular support; their implementation and success would enhance our credibility, engender goodwill with the populace, and give us the latitude needed for decisions that may not be popular but prove to be necessary later on. These proposals, or ones similar, emphasize people over products, people over soulless corporations, and nature and well-being over profit. There is far more respect for the individual in this frame-work than in any neo-liberal conception of the "market" or the "consumer." There is far more respect for human and natural bio-diversity as well.

Three other proposals require slightly more explanation. The first is that an individual must perform twenty hours per week of community service of a nature to be determined by their locality in order to receive welfare. In the state of Maine:

In October 2014, Maine began requiring about 16,000 able-bodied childless adults to work, train, or volunteer on at least a part-time basis in order to continue receiving food stamps. Adults who refused to comply with the new requirements would cycle off after three months of benefits. After implementing these reforms, Maine quickly moved thousands of able-bodied adults out of dependency and into self-sufficiency. By January 2015, the number of able-bodied adults on food stamps had dropped to 4,500 and has continued to decline. These changes drew ire from the Obama administration (note: that means it's working)...

Today, just 1,500 able-bodied childless adults rely on Maine's food stamps program. Those still relying on the program also need less assistance overall, as they are working more, with average benefits dropping 13% since the work requirements went into effect. As a result of these changes, taxpayers are now saving between $30 million and $40 million each year.[13]

Similar such national-level policies in times of greater deprivation resulted in the Hoover Dam, the Autobahn, and the mass re-growth of forests through re-planting. This would also expedite much-needed infrastructure improvements and beautify the landscape, creating more recreational space for the citizenry. This proposal gives men purpose while also improving their surroundings, their environment, and their nations. The essence of the totality of this project is that the cultural, biological, physical, and natural ecosystems of a nation define that nation and are all inextricably intertwined, and that without active cultivation – to say nothing of stopping the exploitation and degradation brought about by the developing neo-liberal system – the death of the living organism that is the nation is guaranteed.

The second proposal requiring some explication is the nationalization of the banking industry and the state regaining control of its own money supply. As Gottfried Feder writes:

Money is only and exclusively a voucher for completed labor issued by a community that has its own state. To issue money-tokens is one of the sovereign fundamental rights of the state. The counterfeiting of the state's money-tokens is subject to the most severe punishments; thus it is a quite forceful social demand that the monetary system be placed under the control of the collectivity.[14]

---

13 Archambault, Josh, "New Report Proves Maine's Welfare Reforms Are Working," May 19, 2016. *Forbes*. Available at: www.forbes.com/sites/theapothecary/2016/05/19/new-report-proves-maines-welfare-reforms-are-working/#bc95fcb3f6ab.

14 Feder, Gottfried, *The Manifesto for the Abolition of Enslavement to Interest on Money*. Joseph C. Hubers Verlag: Munich. 1919. Translated into English by

CONCLUSION (THE RETURNER)

One counter-point made by the proponents of the present system is that *technically* not all central banks are privately-owned. Many are publicly-traded, government-owned, or some hybrid system. While this is true, as the relationship each central bank has with its state, shareholders, and people is often different, it is ultimately irrelevant for the simple fact that the locus of control is the same. All of the globalist states are treated as assets or markets, run as corporations by corporations and financial institutions for themselves (and this can be indirectly – think of lobbyists in the United States), backed by Money Power, ie-the banks and control of the money supply. And besides, just because a company "goes public" obviously does not mean that it is owned by and accountable to the public. It is accountable to the shareholders only, and the majority shareholders to boot. This is to be understood the same way we refer to companies as private entities even if they are publicly-traded. To pretend otherwise is a semantic game only done in bad faith.

The public-private "debate" is a false dilemma, for as long as the fundamentals remain the same, the core of the system stays unchanged. The US government, for example, has not truly had control of its own money supply since 1913. This is unconscionable, and was one of the deciding factors in the severing of America from its orientation as a nation (or federation of several nations as the case may be) to its becoming a *tabula rasa* market.

Money must have a tangible backing, but gold is not the answer for the same reasons it has always been – control of supply. Rather, that backing is labor, for only labor is productive, and thus only labor has value. This does not have to refer exclusively to physical labor, for there are many kinds of invaluable intellectual and creative labors. It does, however, exclude speculation, usury, and other kinds of parasitic activity and it preserves the national interest and accountability to the citizenry.

As a counter-point to the system I am proposing, one might turn to that dusty form of Austrian Economics favored by think-tank libertarians

Hadding Scott, 2012. p. 40.

everywhere. Ludwig von Mises claimed that socialism would bring about chaos and, in a bit of hyperbole, "the end of civilization." It is telling that one of the seminal figures of Austrian Economics, F.A. Hayek, is on record stating, "My personal preference leans toward a liberal dictatorship rather than toward a democratic government devoid of liberalism." A liberal dictatorship? Curious, isn't it, that the free market and individualism are always conflated with democracy and liberty, whereas certain controls are always conflated with tyranny and totalitarianism. And besides, simply going back to the neo-liberal source material is not any kind of alternative, obviously.

In contrast to the autarkic barter system of their neighbors in Germany, Austrian Economics' progenitors were focused on hyper-individualism, the primacy of free trade, the repeal of export subsidies, staunch opposition to "collectivism," the use of the gold standard, and "interest as the charge for the use of capital." Anthony Migchels expands on the problems with libertarians' retreat to the source of neo-liberal economics to combat the modern incarnation of neo-liberalism:

Austrian Economics correctly identifies the manipulation of the money supply as the cause of the boom/bust, a.k.a business cycle. This is the little bit of truth necessary for the rest of the disinformation to have credibility. However, they completely ignore the wealth transfer through interest, which is of much greater significance. Interest has always been the Money Power's main tool. They took power by creating wars, financing both sides, and having Governments go deeply into debt. This is the key issue: interest is a wealth transfer...The US government loses up to $700 billion per year in debt service. That's a TARP every year. All for money that was printed the minute it was borrowed. But Austrian Economics will 'fix' that problem: we'll be paying it for Gold-based credit instead. To add insult to injury: the boom/bust cycle will not change, which is the basic case for gold. Gold has been the standard for a long time and it didn't stop the Money Power from creating asset bubbles and deflationary busts. Even under a full reserve banking system it is quite easy to manipulate the volume in circulation when you control a large part of the World's gold reserves... In the debate you see the Keynes-Austrian Dialectic: Spending versus Austerity. Both ignore interest, which is the hidden common ground... During modern history the financiers behind the throne clearly subjugated Governments. They don't need the State. To them it is a competitor, a dangerous one too. They will use it as long as they can control it, but it is not for nothing they are trying to consolidate their financial power in a World Government of their own. Meanwhile, the gold versus fiat narrative is a distraction which allows them to sabotage all meaningful monetary reform.[15]

This brings us to our third proposal: the abolition of interest altogether. As George Pullman relates, "For the Athenians, the single greatest virtue was autonomy." Athenians who were in debt to the state had their right to vote suspended until they were back in good standing; I think we could implement that here with net takers. In the Athenian mindset, Pullman writes, "To desire is to be beholden and to be beholden is to be other than autonomous...Desire leads to debt and debt to slavery," remarkably prescient considering where we are today. The idea of compound interest as deeply immoral predates Christianity in the Western world; Aristotle declared that because money producing money is unnatural and its natural function is as a medium of exchange to facilitate the transfer of goods, it is unjust to lend it at interest. Similar condemnations were articulated by Plato, Cicero, and others.

In Rome, the Lex Genucia of 342 BC prohibited loans which carry interest. Though adherence to this prohibition waxed and waned, official decrees by Julius Caser and Justinian sought to at least cap interest rates. By the fifth century AD, the Catholic Church was adamant about banning the acceptance of interest-bearing loans for all Catholics, not just the clergy, a stance which increased in intensity throughout the Middle Ages. There is scriptural support for the banning of usury for all three major monotheistic religions, as well as in some ancient Hindu texts, but Judaism has evolved and accepted

---

15 Migchels, Anthony, "Ron Paul's Masonic Jewish Economics," January 4, 2012. Available at: www.henrymakow.com/austrian_economics_is_masonicjewish_e.html.

numerous loopholes, especially as regards charging usurious interest rates to non-Jews, often referred to derisively as goyim. For Charles Eisenstein:

> Abetted by technology, the commodification of formerly nonmonetary goods and services has accelerated over the last few centuries, to the point today where very little is left outside the money realm. The vast commons, whether of land or of culture, has been cordoned off and sold – all to keep pace with the exponential growth of money...The imperative of perpetual growth implicit in interest-based money is what drives the relentless conversion of life, world, and spirit into money. Completing the vicious circle, the more of life we convert into money, the more we need money to live. Usury, not money, is the proverbial root of all evil.[16]

The reality is this: we live under an occupation government fully committed to population replacement and completely beholden to globalist corporate and financial interests. In the face of the preponderance of evidence we have before us, there can be no other conclusion than that the true power players know exactly what is going on and are motivated by two things: malice and greed. It is often difficult for people to accept that our rulers could be *this* corrupt(ed), but they are.

Always looking to open up new markets, the neo-liberal model is one of infinite growth and perpetual expansion. Returning to Feder:

> By Mammonism is to be understood: on the one hand, the overwhelming international money-powers, the supragovernmental financial power enthroned above any right of self-determination of peoples, international big capital, the purely Gold International; on the other hand, a mindset that has taken hold of the broadest circle of peoples; the insatiable lust for gain, the purely worldly-

---

16 Eisenstein, Charles, *Sacred Economics*, Chapter Six. North Atlantic Books. 2011. Available at: https://sacred-economics.com/sacred-economics-chapter-6-the-economics-of-usury/.

oriented conception of life that has already led to a frightening decline of all moral concepts and can only lead to more. This mindset is embodied and reaches its acme in international plutocracy. The chief source of power for Mammonism is the effortless and endless income that is produced through interest.[17]

Without outlawing interest, we will never truly be free. Ending the slavery to interest is not the end, though. We need to get control of technology and physical means of production, from factories to farms. We also need to rebuild families, neighborhoods, and entire communities. We have over one hundred million alien persons who do not belong here. We have foreign entanglements and Iscariotic leaders. We're not going to vote our way out of this, at least not with the way the system is presently constructed. It's not just consumer goods that have become cheaper – it is everything, from the value of citizenship to real and deeply-felt emotions and affinities for nation, people, family, and friends. Everything becomes ersatz and inauthentic, plastic and pliable, in the hands of these people.

To truly grasp the problem before us, you must understand that it is not *just* a political, or even civilizational, struggle; this is the ultimate revolution against the entire rotten edifice of neo-liberalism. It is a revolt against enslavement to our vices and devices, against usury and debt slavery, against the selling away of our birthright for pennies. It is a revolt against Mammonism. It is a revolt against the modern world, but even more importantly, it is the restoration, the Return, which signals the end of the old cycle and a new, harmonious dawn.

---

17 Feder, Gottfried, *The Manifesto for the Abolition of Enslavement to Interest on Money*. Joseph C. Hubers Verlag: Munich. 1919. Translated into English by Hadding Scott, 2012. p. 7.